Leading the Lean Healthcare Journey

Driving Culture Change to Increase Value

"In this book, *Leading the Lean Healthcare Journey: Driving Culture Change To Increase Value*, Pat Hagan and his colleagues tell a compelling story of change at an enormously prestigious institution in its market whose leadership listened carefully to their patients, families and staff and set out to raise quality, safety, and service to new heights.

I have known Seattle Children's for over 30 years and have watched their leaders take Children's from a good pediatric hospital to an emerging international powerhouse in the care, teaching and research related to the most complex pediatric illnesses. My wife, Gail, served as a PICU nurse there for 10 years and would come home daily to tell stories of heroic medicine, compassion beyond comprehension and opportunities to improve systems to deliver excellence reliably.

The story is really about the evolution of thinking by the leadership about the management system necessary to truly create a world class healthcare system. It is a story about leadership deciding that a true commitment to customers (patients) meant going and seeing what was really happening to them at the front line. It is a story about the culture change led by management to publicly acknowledge their defects, thereby giving their people the permission and freedom to fix things right away. It is a story about leadership taking the long view and systematically improving. It is a story of humility and the courage to go outside of healthcare to learn.

I remember when Children's started this journey. I remember Pat finding the Toyota Management System, called CPI by Children's, as intriguing. While there was clearly interest by all, there was a fair amount of palpable skepticism about the applicability of lean to healthcare and another "management fad of the month". The reader gets to enjoy the 10 year story of transformation from the perspective of the staff and clinician leaders that made CPI take root, grow, sustain, and enable all of its staff to soar daily. The reader will also see that while 10 years ago, lean in healthcare was "interesting", today it is essential."

—**J. Michael Rona**, Principal, Rona Consulting Group
(J. Michael Rona is the former president of Virginia Mason Medical Center in Seattle, Washington and introduced the Toyota Management System to Virginia Mason in 2000. He founded the Rona Consulting Group in 2007 to teach healthcare systems how to transform themselves using the Toyota Management System)

Buy this book and gain the confidence to act!

"Joan Wellman and her colleagues provide examples of dramatic performance improvements. Using their practical examples you can be on your way to becoming a leader who transforms your organizations, empowers your team, adds value, and saves lives."

—**Ken Graham**, CEO of El Camino Hospital in Mountain View, CA

"Joan Wellman and co-authors Pat Hagan and Howard Jeffries are true pioneers in the lean healthcare world. Their book, *Leading the Lean Healthcare Journey*, puts lean into the right context for healthcare leaders and change agents. This book presents all of the aspects of a management system that will create alignment and improvement from top-to-bottom, from arrival-to-discharge, each and every day. Engaging and well-written, I recommend it highly."

—**Mark Graban**, author of *Lean Hospitals: Improving Quality, Patient Safety, and Employee Satisfaction*

"The ability for health care delivery organizations to increase their ability to deliver value is not just of national importance, but might be the critical factor for our country to continue its economic leadership position in the world. In *Leading the Lean Healthcare Journey*, Joan, Pat and Howard have made an important contribution to the growing body of literature that lean techniques, but more importantly, the lean management philosophy, can be brought to health care delivery organizations successfully. The result is higher quality, more affordable, and safer care, and a more satisfying care experience for our patients. They have addressed through several case studies the fundamental point that lean is not a set of tools, but a way of leading and engaging an organization's work that can result in real transformation of care delivery."

—**James Hereford**, Executive Vice President, Group Practice Division, Group Health Cooperative

Leading the Lean Healthcare Journey

Driving Culture Change to Increase Value

Joan Wellman

Patrick Hagan

Howard Jeffries, MD

CRC Press
Taylor & Francis Group
Boca Raton   London   New York

CRC Press is an imprint of the
Taylor & Francis Group, an **informa** business

A PRODUCTIVITY PRESS BOOK

Productivity Press
Taylor & Francis Group
270 Madison Avenue
New York, NY 10016

© 2011 by Taylor and Francis Group, LLC
Productivity Press is an imprint of Taylor & Francis Group, an Informa business

No claim to original U.S. Government works

Printed in the United States of America on acid-free paper
10 9 8 7 6 5 4 3 2 1

International Standard Book Number: 978-1-4398-2865-6 (Paperback)

Visit the Taylor & Francis Web site at
http://www.taylorandfrancis.com

and the Productivity Press Web site at
http://www.productivitypress.com

Contents

Preface

Joan Wellman had invited Pat Hagan and Jerry Zimmerman to help her teach her weeklong Lean Leader Training to a group of physician and executive leaders at Children's Hospitals and Clinics of Minnesota. It was July 2008. During the course of the week, we talked a great deal with our "students" about the utility of applying continuous improvement principles to healthcare. After class each day, we took advantage of the long and warm Minnesota evenings to discuss the importance of an organization's leadership to a successful lean transformation, and the different paths taken by different hospitals (and manufacturing companies) on their lean journeys.

Joan noted her early 1990s involvement in the introduction of lean principles to healthcare in the Northwest, citing Bellevue's Overlake Hospital as an example of an early adopter of lean methodology due to the influence of their board chair from the Boeing Company. Later Peace Health, Virginia Mason Medical Center, Group Health, and Seattle Children's also began adapting continuous improvement to their organizations. Leaders at all of these organizations were taking the risk of applying "manufacturing methods" to healthcare practices. Each, however, took different approaches to implementation, some preferring a top-down approach and others a less philosophical "tools-only" path.

As we talked we discussed the Seattle Children's approach, what we called "continuous performance improvement" (CPI), and compared and contrasted it with those of others. At Seattle Children's, CPI was marked by guidance and direction from the top but grounded in the engagement and participation of clinical leadership, middle management, and staff, and we had embraced the philosophy of continuous improvement as well as the tools and methods. Not that we felt this approach was superior to others, but our results were pretty darn good and our people—faculty, management, and staff—were highly engaged in CPI.

As we talked we agreed we had a story to tell and, coincidentally, with the Lean Leader Training modules we were using that week, a structure with which to tell it. The training modules are based on the principles of continuous improvement, and we decided that our story should take the form of a series of chapters based on those principles. To highlight the leadership and involvement of clinicians, management, and staff, the chapters would be written by people who had applied lean principles to improve their own processes, from 5S to load leveling to standard work....

So, two and a half years later, we're published. Most of the chapters that follow describe work at Seattle Children's, but to avoid an exclusive focus on any one organization and the possible concern that it is a "special" case several other healthcare organizations with whom Joan has worked have also provided chapters.

We hope that readers both beginning and well on their way on their lean journeys will find the stories within helpful as they seek to apply the philosophy and principles of continuous improvement to their work.

Joan Wellman

Pat Hagan

Howard Jeffries

Acknowledgments

We would like to thank Tony Payauys, this book's tireless project manager, for his hard work keeping us organized, reminding us of deadlines, and helping us negotiate the world of book publishing. We couldn't have finished this book without him. We would also like to thank Jerry Zimmerman and Cara Bailey for their encouragement from the beginning of this endeavor and for helping us identify where to focus our efforts, and many thanks to Sue Cowan for her invaluable support throughout the project.

We acknowledge that this book represents not only our individual work, but also the hard work of many authors, writing about how dedicated, smart people with great ideas are changing how healthcare is delivered. We are privileged to present their stories in this book.

Finally, we thank Productivity Press for their willingness to publish our work.

About the Authors

Joan Wellman, founder and president of Joan Wellman & Associates (JWA), pioneered the application of Toyota principles to healthcare in 1995. Joan and her associates have provided lean consultation to Seattle Children's since 1997, and to other organizations featured in this book, including MemorialCare Health System, Children's Hospitals and Clinics of Minnesota, The Everett Clinic, and Jefferson Healthcare. Today, JWA supports healthcare organizations as they implement the methods, management systems, and mind-set required for sustained lean transformation. Before working in healthcare, Joan  spent twenty years consulting to lean initiatives in the aerospace, telecommunications, computer, and energy industries.

Patrick Hagan joined Seattle Children's Hospital in 1996 and currently serves as its president and chief operating officer. Over the past twenty-five years, he has held executive positions at children's hospitals in Ohio, Arizona, and Seattle. Pat helped develop and lead Seattle Children's continuous performance improvement (CPI) strategy. This multidimensional approach has contributed to the hospital's success in improving its performance in service quality, clinical access, patient safety, staff engagement, and financial results. Pat has spoken at numerous national conferences about Seattle Children's successful application of its transformative CPI strategy.

Howard E. Jeffries, MD, MBA, is a cardiac intensive care physician and medical director of continuous performance improvement at Seattle Children's Hospital. He is a clinical associate professor of pediatrics at the University of Washington School of Medicine. He completed a residency in pediatrics at Children's Memorial Hospital and a fellowship in critical care at Childrens Hospital Los Angeles. He has published peer-reviewed articles and book chapters, with an emphasis on cardiac intensive care, informatics, and quality improvement. He sits on the advisory board for the Virtual PICU Performance System database and on the Washington State Healthcare Associated Infections Advisory Committee.

Chapter 1

Introduction

This book is about people who have the audacity to seek and implement desperately needed change in our healthcare system. Each chapter tells how determined men and women are studying, innovating, learning, and most of all leading their organizations forward by reducing waste in our healthcare system, a system that is rapidly approaching 20 percent of the U.S. gross domestic product (GDP).

Each of these stories begins with a healthcare leader being curious enough to read, attend training, and visit companies that have proven track records of dramatically reducing waste: lean manufacturing companies in the United States and Japan. Curiosity led these leaders to an understanding that much of what we do in healthcare is waste "cleverly disguised as real work." Curiosity also led to the understanding that quality, cost, patient access, and safety outcomes are not a set of "trade-offs" but characteristics that can be improved concurrently if we are willing to learn from the likes of Toyota.

You can't help but admire these healthcare professionals. At least we can't.

And if you read on, we think you'll agree. Indeed, you'll meet and get to know healthcare providers who are focused on easing patient pain, reducing medical mistakes, increasing accountability, enriching care, and eliminating waste wherever and whenever it surfaces.

We began this journey in 1996, when Pat Hagan invited Joan Wellman to Seattle Children's Hospital to talk with hospital leaders. Pat wanted hospital leaders to understand more about how companies like Toyota and, more recently, Boeing were addressing process speed, product quality, and cost concurrently rather than as separate initiatives. Joan, a lean consultant with experience in a number of industries, had pioneered the application of lean in healthcare starting in 1995. The field of "lean healthcare" was very young at that time, so the very idea that a company like Toyota could provide lessons for improving healthcare was very new to Seattle Children's leaders.

These leaders were not "hooked." Far from it. In 1996, it was uncommon for healthcare executives to look for improvement models outside of healthcare, let alone look to manufacturing companies. Seattle Children's was no exception, and the feedback was "I sure wish that Joan would use more healthcare examples" and "I'm not so sure that we should be applying business models to healthcare."

But the Seattle Children's executive and faculty leadership group (the hospital steering committee) persisted. Pat continued to invite Joan back to facilitate discussions about lean manufacturing and conduct process improvement projects with Seattle Children's organization development staff, Barb Bouche and Margaret Dunphy. Eventually, a comprehensive plan emerged that embraced lean thinking and philosophy.

While there was some initial resistance, the approach began to make sense to people, that is, you can reduce costs and improve patient care at the same time. These outcomes cannot be separated. Our philosophy—and the approach articulated in this volume—makes it clear that patient well-being is critical; that supporting the people who work in our hospitals is essential; and that sustainable, long-term change that is broad and deep is the only answer.

The stories that follow come from Seattle Children's and other organizations that have engaged Joan Wellman & Associates as consultants over the last ten years: the Everett Clinic in Everett, Washington; MemorialCare Health System headquartered in Fountain Valley, California; Children's Hospitals and Clinics of Minnesota; and Jefferson Health System in Port Townsend, Washington. These organizations cover a large geographic territory and vary widely in size and complexity from a twenty-five-bed critical access hospital (Jefferson) to a very large, multihospital system (MemorialCare). These organizations also have very different physician models, including a primarily academic model (Seattle Children's), a primarily private practice–based physician model (MemorialCare), and a physician-owned model (the Everett Clinic). Each organization has "branded" its lean management system differently. Those "brands" include Seattle Children's continuous performance improvement (CPI), MemorialCare's management system (MC21), The Everett Clinic improvement system (TEC-15), and the list goes on.

These different organizational circumstances provide insight into how lean principles apply regardless of organization size, physician model, or words that are used to describe what they are doing. The common thread is an enduring philosophy and strategy that rally everyone in the healthcare enterprise around reducing waste to achieve common goals: improve Quality, decrease Cost, improve Delivery (patient access as an example), improve Safety, and increase Engagement of all organization members in continuous improvement. We refer to these goals as QCDSE.

As you read on, and read carefully, you'll come across some inspiring case studies that demonstrate improved quality, cost, delivery, safety, and staff and physician engagement (QCDSE). You'll learn, for example,

- How median nonoperating time in an operating room was cut from seventy-four to thirty-seven minutes
- How catheter-associated bloodstream infections were significantly reduced
- How the number of operating room documents was steadily sliced from twenty-one to fourteen to eight, freeing the staff to focus more intently on patients
- How a revamped and reorganized work flow in a lab trimmed overtime by 25 percent and boosted productivity by 5 percent
- How a 400-square-foot supply repository costing $4,000 per square foot went from a littered storage space to a seven-figure-generating operating room
- How a research review board cut its approval process down, from 86 days to 46.5 days, by eliminating thirty-five steps
- How a behavioral medicine department was able to overhaul its processes and procedures in order to see more patients
- How a newly thought out registration-to-cash value stream ended up saving millions of dollars
- How a new approach to total parenteral nutrition order writing dramatically reduced errors
- How supervising nurses, who were spending 90 percent of their time reading e-mails, transformed their jobs so they could spend 50 percent of their time on the floor working with staff and caring for patients
- How infections, overutilization, and confusion stemming from the use of peripherally inserted central catheter lines were addressed and reversed

Achieving results like these is anything but easy. Just listen to the people in this book as they struggle to solve entrenched problems. You don't have to read between the lines to realize how hard it is to wrestle with deeply ingrained behaviors that embed waste and foster a lack of sensitive care. And you'll immediately understand how difficult it is to build and maintain a consensus for change in most healthcare organizations.

While this book is filled with new vocabulary, new phrases, and new concepts, please do not be put off by this. It's simply the language of continuous change and continuous rethinking. And—whether it's the 5S's (sort, simplify, sweep, standardize, and sustain); plan, do, check, and act (PDCA); Rapid Process Improvement Workshops (RPIWs), QCDSE, CPI, lean, or value stream—just go with it. Our contributors do a good job explaining what these idioms of improvement mean, and how they work. If you're still confused, we've included a fairly comprehensive and, we think, cogent glossary of terms.

This book is not a "how to" improve healthcare book, or a recipe on how to run an operating room or intensive care unit more efficiently. It is a book about curiosity, learning, and the courage to challenge deeply held assumptions about how we deliver healthcare in this country.

The most fundamental assumption that is challenged in this book is the belief that we need more money to operate an effective healthcare system. The reality is that what we need most is what we can't buy: great leaders. Leaders who, like the authors in this book, have the curiosity and tenacity to look critically at what they are doing and find better, less wasteful ways to deliver safe, high-quality care.

We hope you'll turn the pages and join us in this sometimes rough—but always rewarding—journey.

Patrick Hagan
President and Chief Operating Officer
Seattle Children's Hospital

Joan Wellman
President
Joan Wellman & Associates

Howard Jeffries, MD, MBA
Medical Director, Continuous Performance Improvement (CPI)
Pediatric Cardiac Intensivist
Seattle Children's Hospital

Chapter 2

The Continuous Performance Improvement (CPI) Journey: A Long and Winding Road

Patrick Hagan
President and Chief Operating Officer
Seattle Children's Hospital

Our continuous performance improvement (CPI) journey has been a long and winding road that has stretched out in front of us for more than a decade. We are always close to our destination, but we never quite get there. And that's how it should be. CPI keeps leading you down new paths that need attention, patching, and paving. It's an endless—but immensely satisfying—excursion that takes healthcare organizations and their people to new and never-before-imagined places that offer improved care, greater compassion, and heightened efficiencies that truly benefit patients, clinicians, and researchers.

We started down three separate trails in the late 1990s. The first one was cultural. We simply had to recognize and accept where we were in healthcare—and at Seattle Children's Hospital—ten to fifteen years ago. Our people were bright and uniformly well intentioned, and so was leadership. But our "systems" were inefficient and at times unsafe. We simply weren't where we needed to be. Nowhere near where we needed to be. And that was OK—after all (with apologies to Tom Peters), we were no worse than anyone else. There were hundreds and hundreds of ways we could have been better as an organization, in the way we delivered patient care, and in the experience we offered our people—our doctors, nurses, and staff.

But we were generally complacent. We were a hospital where the sickest kids came for help, yet we were anything but welcoming for young patients and their families. At worst, our attitude was that people—patients and staff—were lucky to be here. But people had choices. They didn't have to come to Seattle Children's. So, if we wanted people to come to us for care, and if we wanted people to come to work, practice, teach, and study with us, we needed to change our culture.

We had traveled down the reengineering avenue, but it was an exclusively cost-focused and cold way to go, and it felt antithetical to our culture and values at Seattle Children's. In looking for other options, we started working with Joan Wellman, an organization change and process improvement consultant then with DeltaPoint. Joan challenged us with success stories of other organizations—stellar enterprises outside of healthcare. She told us we could learn from these companies and how they focused on customers and removed waste that got in the way of their people and their customers.

At first, we found it a bit off-putting to hear of Boeing and jet airplane manufacturing or Toyota and automobile production in the same breath as neonatal care or pediatric cancer. But that eventually led us to an even more important conversation in which we asked ourselves, "Why do we really want to improve?" We started talking about becoming the best children's hospital, not in an immodest way, but as the rationale for striving to continuously improve our performance. We began to talk about wanting to improve every year, continuously, so that we provided the best possible experience for our patients and the best possible environment for our faculty and staff to work and practice. We didn't want to be the "above average" children's hospital, and we certainly didn't want to be the "we're no worse than anyone else" children's hospital. We wanted to be the best children's hospital.

That meant we weren't interested in changing at the margins; we were determined to make fundamental, long-lasting, and long-term changes. But we also believed that a "big bang" approach would be counterproductive, and indeed the best way to generate resistance and opposition. Instead, we proceeded iteratively and incrementally, gradually improving our processes and how we functioned on behalf of the patients, clinicians, and researchers in our world. Using that approach, we gave ourselves time to "prove the concept"—and we did.

We learned from the companies we observed that to achieve this kind of change would require substantive and sustained leadership commitment. Leadership would have to go beyond talking the talk to walking the walk of performance improvement. What we've learned from our experience is that leaders need to be present with their people in observing and supporting their work, and in noting their performance improvement efforts. Leaders need to be trained and knowledgeable in the principles, methods, and tools of CPI, and they need to participate in improvement events. And leaders need to be tenacious and patient: tenacious because there will be resistance to this effort and because that's what's required to keep CPI from becoming the next "flavor of the month," and patient because it will be hard, difficult work; some events will fail; and fundamental improvement takes time.

The second trail we found ourselves on was all about events and circumstances. In the late 1990s and early 2000s Joan, with Seattle Children's employees Barb Bouche and Margaret Dunphy, had led Rapid Process Improvement Workshops (RPIWs) to help us improve our emergency, pharmacy, and supply departments; our lab had employed this methodology as well, working with a different consultant. Initial results were enlightening. But, as we headed down this route, we were routinely, if infrequently, reminded that we really weren't all that great. Our errors and defects caused injury and even death in our hospital, and, worse, we came to the sobering conclusion that we weren't learning from our mistakes. We weren't seizing the opportunities to improve. We had serious systemic issues that absolutely had to be addressed in the name of patient safety.

After a particularly tragic error caused by communication failures between clinical teams, we decided to use the RPIW tool to improve our clinical care processes. Our approach was "simple"—give the clinical teams most affected by the mistakes the opportunity to improve the way they cared for patients. We pulled together the medical director, the chief of nursing, the chairman of pediatrics, and the clinical teams, and we began in earnest the process of continuously improving our performance by giving our people the tools and resources to do so. This was a seminal moment for us. It was the true beginning of directing "from the top"; and we would use this method, which enabled the real work of improvement to occur on the front line. It was 2002.

We asked members of the clinical teams (faculty, nurses, residents, coordinators, et al.) to participate in an RPIW to improve communication among the teams, and to consider changes in the way we were conducting patient rounds. The RPIW team identified multiple flaws in the rounding process, not least of which were a remarkable absence of reliable physician-to-nurse communication and a profound lack of involvement with patient families. The RPIW team pointed out that rounds had become an esoteric conference room process that needed to be redirected to the patient bedside. The team recommended changes in the way rounds are conducted, and this began a journey of continuous improvement in our rounding process that has endured to this day.

Over time, we labeled our work "continuous performance improvement." We framed our work as a CPI "house" representing the elements of quality, cost, delivery, safety, and engagement (see Figure 2.1). Patients and families would "come first" and be the roof of the house, the engagement of our people would be the foundation of the house and of our success, and quality, cost, delivery, and safety would be the pillars supporting the roof of the house, our patients.

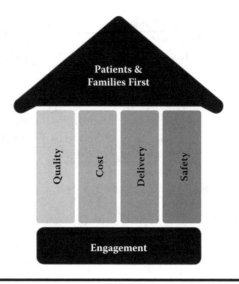

Figure 2.1   The Seattle Children's House. Seattle Children's uses a house to show how we think about evaluating and improving healthcare. Patients and families are our primary customer, as illustrated by the roof. Patients and families are supported by pillars that indicate areas where we strive for continuous improvement: quality, cost, delivery, and safety. The pillars rest on a foundation of engagement: employees, faculty, and referring physicians who are engaged and committed to the care or our patients.

We gradually expanded our CPI focus. In addition to the RPIWs we were running, we started using the Five S's of CPI: sorting, simplifying, sweeping, standardizing, and sustaining. Importantly, we decided to invest in our own process improvement infrastructure. We trained our own people (with Joan's able leadership) and hired others to form a cadre of internal process improvement consultants to help spread the methodology throughout the organization. Today, we have over thirty people in our CPI Department.

Our third trail—after the cultural and circumstantial ones—was intellectual. I finally sat down and read *The Toyota Way*. It was a definite capstone for my thinking about continuous improvement. It woke me up to the kind of overarching philosophy of leadership and management necessary for our hospital to become the best. It was now clear to me that it wasn't *what* Toyota did that was important; it was *how* they did it.

There were several other crystal clear learnings from Toyota: first, our prime focus should be on our customer, the patient; second, we always need to support our people in their work; and, third, we must take a long-term view and be relentless in performance improvement, never abandoning our goals of continuous improvement in response to short-term issues.

This translated into several important principles at Seattle Children's Hospital: we involve patients and families directly in our improvement efforts; physicians and staff are partners to be engaged, not customers to be served; and our goals are multiyear initiatives, not flavors of the month.

By 2007, we had had good—not great—success after several years of incremental CPI development. Having observed and learned from various American manufacturing companies, it became apparent that we needed to experience more sophisticated continuous improvement environments if we were to accelerate the pace of our cultural transformation. We knew other organizations that had traveled to Japan for that experience and recommended it highly. Generally speaking, they had done so to "shock" their culture and jump-start their transformation. Early on, we had consciously decided *not* to invest in Japan trips because we had chosen a more gradual, incremental approach to cultural transformation. But, after several years of experience, the timing to go to Japan seemed right. The trip to Japan wasn't needed to shock our people into CPI awareness, but rather to accelerate our transformation and truly set the wheels in motion for a long-term generational effort.

The decision to take twenty-five of our people to Japan for a two-week "CPI immersion" was a step we had to take. We were ready for it, but it was a high-risk move nevertheless. Right off the bat, there was the fact that none of us had done this before; it was a completely new experience. We had a new CEO and medical director at the hospital; both were only just getting started with CPI and beginning to appreciate what it could do. We also took two board members, and the rest of the group was composed of executive, faculty, and CPI leaders.

The trip went very well—beyond our wildest dreams and expectations. The trip's theme was "learning to see"—and we were focused on observing flow in sophisticated companies and applying their lessons to our work. We learned a huge amount by observing these companies and the way they used the philosophies and tools of continuous improvement. Each successive company we visited had ever-increasing time investments in continuous improvement, from twenty years to Toyota's fifty years of commitment. Each company was therefore more accomplished than the last.

That yielded another profound truth for us—that it takes time and patience to implement CPI, and it truly is a generational effort.

And, finally, we saw something in Japan that stuck with us: the leaders of CPI organizations are teachers and coaches, not bureaucrats; these leaders personally embody the change and transformation of their company.

So far, we've made six trips in all to Japan, and we learn more each time we go.

For example, on the second trip, we visited a piano factory and came to the realization that the art and craft of building these wonderful instruments—with wood, strings, and wires—was very much akin to the craft and art of medicine. We saw pianos being built on a moving line to takt time. It was eye-opening for our physicians as they concluded that it's possible—and desirable—to pursue the craft of medicine to the rhythm of takt time. And as with each of our trips, this experience highlighted the importance and value of standard work for clinical practice. On each trip, our clinicians have learned how standard work is not constraining but in fact frees one to focus more attention on the patient or, as in this case, the piano.

The third trip taught me about the language of CPI. The bottom line is that these Japanese companies do not use shorthand or catchphrases to convey and communicate the generational changes of continuous improvement. You don't hear the word "lean" in Japan. But you do hear about the focus on the customer; the commitment to, and support of, the people; and the long-term view.

Our most recent trip took place in late 2008, just after the financial meltdown hit. This visit was also instructive. We immediately saw and felt the Japanese companies' commitment to waste reduction as the means to cost reduction. They redeployed or further trained their people instead of laying them off. This breeds a true sense of engagement and participation among all staff; everyone in the companies we saw was pulling in the same direction. We were impressed with the concept of "scarcity drives improvement." It wasn't about taking resources away, but about providing workers with the tools to eliminate waste so that work can be done with fewer resources. This makes a big difference. In the toughest times, CPI tools and processes help drive meaningful change.

After each of our Japan trips, our teams were very excited about what they had learned and they were eager to apply it. But we were also very cautious and careful. We didn't want the hospital to become divided between those who had been to Japan and those who hadn't, so we always cautioned against being too "evangelical" upon our return. It was, however, definitely difficult to restrain ourselves.

The lessons from the American and Japanese companies that we visited were many, but high on the list was learning how important it was to "steal shamelessly" from others—their improvements, innovations, and ideas, regardless of where you find them. We had reached the point where all of us—physician and nurse leaders, staff, and executives—were willing and able to apply the lessons of others to our work.

So where are we now, and how did we get here? Looking back on a decade of development, we got here through a series of successive waves of improvement. Not that we consciously proceeded in this fashion; but armed with the clarity that's achieved by peering through the retrospective lens, it's now apparent that there were four overlapping waves of organizational transformation, and we're working on number five.

Our first wave was borne of caution. We began our improvement efforts behind the scenes, without much clinical involvement, let alone clinical leadership. The best example of the first wave was the 5S project in our loading dock–receiving area. Very "offstage" and a classic place for good "before-and-after" 5S photos, it was also an excellent example of a "point" improvement, where the project focuses only on the process at hand and does not take into account the related processes or departments.

Success in our first wave bred the second wave, where we continued with point improvements and began to see more clinician involvement, but without explicit clinical leadership. Projects occurred in places like the laboratory and pharmacy, and began to come to the attention of more folks in the organization. It was at this point, too, that we learned the important lesson that removing waste from our processes not only improved process performance (e.g., lab and pharmacy turnaround times) but also reduced cost. Indeed, improved pharmacy turnaround times directly led to reduced IV wastage, which saved $350,000 per year.

The beauty of this achievement was that, unlike reengineering, we did not focus on cost as a target. We asked our people to help us improve the quality of our service, the access to our services, and the safety of our care. And we demonstrated that when we did these things by removing waste, we inevitably reduced our cost per patient (by 3.6 percent in 2006–2007 and by 6 percent in 2008–2009).

Our third wave saw the emergence of physician and nursing leaders not only heading up point improvement projects but also driving the organization's embrace of continuous improvement. Faculty leaders saw that the core principle of CPI is to apply the scientific method to clinical and operational practices, and they were eager to see this approach applied in their areas.

During this wave, we had point improvement efforts throughout the hospital, and even in our research institute. The General Medicine Rounding RPIW occurred in this wave, as did projects in operative services, the emergency department, and the clinical laboratory; we also instituted multisystem projects like Total Parenteral Nutrition. In research, we improved processes for the institutional review board and the vivarium.

These projects helped us become comfortable with two significant cultural changes—the application of learnings from other companies in other industries, and the routine involvement of patients and families in our improvement workshops. Joan was very helpful with the former, and she motivated us to literally leave the comfort of our conference rooms for the factory floor to advance our learning.

Our ongoing focus on family-centered care helped us with the latter cultural change. We were quite concerned that inviting patients and families into our workshops would reveal our "dirty laundry," and that no good would come of this, but our family support leaders assured us that we needn't worry because our patients and families knew better than anyone else what our shortcomings were. Indeed, we quickly learned the folly of believing that we could "imagine" what our customers wanted, and we found that having them directly involved in our improvement work is invaluable.

The fourth wave was the most distinct, in terms of time and type of improvement activity. It began with the development of our new strategic plan in 2006 and the implementation of "value stream mapping" in our CPI efforts. Our strategic plan identified six specialty "focus" programs (cancer, orthopedics, general surgery, cardiac, neonatology, and transplant) and called for improvements in quality and safety and for growth in patient activity. Over time, each specialty's "value stream" (i.e., the specialty's activity from the patient's perspective)—from referral to outpatient visit to procedures to admission to discharge home—was mapped.

The mapping process is time intensive and involves dozens of people, including parents and patients; it ultimately yields a description of the specialty's work, waste and all, from the beginning of the patient experience to the end. It also yields innumerable opportunities for improvement as well as projects for growth, and it enables those dozens of people (physicians, nurses, management, and staff) to reach alignment on the projects in a way previously not possible. Several of the focus programs have sent teams to Japan to hone their maps and project plans.

Our work is progressing through a fifth wave of CPI activity and organizational improvement as we embrace the concepts of integrated facility design (IFD) and strategy deployment. IFD adapts Toyota's Production Preparation Process model for designing and building new car factories to healthcare building design and construction. As with all CPI efforts, IFD is a multidisciplinary approach, in this case involving architects, general contractors, hospital facility executives, physicians, nurses, other frontline staff, and patients and families. Using this approach with a new ambulatory building and surgery center, we reduced conventionally derived space estimates by thirty thousand square feet with a new design applauded by all—and saved $20 million. We are now applying IFD to a new inpatient facility and expect similar results with excellent design, optimal square footage, and reduced costs.

Strategy deployment is the next iteration of CPI for Seattle Children's. It will involve explicitly connecting staff-level improvement objectives and daily work with our strategic goals. This will require the development and implementation of leader standard work and daily management systems throughout the organization, and will help us continue to spread CPI thinking—everyday improvement—to all of our people in all areas of Children's. Very challenging and very exciting!

In view of the recent financial meltdown and the surprising difficulties of Toyota, one might ask how we've fared and whether our direction has changed in light of these events. The answer is that we believe that CPI is critical to our success, quite literally now more than ever. As we move forward, we will learn from Toyota's mistakes as we have learned from its great successes. As we grow we will strive to grow responsibly, building quality and safety into our improved processes and our new designs. We will continue to focus on our patients and families first, and support our people in their work; and, at the same time, we will take the long-term view in our leadership and in the management of our organization.

In these difficult economic times, we have focused more intently on translating waste reduction to cost reduction, and we have emphasized cost reduction more than we have in the past. Yet, at the same time, we have made the commitment of "no layoffs" and instead repurpose and redeploy our people as our work changes. Our efforts now are directed at preparing for the recovery, and we continue to see improvements and great results in the quality, cost effectiveness, and delivery of our services; the safety of our care; and the engagement of our people.

Naturally—and of course—our journey continues.

Chapter 3

Creating High-Powered Healthcare Improvement Engines

Joan Wellman

President
Joan Wellman & Associates

It is now well known that the United States spends as much as two times more per capita on healthcare than other developed nations. This fact begs the question: what additional value do consumers in the United State receive for the extraordinary financial commitment made to healthcare? It does not appear that we are healthier than our industrialized peers. In fact, a 2008 Commonwealth Fund Report ranked the United States last in quality of healthcare among nineteen comparative, developed nations. Not a stellar track record for a society paying top dollar.

There are plenty of candidates for the root cause of the U.S. healthcare system's woes, including a complex network of third-party payers that do not "add value," public policy that drives patients to emergency rooms rather than to appropriate and safe care in less expensive settings, physicians practicing "defensive medicine" over concern about medical liability, and the list goes on. Many of these root causes are related to public policy and the structure of our healthcare delivery system, factors not controlled by healthcare delivery administrators and physician leaders.

Brutally Honest Leadership

There are an increasing number of U.S. healthcare leaders who, despite the systemic causes of poor performance mentioned above, are demonstrating that they can, in fact, achieve dramatic improvement of healthcare quality, cost, and safety and patient access to services. These leaders are brutally honest about the tremendous amount of work conducted in their organizations that is actually waste cleverly disguised as "real work." Their definition of waste is expansive and includes things that are easy to see such as excessive transportation, patients waiting, and the human cost and financial burdens caused by defects, as well as things that are more difficult to see such as complexity. For the purposes of this chapter, the leaders who are actively removing waste in healthcare are called "lean leaders."

Lean leaders are, at their heart, people developers. They know that their ability to drive out waste depends on using the brainpower of all organizational members. If you ask lean leaders what the most important element of their improvement strategy is, they will tell you, "Developing and respecting people." They actively engage staff, physicians, patients, payors, families, educators, researchers, and suppliers as problem solvers, getting out of the conference room and going to "gemba," or the workplace, to observe and support problem solving.

If you hang out with lean leaders, you will find that they are some of the most dissatisfied people you have ever met. While they are never short of praise and recognition for achievements, what they value most is the reflection that leads to even further improvement. They are constantly learning, constantly experimenting, and not shy about trying things that may not pan out.

Lean leaders do not rout out waste or solve problems in their spare time; they see improvement as central to their job. When a critical mass of these people converges in one organization, the organization can become a "healthcare improvement engine."

Imagining a Different Approach to Defects and Waste

I once told a group of healthcare executives that if they saw high reliability in action in organizations that measure all defects in "parts per million," rather than "parts per thousand" as is often done in healthcare, they would recognize such an extraordinary gap that they would weep. Recently, I took a group of them to see just this kind of organization. Our host company supplies Honda, Toyota, and other auto manufacturers with safety equipment. The visiting group got invited to the plant for a daily 5:00 a.m. "abnormality escalation meeting," starting with production team leaders and supervisors meeting to discuss quality and production problems that occurred on the previous shift. This meeting was followed by the supervisors meeting with production managers and finally the managers meeting with the plant manager. At each level, the managers worked on issues that required action on their part. By 8:30 a.m., everyone who needed to know that they had an issue to resolve was on point to do just that. All of these meetings were held on the factory floor with the plant manager's meeting on loudspeaker at one end of the factory, visible to all.

While the visiting healthcare group did not exactly "weep," they got the point. Their visit debrief described the gulf between what they had seen that morning and their healthcare organizations. They contrasted their world, in which deviation from standards is a daily event and staff feels the need to "protect" patients from safety and quality hazards or apologize to patients and families for long wait times, poor communication, and "everyday" errors. In their organizations, staff has learned to cope with a far from perfect world, with problems so frequent that they go unreported and unaddressed.

The trip to the automotive supplier gave the healthcare visitors the ability to imagine what it would be like if deviation from safety and quality standards and barriers to patient flow were considered defects worthy of "stopping the line for immediate attention." For example, a nurse who notices that the wrong medication has been delivered to a drawer in a medication room would not only correct the problem to protect patients from the defect (which is what nurses spend a good deal of time doing today) but also STOP and NOTIFY someone IMMEDIATELY that a defect worthy of attention has occurred (as opposed to writing up the event and sending it to the quality department later in the shift … if time permits). Most importantly, the nurse would have confidence that when a defect signal is sent, the organization's problem-solving prowess would swing into action.

In this environment, problems would be seen as "treasures" that provide the raw material for improvement. Staff would feel valued for using critical and creative thinking to solve problems. Problem identification and problem solving would be accelerated to the point that the healthcare organization is a "learning and improvement engine."

Imagine further that if you ask the executive team to not limit the description of its organization's mission to the "what" (i.e., the delivery of healthcare), they would also tell you that their mission is to *improve how patient care is delivered*, and that the *how* is central to ensuring sustainable high-quality care to their community.

Beginning to Build the Engine

Most healthcare organizations have begun their improvement journeys, and over the last decade there have been hopeful advances in the application of improvement tools and methods to some tough problems. These advances, sometimes aided by lessons from other industries, are the topics of great interest at national conferences with titles such as "improving access in ambulatory operations" or "reducing length of stay for heart failure patients." At various points during the year, improvement projects go before the board quality committee or the process improvement steering team with well-deserved congratulations all around.

Figure 3.1 Gears of the healthcare improvement engine. When everyone shares the same frame of reference, the wheels of progress can turn faster.

So what's the problem? It lies in the episodic approach to improvement, that is, improvement as a series of unconnected "projects" rather than a way of organizational life. It also lies in the pace and intensity of improvement. Our current rate of improvement simply will not close the gap between what we are paying for healthcare in the United States and the value we receive. Finally, the problem lies in the focus on tools and methods rather than on the mind-set of organizational leaders and the management systems that create the "improvement engine (See Figure 3.1)"

It's Not about the Tools and Methods

Unfortunately, many healthcare organizations suffer from "methodology incongruence," where frontline managers are confused by the various specialized departments requesting adherence to initiatives led by that department. Clinical education wants to use storyboards, finance wants to use cost reduction methods, quality wants to deploy e-feedback, compliance wants tracer rounds, process improvement wants to engage people in Six Sigma, and the list goes on. This incongruence can make for an improvement technology alphabet soup that confounds some of the most sophisticated change agents.

There are really only two critical "must haves" regarding improvement methods and tools.

1. Whether using Rapid Process Improvement Workshops (RPIWs), Six Sigma tools, value stream mapping, tracer rounds, or root cause analysis, any method worth engaging must drive rigorous, rapid, and frequent plan, do, check, and act (PDCA) cycles (See Figure 3.2). The PDCA cycle is not a method or tool per se;

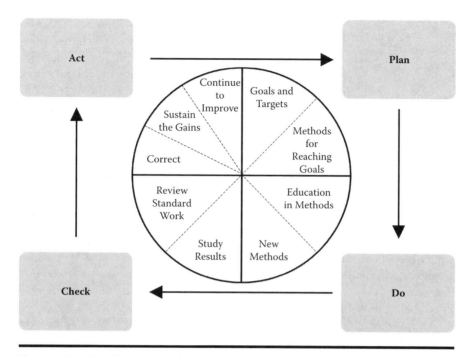

Figure 3.2   The PDCA Cycle. The PDCA cycle is not a method but a way of thinking. Adopted from Kaoru Ishikawa, *What Is Total Quality Control? The Japanese Way* (Englewood Cliffs, N.J.: Prentice Hall, 1991).

it is a way of thinking. By completing the entire cycle, and not leaving the check and act parts of the cycle to chance, organization learning can be accelerated.

2. Improvement methods must be accessible to organization members. Too much variety or complexity distracts rather than enhances progress.

This is not to say that tools and methods are not necessary. The organizations with case studies in this book all use lean tools and methods with a common vocabulary and set of tools. A standard set of improvement tools and a commonly shared vocabulary of improvement are critical, but they are not sufficient to achieve the results described in this book.

It Takes a Leadership Mind-Set

So if it's not about the tools and methods, what drives the improvement engine of the healthcare improvement engine? Most important is a leadership mind-set that expects everyone in the healthcare organization, including executives, to actively apply scientific thinking (PDCA) to remove waste and variation. Managers in these organizations are not willing to accept organizational silos which create hardship for their patients as "a fact of life." They are not complacent about the fact that defects are occurring hourly in their organizations or that waste is making their services more expensive and less safe for patients. They are curious and constantly learning. They treat problems raised by patients, staff, and physicians as "gems" to be solved rather than irritations. Most importantly, they are willing to become students, then practitioners, and finally teachers and coaches of the methods and principles that will remove waste and defects.

To illustrate the difference that mind-set, management systems, and methods can make, let's take a look at two hospitals and explore the differences in the mindsets of Hospital A and Hospital B when it comes to improvement.

The CEO of Hospital A was introduced to the concept of a lean enterprise, and he liked the idea a lot. But he didn't want to engage his senior managers in the process of change because they were busy. So, he went outside and recruited a high-profile industrial engineer who understood the principles that have helped Toyota and a number of manufacturing organizations improve their enterprise. The industrial engineer reported directly to the CEO; as a result, the entire hospital knew that its leader was serious about implementing change.

The new recruit's first assignment was the operating room (OR). And he went ahead and did solid engineering work. He mapped the process, did time observation studies, and zeroed in on ways that the OR could run more smoothly. But several months later, he left the hospital, frustrated and with little to show for his hard work. Most of his recommendations weren't implemented, and those that were simply weren't sustained.

What happened? Why did this experienced outside expert fail to help Hospital A become a lean enterprise—or even move toward becoming a lean enterprise?

The first reason for this lack of success has to do with the people at the sharp end of the process. These are the frontline players—the doctors and nurses—who are deeply involved in the hazards and constantly immersed in the vulnerabilities of care. These people must be intricately and emotionally engaged in any change effort within a hospital. Outside experts—no matter how deep or rich their experience may be—will never convince clinicians that they understand the essential nuances and lifesaving technical work that goes on in the OR, in the intensive care unit (ICU), and at a patient's bedside. Hospital A failed to realize that lean healthcare organizations must, therefore, make those at the "sharp end," the content experts in the work, their greatest source of finding and solving problems. This requires a significant change in management mind-set and investment strategy: lean organizations invest significant time and money in the development of people.

The second factor behind the failure is that many hospital CEOs want quick and big fixes, so they turn to compelling outside experts—but they do so without considering how difficult, time-consuming, and expensive it is to integrate these new hires into the actual cultural and technical fabric of the healthcare organization. While outside experts may be critical to success, their best role is as coaches and mentors of content experts, not as the primary "change agents."

The third variable that contributed to Hospital A's misstep revolves around the CEO's assumption that if he brought in the industrial engineer, it would be helpful to his leadership team, who were "too busy" to be involved. What the CEO of Hospital A did not realize is that without executives and managers changing the way they manage, how they spend their time, and what gets their attention, improvement progress would be slow and episodic.

Hospital A obviously went down the wrong path and ended up in an organizational cul-de-sac that did very little—if anything—to advance the cause of continuous improvement.

Now let's talk about the mind-set at Hospital B, which is starkly different from that of Hospital A. The best way to understand what went on in Hospital B is by looking at its pharmacy, which changed dramatically over a four-year period.

On one visit, the pharmacy staff had implemented 5S (sort, simplify, sweep, standardize, and sustain). By the next visit, it had standardized the workflow and balanced the work to meet demand and achieve shorter lead times. And, when it came time to design a new physical space, the team laid out a U-shaped work cell and limited the work in process inventory. The pharmacy also demonstrated its new and improved inventory-ordering signals and work-leveling tool.

The key takeaway here is that the process of improvement within Hospital B's pharmacy just didn't stop. The team constantly upgraded safety, steadily cut waste, and consistently reduced lead times. And, over time, it became clear that the staff was redefining what it called "good." That new definition didn't come from a healthcare industry average for order turnaround times and medication safety; it came from the team's vision—operating a waste-free process with zero defects in a lean enterprise.

The pharmacy director at Hospital B said it all when he was asked how, with all the competing demands on his team, he was able to develop a learning-focused mind-set in his organization.

"The hospital leaders have told me that improvement is what my job is," said the pharmacy director. "At first, I was the sponsor, process owner, and the person making sure that the follow-up was done. Now, we've developed our staff, and they do what I used to do, so we can address projects concurrently. We've spread the wealth of knowledge ... it's permeated the organization."

That's a far cry from Hospital A, which went out and tried to buy the change management talent it needed to solve its problems.

Hospital B mobilized its leaders and transformed them into coaches, teachers, and role models who helped inspire and motivate managers like the pharmacy director with a "lean state of mind." Hospital B's pharmacy director understood that change was his job, because his boss helped him see that; and the pharmacy director's boss got his lean education and mandate from *his* boss. The point here is that with the right mind-set, all managers can become dynamic change agents in a hospital and do what they've never done before—what they might think is impossible.

The moral of this story is that the more educated senior people are about lean principles, the greater the opportunity for a hospital to achieve continuous improvement. When leaders—all the way up to the board—share a mind-set about improvement, the work goes faster because everyone in the organization is on the same page.

The Management System Provides the Dance Steps

On Seattle's Broadway Avenue, dance steps instructions to the tango, waltz, fox trot, and other ballroom dances are laid as brass footsteps in the concrete sidewalk. These dance steps are reminiscent of the next ingredient of a healthcare improvement engine: standard "dance steps" for managers that ensure success is not left to the chance that managers and leaders will have that "certain something it takes to lead." In high-velocity improvement organizations, the dance steps are clear and form the basis for not only continuous improvement of processes but also continuous improvement of the organization's management.

The dance steps are laid out in three basic management systems, all based on the PDCA cycle.

1. **Strategy deployment**: This is a method for ensuring that strategic initiatives are developed with high levels of intelligence of what is happening at the "ground level." Strategy deployment establishes a learning system which ensures continuous improvement in the organization's bandwidth to achieve strategic results. This is the PDCA of senior management. This is also referred to as "hoshin planning" or "policy deployment."

   One of the most rewarding parts of our consulting work is watching clients reflect on how much they have learned after their first and subsequent years of using strategy deployment. The check and act phases of executive PDCA drive thoughtful, frank reflection, leading to better and better execution versus a "blame game" that can easily take center stage when goals are not reached.

2. **Cross-functional management**: Sometimes referred to fondly as the system that ensures that *the fact that we are a complex, multidepartmental, multisite organization with complex organizational relationships is not our patients' problem.* Cross-functional management uses value stream management methods to ensure that patients experience ever improving results in quality, cost, access, and safety as they move throughout their continuum of care (See Figure 3.3).

3. **Daily management or the daily engagement system**: Everyday problem solving, checking, and coaching on standard work, work balance, staff huddles, visibility walls, and metrics are all ingredients of daily management.

Functional Departments

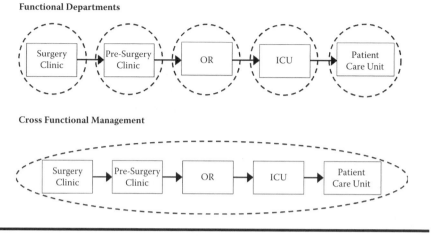

Cross Functional Management

Figure 3.3 A cross-functional management system. Cross-functional management focuses on loyalty to the customer rather than loyalty to functional silos.

This is the glue that ensures reliability, holds improvement gains, and provides insights for "what needs work" (See Figure 3.4).

Let's imagine what it would be like to have all three of these management systems in full working order. Strategic goals would be clearly set, articulated, prioritized, and deployed. And there would be lots of discussion throughout the organization at every

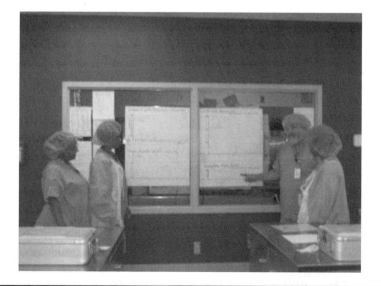

Figure 3.4 The daily management huddle. Getting on the same page. Daily management huddles provide teams a chance to "check in," verify expectations, and more.

level—not just about the goals themselves but also about the means to actually achieve them. Just as importantly, frontline supervisors and managers would be released from the tyranny of putting out daily fires, and instead they would spend much more of their time actively engaging, coaching, and huddling with staff members. This would enable a host of staff-inspired ideas to surface and be put to constructive use.

Prior to implementing daily management, the typical supervising nurse spent 90 percent of any given shift in meetings, in the office answering e-mails, or on the phone; once daily management was adopted, however, the ratio shifted dramatically, and the supervising nurse now spends nearly 50 percent of the time on the floor, auditing, coaching, engaging, balancing workloads with demand, and getting and implementing ideas from the staff.

How to Get Started

Healthcare leaders who realize that this journey involves methods, mind-set, and management systems, and are ready to embark should start with a series of hard questions.

- **Are we serious about change?** This is not a trick question. "Serious" means that hospital executives want their organization to become the best it can possibly be and are willing to spend the time and resources required. "Change" refers not only to processes and people—but also to how leaders spend their time and attention.
- **Are we willing to be students?** An afternoon of lean lectures, a week of lean training, or participation in a couple of lean events will not help any hospital reach the tipping point for lasting change. The baseline investment here is 3–4 years of learning through application, reflection, and the coaching of others.
- **Do we have the patience, tenacity, and focus to see this through over the long term?** This may be the toughest question of all. The type of change outlined in this chapter isn't just about joyful case studies that yield 50 percent improvement. It's also about the experiments that fail, which usually bring the organization's naysayers out in full force. And it's about learning to lead through rugged moments, a willingness to take on intractable problems that have lingered for years, and active learning that engages people in making change rather than merely talking about change.

If the answers to these three thoughtful and thought-provoking questions are "yes" or reasonably close to "yes," then senior leaders should begin a frank assessment of their healthcare organization's current situation. This self-analysis will help guide executives as they contemplate the scope and plan of work, the speed and ambition of the change plan, the people who should be involved in the process, and how the progress and results should be communicated.

To get going in this assessment of the current situation, it will help to frame the discussion around these eight questions:

1. **What is our organization's sense of urgency?** Organizations that have taken a deep dive quickly have a high sense of urgency, often based on financial, quality, access, or safety concerns. Leaders in these organizations hold a strong conviction that a new way of managing and an all-out effort are required.

2. **Is our leadership team convinced that healthcare must look for models from other industries?** Leadership conviction varies widely when it comes to the need for disruptive change, both in the technologies of improvement and in the content of the improvement. This is particularly true if the change models are coming from progressive and successful companies like Toyota, which are outside of healthcare.

3. **What is our organization's appetite for risk taking?** Any new approach or direction involves risk. As more healthcare organizations embrace learning from lean and achieve sustainable results, the perceived risk of using this business approach is decreasing, but anxiety is usually high on issues such as physician buy-in, the teaching mission, and time and resource demands in order to generate lasting change.

4. **How much willingness is there to invest resources?** It takes resources to improve. Organizations vary widely in their ability and willingness to invest in improvement. Most of this investment is in the time and energy of people.

5. **How are the roles of leaders perceived?** One of the toughest pills to swallow is the deep involvement of leaders in the change process. Not only must leaders become educated in the content, thought process, and technologies of lean, but also they must become practitioners and coaches. This is a far cry from the typical delegation of improvement to the process improvement department, and it has profound implications for leaders, including how they spend their time.

6. **How do our frontline managers currently spend their time?** It is not unusual for nursing managers to have sixty to one hundred direct reports and spend much of their day struggling with human resource issues. In a lean enterprise, just as there is standard work for processes, there is standard work for managers. This work includes using a daily management system to make work progress transparent and enable engagement in proactive process control versus reactive firefighting. This may not be something that comes naturally to healthcare, but it is a critical element of sustainable improvement.

7. **What stories exist about the successes or failures associated with past improvement initiatives?** Some organizations are still talking about what happened during the days of reengineering or any improvement technology that has come and gone. The degree of healthy—or not so healthy—skepticism

will make a real difference in how an organization launches and proceeds on its lean journey.

8. **What is the current level of staff and physician engagement?** "Engagement" in this sense refers to the psychological commitment to an organization's mission and the commitment to advance the work of the organization itself. Organizations that have high levels of cynicism and disengagement need to chart a more gradual course than those with high levels of engagement.

The questions above helped shape strategies adopted by the three organizations described below. In each case, executives used the understanding of their current situation to shape how they would introduce lean to their organizations and what they would emphasize in the first years of work.

Pat Hagan, for example, adopted an evolutionary strategy in order to bring lean principles to his organization. At the outset, Pat was aware that process improvement in his organization was directly tied to the highly unpopular reengineering work done by Seattle Children's in the mid-1990s. The reengineering work had sparked widespread cynicism that hospital administrators were focused primarily on cost reduction at the expense of clinical work. It took slow and steady progress to prove that this time around, there would be a balanced approach focused on.

"At the beginning of the journey, we were in the aftermath of the reengineering era," explains Hagan, "and that made us gun shy about addressing any process improvement activity, particularly with cost as a focus. We knew, however, that there were safety, service, and process improvement issues that needed to be addressed and we were looking for ways to do that. We began with point improvements in nonclinical areas, and we discovered that this approach worked. By improving quality and safety, we could and did reduce cost. We also found that we could learn a lot from other industries. We took our time to prove the concept, and, in doing so, we engaged our faculty and staff in the work to a degree that became our strength."

Seattle Children's conducted its first proof-of-concept Rapid Process Improvement Workshop in 1998. Six years later, Hagan went to the board of directors for support of an all-out lean effort. And several years after that, when Seattle Children's reached a plateau in its learning, it began to send physician and operations leaders to study in Japan. At Seattle Children's, the steady and balanced approach went a long way in developing the leadership mind-set and cultural changes which are foundational to many of the case studies described in this book. Their lean mind-set permeates everything they do today from the design and construction of their facilities, to supply chain management, to their research mission. There isn't a part of their enterprise that doesn't think in terms of "continuous performance improvement."

Jim Hereford, the executive vice president of strategic services and quality at Group Health Cooperative, adopted a different strategy, focusing early on transforming the management system. As he puts it, "Anyone can improve a process; that isn't hard. It's getting it to persist and to demonstrate it at scale that is difficult.

It won't work to use old-style management. You have to change the management system."

Like Seattle Children's, Group Health began with point improvements. But after some early struggles and successes, Group Health expanded its efforts in 2005. Executives at the organization realized that it wasn't enough to change processes; they also had to translate strategy into action and transform the work of managers at all levels.

"After our initial comfort level with point improvement, we knew we had to bring this to scale," recalls Hereford. "In order to be truly successful, managers needed to have a different mental model of who they were and what their role was. We became convinced that our vision would be limited if we didn't change our management system."

Today, Group Health incorporates the three elements of a lean management system into their work: strategy deployment (hoshin kanri), cross-functional management, and daily management.

Tammie Brailsford, the COO of MemorialCare, a large hospital system in southern California, took yet another path when MemorialCare began its lean journey in 2007. MemorialCare had a healthy sense of urgency and a leadership team that was willing to take on some risks when they began. The first year, MemorialCare completed seventeen point improvement projects, launched their lean office, launched a value stream, engaged 245 employees in lean events, and realized an economic benefit of $700,000. In their second year, they completed forty-seven improvement projects, launched four more value streams, and engaged 1,823 employees in their lean efforts. While this may seem to be a rapid start-up strategy, Tammie Brailsford and her colleagues were careful to position lean as part of an ongoing organization change, called MC21, that was in place prior to the time that executives were trained in lean principles. MC21 represents the MemorialCare of the future and, with the incorporation of a lean mind-set, methods, and management systems, is on track to deliver $3.4 million in savings by the end of 2010. MemorialCare's goal is to have their costs at or below Medicare reimbursement rates by 2014, a $2,800 reduction per discharge over today's rates.

Whether Seattle Children's evolutionary strategy, Group Health's management system–focused strategy, or MemorialCare's aggressive cost reduction strategy, each of these organizations has thought carefully about the organization's integrated plan to achieve the transformation it is hoping to achieve.

After a strategy is selected, it's essential that a master plan be crafted and adopted. A master plan details how lean technologies will be learned and deployed as well as how the necessary management systems, philosophy, and leadership competencies will be developed—from frontline supervisors to senior executives.

Ultimately, the master plan drives the transformation of a lean enterprise from a "proof of concept" phase to lean as a "management system." With thanks to Malcom Gladwell for his characterization of *the tipping point*, the lean transformation tipping point is shown in Figure 3.5.

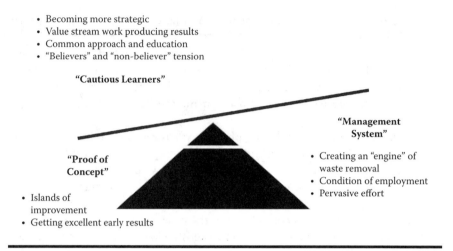

- Becoming more strategic
- Value stream work producing results
- Common approach and education
- "Believers" and "non-believer" tension

"Cautious Learners"

"Management System"

"Proof of Concept"

- Creating an "engine" of waste removal
- Condition of employment
- Pervasive effort

- Islands of improvement
- Getting excellent early results

Figure 3.5 The Tipping Point. Three phases of change characterize the transformation to a lean enterprise. Early learning in the "Proof of Concept" phase captures people's attention to start the journey. The second phase begins the hard work of deeper change with work deep into values streams. In the third phase, "Management System," there is no doubt in anyone's mind that this is the "way we run this place."

The list below emphasizes the systemic nature of this journey and describes each element once the organization has reached the tipping point.

- **Leadership engagement** (executive, upper, and middle management). Lean leadership is a condition of employment and promotion, and incentives are tied to value stream improvement. QCDSE is targeted and tracked for every value stream. Lean is seen as the "right thing to do" for patients, families, staff, and the community.
- **Leadership development**. Lean expertise is central to leadership development, and hospital leaders are required to demonstrate the technical, cultural, and political aspects of change. Succession planning candidates are expected to demonstrate lean leadership and may be asked to rotate into the department supporting lean, often referred to as the "lean resource office."
- **HR system**. Recruitment, orientation, succession planning, perfomance appraisal and development are all integrated into lean initiatives.
- **Financial system**. Accounting is linked to value streams, and all major capital expenditures are subject to lean analysis and improvement prior to authorization. Capital building projects are subject to Integrated Facility Design (see Chapter 19).
- **Operating system**. Daily management and cross-functional management are practiced once the tipping point has been reached. Organization metrics should also reflect flow, including patient routing.

- **Methods and tool integration**. Lean tools and methods are used for virtually all processes and projects within the healthcare organization, and leaders have well-developed skills that enable them to choose the right tools and methods for the right projects and processes.
- **Infrastructure and lean resource office**. A dedicated team of internal experts is well established, primarily internal hires and succession-planning candidates, who rotate into the lean office for 18–24 months. Each of these professionals operate with a common training and framework.
- **Physician engagement**. Physicians see lean as directly tied to long-term clinical and financial success; physician leaders are promoted, in part, on the basis of their lean engagement and success.
- **Board engagement**. The board attends lean training, engages in lean events, and has a long-term view of the importance of continuous improvement work. Directors evaluate CEO candidates for their ability to lead a lean healthcare organization.
- **Patient and family focus**. Patients are involved as full-time participants in lean events and are an important voice in the change process.
- **Supply chain and supplier development.** Suppliers are involved in value stream work throughout the organization. The right supply in the right amount in the right place at the right time is a reality.
- **Pace and intensity of lean effort**. During the "management system" stage, there should usually be 4–8 lean events per month with daily problem solving everywhere
- **Visual systems**. There are visual systems for all value streams, that tie directly to the daily management system.

Implementing lean using a thirteen-component master plan can certainly pave the way for a healthcare organization as it tries to reach the tipping point and transform itself into an improvement engine.

The first sign of progress will be the contagion or attraction to change among staff members. This usually occurs during the "proof-of-concept" phase, when the work yields initial results. In the end, it's very hard to argue with a 50 percent reduction in waste in project after project.

The next eye-opener takes place when there's a basic understanding of what actually constitutes waste. The resulting mobilization of talent, expertise, and energy leads to an even greater removal of waste. This frequently happens during the "cautious learners" stage and leads to serious learning.

Lean healthcare organizations ultimately reach a point of no return, when they can't turn back and the mind-set of staff members has been radically changed. At this juncture, the operational process and principles that drive waste reduction are in place and the hospitals are deeply into the management systems phase.

So many challenges, so much complexity, and a vast amount of ongoing hard work surround this quest for continuous improvement. But, after watching healthcare organizations apply lean principles over the last fifteen years, one realization is fairly clear, and it's simple: leadership in the healthcare industry today can't be effective, and can't help patients, if it's not focused on building high-powered improvement engines.

Chapter 4

What We Need Most We Can't Buy: Leadership and Culture Change Engaging Everyone in a Patient-Focused Culture

Patrick Hagan
President and Chief Operating Officer
Seattle Children's Hospital

Cara Bailey, BA, MBA
Vice President, Continuous Performance Improvement
Seattle Children's Hospital

"We tried this 12 years ago."
"Sounds just like reengineering to me."
"It's a scheme to cut jobs."
"I'm waiting this one out."
"Another flavor of the month…."
"This, too, shall pass."

How often do you hear those remarks whispered in your organization? These are not just the utterances of a skeptical workforce; they are the voices of your culture.

Organizational culture, the way things are done "around here," is the context in which improvement occurs. Culture includes the commonly held beliefs and assumptions about the organization's mission, its hierarchy and power structure, and its tolerance for differences of opinion. It includes stories that are told about its history, its triumphs, and especially how its leaders have behaved in tough times.

It has been widely acknowledged that *culture eats strategy for lunch.* No matter how carefully crafted an organizational strategy is, its culture will enable or hinder the execution of that plan. This is particularly true in the implementation of the management system and philosophy of continuous performance improvement (CPI). Regardless of the state of an organization's culture, it is critical to begin the journey to continuous improvement with a realistic understanding of the beliefs and assumptions defining that culture.

At Seattle Children's Hospital (SCH) we began the quest to understand our culture in 2003, when we engaged the Bard Group, a consulting organization specializing in physician and hospital relations, to help uncover the unwritten "simple rules" that informally define the way things get done at Seattle Children's. After a series of interviews and discussions with faculty physicians and administrative leaders throughout the organization, we uncovered the simple rules at the heart of the culture. The top seven unwritten simple rules identified at Seattle Children's are as follows:

- You're only accountable to your boss or silo—not the institution.
- Value peace: avoid confrontation. Challenging an issue is a personal attack.
- Don't set priorities—everything is a priority.
- New ideas must be fully developed to be considered.
- "Plan-do" is more valued than "check-act."
- Get buy-in for all decisions—participation is required for commitment.
- Add new initiatives without reorganizing the systems and processes upon which they are based.

Imagine the implications of these simple rules on the ability to implement and sustain a continuous improvement strategy! Importantly, once we identified these rules we didn't set out to "break" them. But we did publicize and openly discuss them, and made it clear that they could not be tolerated if we were to be successful.

Changing a Culture

If continuous performance improvement is to create meaningful and sustainable change in an organization, it must be much more than a set of analytical and process improvement tools. CPI must become integrated into the culture of the organization—it must become the new "way we do things around here." It must become the philosophy and management system that guides the short- and long-term management strategy. This means leaders must intentionally take action that will, over time, change the culture.

As described in Chapter 2 and depicted in the Seattle Children's CPI "house," staff engagement is the foundation of continuous performance improvement. The roof of the house represents the ultimate focus of all improvement efforts, patients, and their families. These two concepts, engagement and patient- and family-centered care, shape the work of leaders in crafting a culture capable of meaningful and sustainable improvement.

As leaders at Seattle Children's, we recognized we had cultural challenges to both concepts. Although staff engagement was generally high, as measured by the Gallup Organization's workplace survey, memories of a "reengineering" effort in the early 1990s that resulted in staff layoffs were still strong in the cultural lore of the organization. And although Seattle Children's had been a leader in efforts to understand patient- and family-centered care, feedback from families indicated that there were major service deficiencies. This dissatisfaction was echoed by referring physicians who described significant problems in access, communication, and follow-up, and confusing systems and processes. Although they acknowledged Seattle Children's as the quality leader for pediatric care, survey results demonstrated that access and communication were more important than quality in their decisions on where to refer their patients.

The service culture at Seattle Children's Hospital was accepting of these circumstances—in fact, many families described a staff attitude of "You're lucky to be here; we're well worth the wait." Our quest was to change that to "We're happy to serve you—how soon can you get here?"

Critical Success Factors for Cultural Transformation

Intentionally changing the culture of an organization requires more than leadership commitment—it requires a relentless and unwavering focus on the desired outcomes. Several elements are critical to this cultural transformation, including the following.

Executive and Faculty Leadership

It was the Hospital Steering Committee—the executive and faculty leadership group—that determined the need to uncover the unspoken assumptions (i.e., the simple rules) in Seattle Children's culture that were hindering its progress. This same group studied the philosophy and methodology of continuous performance improvement, and came to understand the leadership rigor and discipline that would be required for its successful development and implementation. And it continues to be executives and faculty leaders together who spearhead the improvement efforts, acting as sponsors and management guidance team members for our improvement work.

Community Physician Participation

As the primary referrers to Seattle Children's Hospital's specialty services, and as members of the medical staff, community physicians cannot be left out of the cultural transformation process. Community physicians provide a critical perspective on the opportunities for improvement, the competitive environment, and the experience of their patients with the care provided. Community physicians should be engaged directly in improvement projects on processes that are important to them, and should be compensated appropriately for their time and effort.

Patient and Family Participation

Hearing the perspective of patients and their families directly during CPI events is the most powerful element in overcoming staff resistance to process change. At first we worried about revealing our "dirty laundry" to patients and families in improvement workshops, but we soon realized they lived with and knew our foibles quite well. We learned not to imagine what our patient and families thought, but to directly ask them. In fact, without the direct involvement of patients and families, a team makes assumptions about what is important to the customer—assumptions that are often misguided if not simply wrong. (See Sidebar 4.1.) We have many examples at Seattle Children's of family involvement that has changed the outcome of a process improvement effort. Appropriately recruiting and preparing patients and families for this role are key to a successful experience. (See Sidebar 4.2.)

SIDEBAR 4.1

DON'T ASSUME YOU KNOW WHAT FAMILIES WANT...

In 2007, a team from the cancer value stream was working on improving chemotherapy start times for patients. The process for admission was lengthy, beginning with patients' visit to the outpatient clinic for blood tests necessary to determine whether their lab values were appropriate to be admitted to the hospital for chemotherapy. Patients who met the appropriate clinical criteria were then admitted to the inpatient cancer unit. During this process, families waited for hours while lab tests were run, reported, and confirmed; chemotherapy orders were written; the inpatient bed was prepared; and medications were prepared and dispensed by pharmacy. Many hours later, and often in the middle of the night, patients received their first dose of chemotherapy. The process had been purposefully designed so that families, particularly those coming from long distances, could accomplish the lab test and then begin the inpatient stay in one visit. The assumption was that families would not want to do the outpatient testing one day, and then return the next day for their inpatient admission. During the improvement workshop, however, families told the team that the one-day process was not as important to them as the ability to predict when they would be admitted, and to reduce the total time spent waiting around the hospital for the next decision to be made. This led the team to develop a two-day process as an alternative: patients could have their lab work and clinical evaluation done one day, then return at an assigned time the next day for admission with their meds made and ready to be administered if they met the clinical criteria. The newly designed process reduced total wait time for families, improved the reliability of chemotherapy start times, and has become the option of choice for families.

SIDEBAR 4.2

Patients and Families Know What's Important—Just Ask Them

Getting an appointment in a timely manner with Seattle Children's specialty providers had been a long-standing problem, due to the limited supply of pediatric specialists and clinic-specific requirements for preappointment screening and patient preparation. In an effort to address this issue, ambulatory service leaders began a series of scheduling improvement workshops to address process barriers to access. One of the first events was to address orthopedics clinic scheduling. One of this team's assumptions was that each patient needed to be carefully screened and matched with the particular subspecialist who might best address the unique patient needs—and that families would want the "perfect appointment," even if they had to wait many weeks to get in to see that provider. When families were interviewed during the improvement event, however, they had a different perspective. They told the team that their first priority was getting into the orthopedics clinic to be seen by a clinician; they wanted to get the cycle of care started, and were more than willing to return to see a specific physician if that was determined to be necessary. This insight led the team to think differently about what constituted the "perfect appointment," enabling them to simplify scheduling rules and open up more appointment slots with a wider variety of providers. Along with other process improvements in the clinic, this change has improved clinic access from twenty-seven to eight days.

Staff and Faculty Engagement

Staff and faculty are often initially skeptical of the power of continuous performance improvement to change their work lives for the better. They've experienced many organizational initiatives over the years, very few of which they remember as being ultimately successful. It is not until they actually participate in a CPI event, working on a process or outcome that is important to them and to their patients, that they begin to believe that CPI can be effective. "Proving the concept" through workshop participation is incredibly compelling and highly effective. It is these staff and faculty members who ultimately and more credibly speak to their colleagues about the benefits of the CPI philosophy and approach. These are the people who begin to change the culture, and indeed begin to clamor for increased use of CPI methodology.

Board Support

If continuous performance improvement is to become the philosophy and management system for the organization, the board must be engaged at many levels. First of all, they must be educated about what CPI is, what the benefits are, and the investment that will be required in terms of organizational infrastructure to support it. Involving board members in workshops and other CPI events is an effective way of showing them firsthand what CPI is about, and gives them a chance to witness the focus on the patient and enthusiasm of the staff. Ultimately, involving the board in its own CPI effort is most powerful, as demonstrated in a governance CPI project at Seattle Children's. (See Sidebar 4.3.)

SIDEBAR 4.3

THE HOSPITAL BOARD APPLIES CPI TO GOVERNANCE

In late 2004, the Governing Board of Seattle Children's realized that its structure and processes were no longer effective in meeting the governance needs of a growing health system. Through a series of retreats, board members concluded that they needed to make some radical changes to enable them to be more efficient and effective in their work, to focus on "value-added" governance work, and to recruit and retain a broader diversity of trustees.

The board members were familiar with the continuous performance improvement philosophy and tools being applied in hospital operations; they had approved the resources to support CPI infrastructure in the organization, and had seen the initial success of the CPI program. Therefore, they wanted to apply the concepts to their own process redesign project, and a governance team was formed to evaluate committee structure, process, and outcomes. Facilitated by Joan Wellman, the group agreed upon design principles which included focusing on governance responsibilities and reducing waste in their processes. The result was a reduction in the number of board committees from forty-two to fifteen, and the average number of committee assignments per trustee from eight to three. Using the quality, cost, delivery, safety, and staff and physician engagement (QCDSE) framework, they added a quality committee, defined consistent staff roles for board support, and implemented clear roles and training for committee chairs. Board member satisfaction with governance effectiveness improved by 84 percent in one year, and they were successful in recruiting a more diverse trustee membership. They continue to plan, do, check, and act (PDCA) their design through ongoing assessments of governance effectiveness.

Financial Investment

Leaders who are committed to transforming the organization into a continuous improvement culture must recognize that the transition will require a substantial financial investment. Initially this means utilizing external consultants, but to be enduring CPI requires the development of internal expertise—one must "learn to fish." Therefore, investing in in-house CPI resources and providing education and training for all leaders and staff are of paramount importance. The investment also includes ensuring that financial incentives throughout the organization are aligned to support CPI. For example, this may mean budgeting for "backfill" costs of staff who are participating in workshops so that individual departments aren't penalized for labor cost variances, as well as ensuring that community physicians and faculty are appropriately compensated for their time spent in CPI activities. The investment is substantial—our board originally approved a $10 million budget over three to five years, and we now invest $6 million per annum ($\approx$ 1% of our operating budget) in CPI.

Infrastructure Support

Continuous performance improvement requires well-trained internal experts who can guide the work at the local level and ensure adherence to the methodology of improvement. In the hospital setting, it also means aligning traditional quality improvement, patient safety, customer service, and staff and leadership development resources with CPI. Our $6 million annual CPI budget encompasses all of these functions and includes a thirty-person CPI department. The long-term goal of these internal experts is to build expertise and improvement capability at the local level, so that this philosophy and methodology are fully integrated into the organization.

Values

Most organizations have an articulated set of values that guide their work, and leaders must tie the continuous improvement philosophy to these core values. This anchors the CPI efforts in something that is familiar and enduring to staff. At Seattle Children's, these values and the behavioral expectations that define them are embodied in an acronym called ART—Accountability, Respect, and Teamwork. Children's leaders and staff refer to ART-ful behavior, in terms of both how they treat each other and how they interact with patients and families. CPI supports their ability to demonstrate these core values in their daily work.

Revealing the Simple Rules

As noted in the first section of this chapter, understanding the current state of your organizational culture is crucial to intentionally transforming it. Making the "simple rules" that describe individual and group behavior obvious enables leaders and staff to hold each other accountable for breaking out of the old patterns.

Stealing Shamelessly

Good ideas come from everywhere, inside or outside the industry, and leaders in continuous improvement should be quick to seek new ways to approach old problems. In most organizations, however, using ideas from outside one's company, let alone outside one's industry, is very difficult. Part of the leadership and then broader cultural transformation of a company is the growing appreciation for the power and value of ideas from "outside." The degree an organization has moved from "not invented here" (i.e., don't learn from others) to a willingness to "steal shamelessly" (i.e., learn from others) is a good measure of the depth of its cultural transformation.

Methods for Cultural Transformation

Beyond these critical success factors at SCH, there have been three key methods important to the success of CPI. Our leaders fit these methods together to create what we call continuous performance improvement.

Learning from Toyota: The Philosophy of Continuous Improvement

As Seattle Children's leaders began to study the Toyota Production System (TPS), and to see the adoption of TPS at local manufacturing sites such as Genie Industries and the Boeing Company, we came to understand that the transformative power of TPS was in the philosophy and system, not just its tools. As

Jeffrey Liker articulates in *The Toyota Way*,[1] Toyota's success is rooted in its business philosophy and approach. Liker has categorized the principles that Toyota embodies into four categories: philosophy, process, people and partners, and problem solving. Unless all of these concepts are addressed systemically, CPI will fulfill the prophecy of the skeptical employee as a "flavor of the month." We have adapted Toyota's thinking into our CPI philosophy, the elements of which are as follows:

- Focus on the patient and family.
- Support our people in their work.
- Take the long-term view.

Learning from the Gallup Organization: Engagement Matters

Seattle Children's began using the Gallup Organization's workplace survey tool and concept of engagement in 2001. Key to this approach is an understanding of the difference between employee satisfaction and employee engagement. Employee satisfaction connotes whether the person is "happy" with a job and the working conditions, whereas engagement is a much richer concept. According to the Gallup Organization's research, engagement is the degree to which the employee is psychologically committed to the organization and its mission, and the overall staff engagement in an organization is predictive of important business outcomes, such as customer satisfaction, profitability, and safety. This concept ties directly to the fundamental principle in the Toyota Production System of supporting the people who are doing the work.

Such support requires a leadership commitment to deeply understand the problems that workers encounter in their daily work lives. This means leaders must be visible in the workplace, and constantly asking what they can do to remove barriers for staff. The focus remains on the patient and family as the "customer," but acknowledges that the care and service provided are direct reflections of the ability of the staff and physicians to get their work done without unnecessary hassle (i.e., waste) in the organization's systems and processes.

Learning from the Studer Group: Hardwiring Matters

Beginning in the late 1990s, Seattle Children's leaders took steps to address the service deficiencies identified by patients, families, and referring physicians, but found sustained success elusive. In 2004, as our continuous performance improvement philosophy was taking shape, we discovered the work of Quint Studer and his colleagues.[2] As senior vice president and COO of Holy Cross Hospital in Chicago, Studer successfully transformed the culture of service from one that was producing patient satisfaction scores in the fifth percentile to one that was achieving satisfaction scores in the ninety-fourth percentile. He then replicated these results as administrator at Baptist Hospital in Pensacola, Florida. Success in service improvement was also reflected in stronger clinical and financial results. Along the way, he discovered several key actions (the Nine Principles[SM]) that, if done consistently, can lead to this kind of organizational transformation. Fundamental to achieving and sustaining these principles and the specific interventions he prescribes is a concept Studer calls "hardwiring." This requires that leadership implement the key concepts in a standard way, and that adherence to these interventions is audited and reported to leadership on an ongoing basis. Only by hardwiring such behaviors does the organizational culture change in a way that will transcend the tenure of a specific leadership team.

At Seattle Children's, we used our learning from the Studer Group to continue building our continuous performance improvement philosophy, leadership expectations, and tools. The principles and actions supported by Studer's research and experience integrate well with the Toyota Production System's focus on the customer, supporting the staff, and creating the standard work and expectations for leadership. The link to the concepts of engagement, as articulated by the Gallup Organization, is also very strong. By integrating these three methods, we have created a robust leadership philosophy that has helped transform our organizational culture.

Tools for Cultural Transformation

Changing the culture to support continuous performance improvement requires the buy-in of a critical mass of those working within the organization. The belief that the CPI philosophy and management system works requires experiencing it at the individual and work group levels—something that can be achieved only through direct involvement in continuous performance improvement initiatives and education.

Participating in CPI Activities and Experiencing Results

There is no substitute for direct involvement in CPI activities, such as rapid process improvement workshops, process design events, value stream mapping, A3 problem solving, and 5S events. Well-designed CPI initiatives address issues that are important to the staff working within the process, are well scoped, and have measurable targets. Participants represent all roles in the process, and management supports their active involvement in the improvement effort. In these activities, a didactic review of concepts is integrated with process walks and analysis, and enables integration of theory and practice for participants. Most importantly, well-scoped and executed events enable participants to achieve the targets and experience success in a time frame not possible without CPI methodology.

Participating in CPI activities enables staff and physicians to directly experience the power of the rapid improvement methodology. However, even those in the work area who are not directly involved in workshops are engaged in the improvement activity and given the opportunity for input into process design during the course of the CPI event through tie-in meetings and feedback sessions during implementation. Following CPI principles, the targets and outcomes for events should be visible to all staff working in the area. A successful event is noticeable to staff and physicians because it produces a visible improvement for patients and/or makes the work easier or less complex for staff. Experiencing results that matter to patients, families, and staff engenders support for the CPI philosophy and its role in the organization.

Learning Strategies

Although direct participation in CPI activities is the best way to engage people throughout the organization in the methodology, events must be supported by the overall learning strategy. Continuous performance improvement concepts are new to most people in healthcare, and specific learning experiences that cover these topics build the foundation for spreading the knowledge throughout the organization. These strategies should include both didactic and experiential elements, and should be designed in accordance with adult learning principles.

Human Resource Systems

Human resource systems must be designed to support CPI as the organizational philosophy and management system. This means that CPI should be integrated into recruitment, orientation, development, and performance management within the organization. Becoming proficient with CPI concepts and embracing the philosophy are key to advancement, and leadership development tracks are designed with CPI at the core.

At Seattle Children's, there are several examples of how CPI is being incorporated into human resource systems. Willingness to embrace the CPI philosophy has become an integral part of faculty recruitment; all leaders are expected to participate in CPI leader training, and CPI is an explicit part of leader performance evaluations.

Leadership in a Continuous Performance Improvement Culture

Organizational culture is always evolving; whether that evolution is positive or negative is dependent on the actions of its leaders. To truly transform organizational culture to embrace continuous performance improvement, leaders must intentionally behave in ways that support the philosophy of focusing on the patient and family, engaging staff and physicians as partners, and taking a long-term view. The most important leadership behaviors are described below.

Leadership Presence

Two tenets of the CPI philosophy relate to leadership presence: (1) improvement occurs not in the conference room, but where the work is being done; and (2) supporting staff doing the work is essential to improving the care experience for patients and families. In order to support these tenets, leaders must regularly go to the place the work is being done, observe the key processes, and engage staff in understanding the barriers and enablers within the processes. Leaders can't develop this understanding by sitting in their offices, or merely hearing reports about progress and challenges. They must be visible, interactive, and supportive. Leadership presence at the work site is not, however, about micromanagement. It is about setting clear expectations at all levels, and then supporting the next level of leadership and staff to achieve the goals.

Knowledge

Leaders become teachers of the continuous performance improvement philosophy and concepts, and in order to do that, they must first become students. CPI concepts are both elegantly simple and, at the same time, difficult to integrate into the fabric of the organization. Therefore, CPI leaders are on a long-term path to develop and deepen their understanding of the CPI philosophy and methodology.

Leadership Participation

Leaders in an organization that embraces CPI must actively participate in improvement activities, serving as sponsors, management guidance team members, or participants. This participation serves several purposes. First of all, it reinforces the CPI concepts of support for those doing the work and understanding the work through direct involvement and observation. As importantly, direct participation in CPI activities is the best way to deepen the leaders' understanding of the CPI concepts and their application within the processes for which they are responsible. And it demonstrates clearly that "we're all in this together."

Tenacity

Intentionally changing organizational culture is very hard work and takes many years to accomplish. Resistance to this change comes in many forms—some blatant, most much more subtle. Leaders who commit to the cultural transformation the CPI philosophy demands must be prepared to continually recognize, confront, and overcome that resistance. To those who say, "This too shall pass," leaders must reply, "Resistance is futile."

Patience

Adopting the continuous performance improvement philosophy and management system is long-term, generational work. One of the counterintuitive aspects of this philosophy is that it must be based on a sense of urgency to drive improvement, every day, at all levels of the organization. Yet that urgency must be tempered with the understanding that dysfunctional processes, systems, and culture did not evolve overnight, and that sustainable improvement will, likewise, take time. It will be the ongoing work of leadership. Therefore, the tenacity to push through resistance must be coupled with patience, and the conviction that transformational change is only evident over the long term. Studying companies that have been implementing continuous performance improvement for many years, indeed generations, bears this out.

Implications for Leadership Development

Successfully transforming organizational culture to support a continuous performance improvement philosophy depends on effective leadership. As described above, many of the required leadership competencies and behaviors in a CPI management system are quite different than those required in a more traditional work setting. The leadership development strategy, therefore, must also be tailored to foster, model, and reward the new behaviors. The leadership learning should be intentionally designed and cascaded throughout the organization.

At Seattle Children's, CPI learning activities began with the executive and faculty leadership group, and included reading, lecture, discussion, and experiences at local manufacturing sites that had successfully implemented CPI. Through dialogue with leaders from these manufacturing sites, we learned not only key concepts but also what it takes to truly lead in an organization that embraces CPI. We learned firsthand about the importance of our presence, participation, knowledge, tenacity, and patience. These experiences served to provide us with the information we needed to commit to the cultural transformation it would take to make CPI the organizational philosophy.

The long-term leadership development strategy at Seattle Children's is to build CPI capability at all levels of the organization. Our leadership development strategy includes a mix of experiential and didactic activities designed to deepen understanding of CPI concepts. Over time, leaders are expected to develop the skills necessary to engage in basic problem solving using these concepts. As the leaders progress in their skill development, they are able to coach others and to lead more complex CPI activities. (See Figure 4.1.)

As we continue to build our CPI management system, leadership competencies necessary for success in our transformed organization will be iteratively redefined to reflect the role of leader as teacher, coach, and mentor. Integrated into leader recruitment, selection, development, and succession planning, these

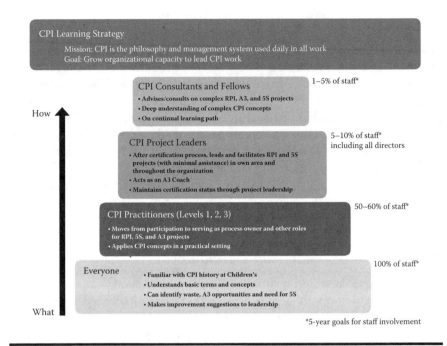

Figure 4.1 CPI Learning Strategy. Continuous performance improvement for all levels of the organization—a look at the core competencies at every level.

competencies will form the basis for leadership expectations at SCH as over time we become incrementally more sophisticated at continuously improving our performance.

Conclusion

The continuous performance improvement philosophy requires taking a long-term view, and nowhere is this more evident than in the work needed to shape organizational culture. The good news is that culture is constantly evolving; the work of leadership in an organization committed to CPI, then, is to take action to *intentionally* shape that culture. We've learned at Seattle Children's that, by getting clinical and executive leadership buy-in, understanding and building on our current culture, and holding a vision of what it needs to look like, we are truly beginning to transform the "way things are done around here."

Notes

1. Jeffrey Liker, *The Toyota Way* (New York: McGraw-Hill, 2003), 6.
2. Quint Studer, *Hardwiring Excellence: Purpose, Worthwhile Work, Making a Difference* (Gulf Breeze, FL: Fire Starter Publishing, 2004).

Chapter 5

Transforming Doctors into Change Agents

Jeffrey Avansino, MD
Department of Surgery, Division of Pediatric General and Thoracic Surgery
Seattle Children's Hospital

Ken Gow, MD
Department of Surgery, Division of Pediatric General and Thoracic Surgery
Seattle Children's Hospital

Darren Migita, MD
Department of Medicine
Seattle Children's Hospital

Dr. P is a new intern on the pediatric hematology-oncology service. It is his third day on this service and only his second month as a resident. Dr. P is thus still learning the ins and outs of the hospital. Having just finished rounds, he is trying to prioritize the many tasks he has to complete in the next few hours prior to evening sign-out.

One of Dr. P's patients is a new admission for leukemia. During rounds, Dr. P was asked by his attending to make sure the patient received a central line in the next 24–48 hours so that therapy could be initiated without delay. With little guidance, Dr. P set out to accomplish this task.

After talking with the scheduler, the surgical resident informed Dr. P that the patient would not receive the line for a full week. Dr. P related this scheduling delay to the team the following day on rounds. Despite a call from the attending, the line still could not be placed sooner due to scheduling in the operating room.

Dr. P was now sent on a second mission, when he tried to obtain a peripherally inserted central venous catheter (PICC) line. This task was even more daunting and confusing than the first. A nurse was available to place the line, and an interventional radiologist was able to do the procedure, but a general anesthetic was required.

Dr. P called the line nurse to evaluate the patient; the nurse, in turn, felt that the line placement would be an appropriate task for the interventional radiologist, who was willing to put the line in the next day.

Circuitously, then, the patient finally received a PICC line—a full two days after the decision for PICC insertion was made. And five days later, the general surgery team was able to find the patient a time slot on the operating room (OR) schedule, and a tunneled central venous catheter was placed.

Within a week, the patient had two procedures and received two anesthetics, ultimately receiving the definitive procedure a whole week after it was initially requested. These system, communication, and scheduling challenges are unfortunately all too common in clinical scenarios.

Providers, especially those who have been practicing a while, typically know how to navigate the convoluted system by circumventing the roadblocks and using back doors to get things accomplished. Obviously, this process for getting things done is disturbingly variable and unreliable, and it's highly dependent on the people, services, expertise, and circumstances involved. Such variability inevitably leads to inconsistent, unpredictable results with frustration ensuing all around. In the wake of this shaky process, teamwork too often dissolves, and providers find themselves losing their focus on patient care.

Clearly, this confusing process begged for change and improvement. And our response to this challenge demonstrates how the impetus behind our continuous performance improvement (CPI) efforts has been to enrich the lives of our patients, enhance the efficiency of delivery of care, and ensure quality and safety.

In 2005, Seattle Children's Hospital decided to map out the line placement process, or value stream. A group of general pediatric physicians, nurses, residents, surgeons, and anesthesiologists gathered together for three days to review the current state of this process and lay out a plan of action. Not surprisingly, each discipline had its "story" about how difficult it was to get this work done. The conversations were emotional and often difficult, but no one ever lost sight of the fact that patients deserved better and that physicians and staff needed relief from the stress exemplified by Dr. P's story.

An analysis of the current process conducted by this team found that, at most, only 15 percent of the time staff and physicians were spending trying to get lines placed for patients was "value added" to the patient; the rest was wasted time and resources that did nothing to advance patients' care. In response to these findings, the team outlined their "ideal state" for vascular access and went to work chartering projects that would become the improvement roadmap for line placement at Seattle Children's.

Two of the many projects completed are discussed below. Both projects began with Rapid Process Improvement Workshops (RPIWs), five-day events with full-time participation of physicians, nurses, and administrative managers.

Many physicians will say that they are just too busy to get involved. In an academic institution, the division of time among clinical, research, and academic duties makes physicians reluctant to add more to their overloaded plates. Others have been practicing medicine "their way" for decades, and change represents a threat to their tried-and-true method of delivering care. In addition, the very physicians who have the actual power to make change are likely far removed from the daily challenges faced by our intern, Dr. P, in the example above. As a result, these physicians might not recognize the need or urgency to change existing processes.

So how does a provider take up the reins and surmount these obstacles to deliver effective change?

The examples below illustrate two change processes surrounding the governance of PICCs and a reduction of lead time in the scheduling of surgically placed tunneled central venous catheters. Both of these stories encompass many of the CPI principles described elsewhere in this book. What this narrative is really about is creating, implementing, and embedding change in the intrinsic fabric of our healthcare institution.

Case Study 1

A PICC is a type of central venous catheter (CVC) that was developed in 1975 to provide a secure method of administering intravenous medications to patients in both inpatient and outpatient settings. PICCs differ from peripheral IVs (PIVs) in that they are longer, and terminate in the large vessels close to the heart. Due to their "central" location, these catheters are more secure and, oftentimes, obviate the need for repeated needle sticks for blood draws or frequent replacement that commonly occurs when more ephemeral PIVs are used. Additionally, total parenteral nutrition (TPN), which takes place when the patient is fed intravenously and no food is given by other routes, can be administered in higher concentrations when a catheter is located centrally. PICCs can be placed at the patient's bedside with less need for sedation than more invasive surgically placed catheters.

The convenience of PICCs led to a dramatic increase in their usage soon after their introduction. However, as the medical community gained more experience with these devices, we learned that PICCs are not without significant complications. Up to 50 percent of PICCs require radiological guided insertion techniques requiring anesthesia, 0.7 percent experience fracture of the line, 7 percent become occluded, and 58 percent migrate 20 mm or more from their original placement. Other complications include deep venous thrombosis, vessel rupture, and catheter-associated bloodstream infections (CABSIs). Between 30 and 46 percent of all PICCs are removed due to a complication prior to the completion of therapy.[1]

Given that nearly eighty thousand CVC-associated bloodstream infections (BSIs) occur in intensive care units each year in the United States, that the reported mortality from a CABSI may be as high as 12–25 percent, and that central line infections are far more likely than PIV infections (2 percent versus 0.04 percent), placing a PICC can no longer be considered a benign procedural intervention.[1]

At Seattle Children's Hospital, we were faced with three major issues surrounding PICC lines: infection, overutilization, and confusion regarding the PICC-ordering process. These problems were all rooted in the same fundamental issue—failure to standardize work methods.

In order to eliminate wasted time and energy, increase the margin of safety for our patients, and establish a new baseline for continued improvement, we needed to draw upon the principals of standardization, error proofing, waste reduction, and andons, which are lights that serve as visual signals.

Keeping these principals in mind, this endeavor was subdivided into four key projects:

- Six questions to ask each day for patients who have a CVC[1]
- PICC clinical criteria—the creation of insertion standards for PICCs[1] (See Table 5.1)
- Creation of a vascular access service (VAS) from preexisting staff[1]
- Creation of a PICC order set[1]

Completion of these projects resulted in a sustained 33.4 percent reduction in PICC placements, as well as improved provider satisfaction with the ordering process as measured on a Likert scale (See Figure 5.1). The data also show that overall provider satisfaction scores increased from 2.68 out of 5 to 3.55 out of 5 over a nine-month period.[1]

Central catheters require day-to-day management; if this does not occur, they may be retained for longer than necessary, thus increasing patient risk. Moreover, opening the line to administer intermittent medications or to draw blood further increases the potential for infection. Since each day that a patient has a central catheter represents a day of risk, our mission was to standardize the daily attention paid to central catheters.

To support this process, six questions were reproduced on daily progress notes in the intensive care units (ICUs) in a checklist format. In addition, medical unit RNs were required to give a synopsis of their patients' central lines on intake forms as well as on daily progress notes. The six key daily questions were as follows:

1. Can the line be removed?[1]
2. Can we change intravenous medications to oral?[1]
3. Can the patient be fed enterally (i.e., no TPN)?[1]
4. Can we decrease blood draws?[1]
5. Can we bundle tubing changes with blood draws?[1]
6. What does the dressing look like today?[1]

Table 5.1   Peripherally Inserted Central Venous Catheter (PICC) Criteria

Indication for Placement	Criteria	Rationale
General	Use peripheral IVs (PIVs) whenever possible. Medically complex patient requiring central venous access—decide on PICC placement early. Patient requires home IV therapy. Documentation of long-term vascular access plan required.	Central venous catheters (CVCs) increase the risk of bloodstream infections (BSIs). An infected PIV is easier to identify than an infected CVC. An infected CVC carries a greater risk of complication than an infected PIV. Documentation of long-term vascular access plan facilitates site preservation.
Total parenteral nutrition (TPN)	Anticipated duration of TPN use > 3 days.	TPN is an independent risk for infection.
Antibiotics	Antibiotic therapy ≥ 7 days from placement of PICC.	The risk of CVC infection outweighs the benefits of short-term PICC usage for antibiotics.
Chemotherapy	Selected standard risk acute lymphocytic leukemia (ALL). Oncology patients: Unable to schedule a surgical central line.	Multiple infusions and blood draws during chemotherapy. Avoidance of surgical line placement, especially during steroid dosing.
Vasopressors	Acceptable for unstable patients in intensive care unit (ICU) settings.	Intermittent temporary need for central venous access.
Anticipated need for hemodialysis.		
Contraindications to PICC Placement		
Do not place PICC for TPN if the patient can be fed enterally or if peripheral parenteral nutrition can be used.		
Do not use PICC for antibiotics that have a good oral availability (e.g., Clindamycin, Rifampin, Flagyl, or Cipro).		

(continued)

Table 5.1   Peripherally Inserted Central Venous Catheter (PICC) Criteria (Continued)

Indication for Placement	Criteria	Rationale
Documented bacteremia or high suspicion of bacteremia requires 72 hours of negative cultures (2 separate complications, 24 hours apart, and at least 24 hours of maturity in the lab) prior to PICC placement. (For selected populations, this may not be possible.)		

Source: Darren Migita, Ken Gow, and Jeff Avansino, "Transforming Doctors into Change Agents," *American Academy of Pediatrics* (April 1, 2009): 1155–61. Reproduced with permission from *Pediatrics* 123:1157–61. Copyright © 2009 by the AAP.

Prior to this work, PICCs were an unregulated procedural intervention. There were no standards for their placement and it was not uncommon for a PICC to be placed—only to be removed a few days later. In these cases, the patient was exposed to all the above-mentioned risks of a central catheter when a simple PIV would have sufficed. This, in itself, was viewed as an error of clinical management.

By convening a panel of local experts, we were able to achieve consensus on specific criteria for PICC placement. Members of this team included interventional radiologists, general surgeons, infectious disease experts, nurses, and pediatric hospitalists. Specific contraindications for PICCs, based on the best available medical

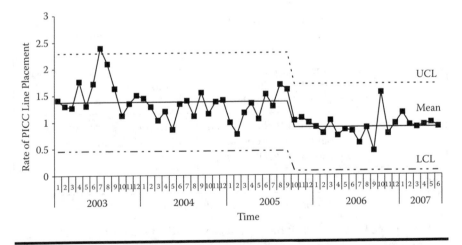

Figure 5.1   Peripherally inserted central venous catheter (PICC) volumes. Rate of PICC line placement per 100 census days. *Source:* **Darren Migita, Ken Gow, and Jeff Avansino, "Transforming Doctors into Change Agents,"** *American Academy of Pediatrics* **(April 1, 2009): 1155–61. Reproduced with permission from** *Pediatrics* **123:1157–61. Copyright © 2009 by the AAP.**

evidence, were also identified and compiled. Although achieving consensus was a somewhat arduous process, gaining general agreement proved to be a critical factor during the implementation stage of these criteria. In creating consensus, the vital groundwork for change was established, and the substance of change in this case was the implementation of a new reliable work standard.

From a patient's perspective, the PICC clinical criteria were constructed to help ensure that PICCs were placed when the benefits outweighed the risks. Patients who did not meet these criteria would instead be candidates for PIVs.

Prior to this work, PICCs were ordered via computerized physician order entry (CPOE) and placed by either interventional radiology (IR) or an RN-staffed "IV team." The ordering provider was responsible for determining the mode of insertion (IR versus bedside), contacting the proceduralist, coordinating PICC placement with other procedures requiring anesthesia, and coordinating care directly with the patient's primary nurse.

Significant dissatisfaction with the protracted PICC-ordering process resulted. Moreover, given that Seattle Children's is a busy teaching hospital, completion of this multitude of tasks in a timely manner was often difficult. Trainees might be unfamiliar with navigating a complex system, which, in turn, would lead to delays, errors, and dissatisfaction. In short, waste abounded in the forms of rework, waiting, and complexity.[1]

To target these problems, we created a vascular access service (VAS) composed of seven RNs whose function was to place PICCs and coordinate the above-mentioned maze of tasks. These nurses were previously part of the RN-staffed IV team, and the creation of the VAS did not require adding new people.[1]

The VAS is now automatically notified by pager once an order has been placed via CPOE, thus ensuring that the process begins in a timely fashion. By centralizing this work within a small group, individual variation was markedly reduced, and the maintenance of the new standard work method was preserved. The VAS fulfills the requirements of a reliable method—the PICC placement process was consciously developed, always followed, and clearly owned, and had a strong foundation for continued future improvement.

The CPOE-based PICC order set (See Figure 5.2) unifies the work of the projects discussed above. The order set contains the data the VAS needs to verify that placement meets criteria, to insure there are no contraindications to placement, to avoid placement in certain extremities, and to coordinate PICC placement with other procedures requiring anesthesia. This computerized order set cannot be signed unless all required fields are completed—a vital error-proofing measure.

Because the VAS reviews each PICC request and proceeds to placement only if criteria are met and no contraindications are present, the order set serves as an andon that warns of a potential clinical error. The VAS also has the authority to hold a PICC placement by "stopping the line," thereby preventing an error from becoming a more serious and entrenched defect. The response to the andon is graded, too. And if the VAS staff member cannot resolve the issue by inserting a PIV rather than

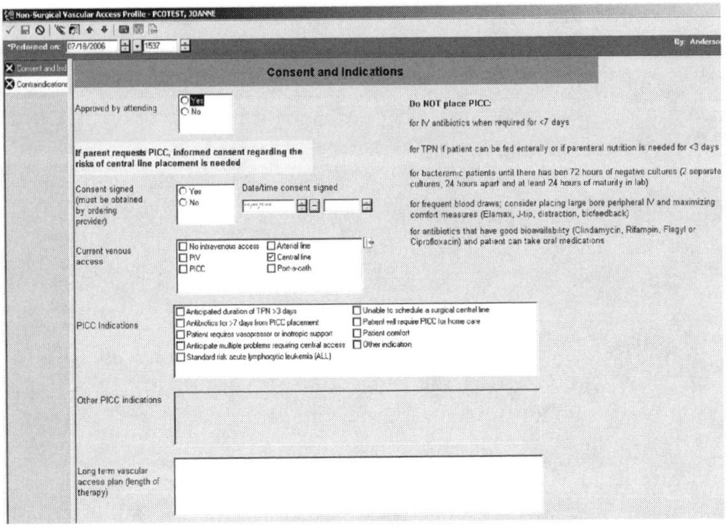

Non-Surgical Vascular Access Profile - PCOTEST, JOANNE

*Performed on: 07/18/2006 1537

By: Anderso

Consent and Ind

Contraindications

Consent and Indications

Approved by attending — Yes / No

If parent requests PICC, informed consent regarding the risks of central line placement is needed

Consent signed (must be obtained by ordering provider) — Yes / No

Date/time consent signed

Current venous access — No intravenous access; PIV; PICC; Arterial line; Central line; Port-a-cath

PICC Indications — Anticipated duration of TPN >3 days; Antibiotics for >7 days from PICC placement; Patient requires vasopressor or inotropic support; Anticipate multiple problems requiring central access; Standard risk acute lymphocytic leukemia (ALL); Unable to schedule a surgical central line; Patient will require PICC for home care; Patient comfort; Other indication

Other PICC indications

Long term vascular access plan (length of therapy)

Do NOT place PICC:

for IV antibiotics when required for <7 days

for TPN if patient can be fed enterally or if parenteral nutrition is needed for <3 days

for bacteremic patients until there has ben 72 hours of negative cultures (2 separate cultures, 24 hours apart and at least 24 hours of maturity in lab)

for frequent blood draws; consider placing large bore peripheral IV and maximizing comfort measures (Elamax, J-tip, distraction, biofeedback)

for antibiotics that have good bioavailability (Clindamycin, Rifampin, Flagyl or Ciprofloxacin) and patient can take oral medications

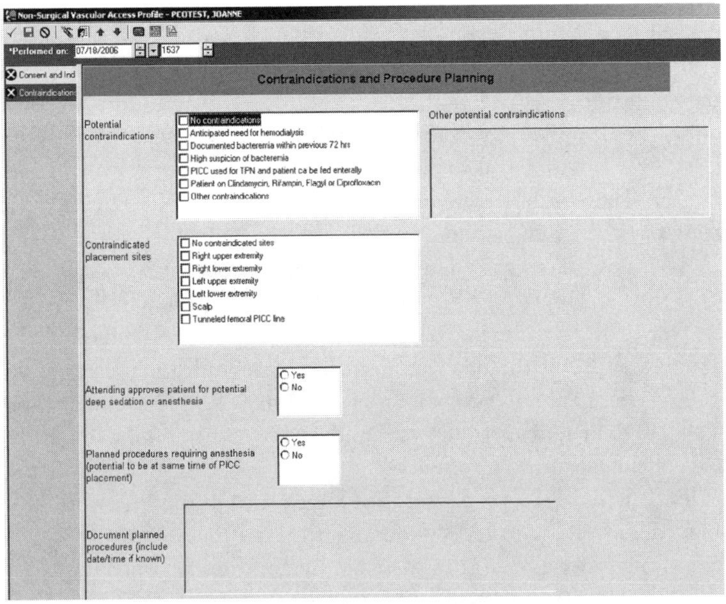

Non-Surgical Vascular Access Profile - PCOTEST, JOANNE

*Performed on: 07/18/2006 1537

Consent and Ind

Contraindications

Contraindications and Procedure Planning

Potential contraindications — No contraindications; Anticipated need for hemodialysis; Documented bacteremia within previous 72 hrs; High suspicion of bacteremia; PICC used for TPN and patient ca be fed enterally; Patient on Clindamycin, Rifampin, Flagyl or Ciprofloxacin; Other contraindications

Other potential contraindications

Contraindicated placement sites — No contraindicated sites; Right upper extremity; Right lower extremity; Left upper extremity; Left lower extremity; Scalp; Tunneled femoral PICC line

Attending approves patient for potential deep sedation or anesthesia — Yes / No

Planned procedures requiring anesthesia (potential to be at same time of PICC placement) — Yes / No

Document planned procedures (include date/time if known)

Figure 5.2 PICC order set. The PICC placement order set directs the physician to provide the minimal necessary information the vascular access service (VAS) requires to place the PICC. *Source*: Darren Migita, Ken Gow, and Jeff Avansino, "Transforming Doctors into Change Agents," *American Academy of Pediatrics* (April 1, 2009): 1155–61. Reproduced with permission from *Pediatrics* 123:1157–61. Copyright © 2009 by the AAP.

a PICC, the case is escalated to either the medical director of line management or to the RN director of VAS, one of whom is available at all times.[1]

Case Study 2

One of the problems that arose at Seattle Children's was that services referring patients to general surgery felt that the lead time for inserting a tunneled central line was too long. As a result, an unnecessary number of patients were having PICCs placed so that therapy could be initiated as quickly as possible. However, since PICCs are not meant for long-term access, this process routinely led to a second procedure that inserted a more permanent form of IV access—again exposing the patient to infection and catheter-site issues.

The general surgery division saw this as an opportunity to address long-standing issues related to scheduling tunneled central lines; it was also an opportunity to provide a better level of service to the referral groups and, ultimately, to our patients.

In reviewing the salient data, we noted that the average lead time from central catheter order to central catheter placement was eight days. After identifying the processes that resulted in the current eight-day lead time, we created a guiding coalition of various representatives involved with the catheter placement process (referring services, schedulers, surgeons, and nurses). Together, we were able to distinguish steps in the process that were crucial and provided value for the patient from those that were redundant and/or did not provide value. We then brainstormed and explored strategies to improve the process with the explicit goal of reducing lead time.

We agreed to revise the line order sheet, to improve the mechanisms for request handling, and to broaden access for line insertion in the operating room schedule. For example, we asked the referring service to specify the type of line that would be needed on the order sheet. This would prevent placement of the incorrect type of line, which could result in a second procedure.

Once the new process was delineated, it was rapidly implemented with a concomitant period of observation to assess for positive change. This postimplementation assessment is critical to measuring success and fine-tuning the new process.

Fortunately, after the changes were implemented, the lead time to insertion of a central venous catheter was reduced from an average of eight days to six days over the next year. This was studied the following year and, as the next few pages will explain, significant improvement was made (See Figure 5.3).

Also, as a likely result of the improved process for scheduling surgically placed central venous catheters, the percentage of PICCs lines placed in patients was strikingly reduced from 78 percent to 15 percent. And, equally important, the referral services considered the changes an important improvement for their patients. In fact,

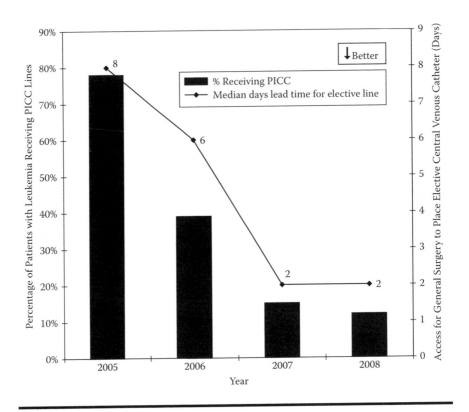

Figure 5.3   Reduction in percentage of patients receiving PICC lines, and reduced lead times for placement of tunneled central venous line. An improved process for scheduling surgically placed central venous catheters is the leading influence of the reduction in PICC lines placed in patients. *Source*: Darren Migita, Ken Gow, and Jeff Avansino, "Transforming Doctors into Change Agents," *American Academy of Pediatrics* (April 1, 2009): 1155–61. Reproduced with permission from *Pediatrics* 123:1157–61. Copyright © 2009 by the AAP.

everyone involved in the CPI work agreed that these changes were a marked improvement over the original process. Finally, because a diverse coalition was involved in designing and implementing the new process, all participants felt invested.

Easier access to the OR for catheter insertions was considered a success, but this also increased pressure to find extra time within an already crowded operating room schedule. Also, with a more urgent need for catheters, a concern arose that the necessary operative information for the attending surgeon would be lost in the flurry. But there is no need to choose between rapid delivery of services and providing quality care. By developing a system that works for everyone, we can have the best of both worlds.

In addition, we originally thought that the degree of need for line insertion could be ascertained in a speedy consult-type fashion. But standard consults require patients to be seen in clinic or in the hospital by either the surgeon or a physician extender, so we agreed that this step would add unnecessary lead time.

This provided an opportunity to eliminate waste by shifting the responsibility for a patient's preoperative management (such as transfusions of platelets or packed red blood cell levels and addressing neutropenia) to the referring team. Structured this way, the patient continues to be cared for by the original team with the most intimate knowledge about him or her. This also means that parents don't receive mixed messages—something that often happens when pediatric patients are handed off to another team.

Another working group was brought together to respond to scheduling issues that were hindering the placement of surgical central lines in the operating room. Ideally, an increase in operating room time would solve this problem, but this wasn't possible because of limitations in available operating rooms and time allocated in the OR to individual surgeons (block time). So the challenge was to try to do more with the same amount of time.

Many of these issues came to light in our discussions.

First, in looking at the average number of central venous line requests in a week, we saw that this matched up with the number of block times available to the surgeons. This provided the surgical team with the option to "level-load" central line insertions so that each surgeon would be performing a similar number of line placements (and so that one surgeon was not placing all of the lines), while the number of line placements would be evenly distributed over the course of a week.

This even distribution is essential because central line insertion always requires additional components that must be available, including fluoroscopy, a radiology technologist, and appropriate operating room staff. As a result, we established that each block time in the operating room would reliably reserve one slot for possible line insertions, effectively planning for the unplanned.

Second, the line insertion requests had always been held up by the need to schedule this with the family. While most of the contact numbers were correct, this was not always the case. Also, many parents were non–English speaking, so time was routinely required to secure appropriate translators. In addition, some families had to be called several times before a date for surgery could be established.

All of these areas of delay were identified as waste that needed to be eliminated.

In discussing how to reduce this lead time, it was agreed that an online calendar should be created to indicate "open" OR time for central venous procedures (either insertion or removals). The referral services would be granted permission a priori by the surgery division to schedule patients at the precise date that the line was deemed necessary. This improvement quickly reduced lead time for scheduling. And families knew the date of the surgery right away, before leaving the referral service's offices. Also, by placing the scheduling responsibility back with the referral services—the providers who knew the patients best—they were empowered to decide which patient had priority when more than one patient was initially assigned to the same date. This removed the attending surgeon from the awkward role of "referee" for patient priority. The net result is that each of these improvements successfully leads to greater overall satisfaction for every player: the referral services, families, schedulers, and surgeons.

Third, by bringing together everyone involved in scheduling a case, the group discovered that much of the scheduling communication that typically occurred was, in fact, redundant. For example, the attending surgeon received information from two different sources: a central venous access device (CVAD) sheet and a separate form that one of the divisions was also using for requesting lines. In tracking this second form, the group found that it was not providing additional value-added information, and that it might lead to confusion if it didn't fully match the information on the other form. By eliminating this redundancy, the CVAD emerged as the only form that was necessary. The unique information on the second form was added to the CVAD form to augment and optimize it. The form was then finalized and placed in a central online site for universally easy access. The form, completed by the requesting team, was sent to the surgeon so it could be viewed prior to the scheduled date of procedure, thereby allowing time to sort out any issues that might need clarification.

In summary, we were able to solve several catheter-scheduling issues very quickly and effectively by looking at areas of waste and choosing to focus on opportunities. By providing the referral services with the ability to schedule cases for their own patients, we provided them with an increased sense of empowerment. Also, because they were able to choose dates for surgery, they were better able to coordinate overall patient care (timing of chemotherapy, timing of radiotherapy, timing for diagnostic imaging, stem cell harvest, and optimizing surgery to time based on blood levels).

This empowerment created a sense of ownership by the referral services. It also highlighted the power of flexibility since the referral services were being asked to perform several steps of scheduling that had been previously performed by surgery scheduling. In addition, because the cases were more "level loaded," schedulers had a much-reduced need to ration resources for the procedures. For the patients, referral services, and operative services, all of these changes were perceived as a resounding "win–win–win." And, as a demonstration of this success, we found that after implementing the new process, the overall satisfaction rate among referral services rose impressively from 49 percent to 71 percent.

The ability to implement or embed change like this is inevitably the result of a committed team that is involved in the process. And paramount to successful outcomes are the people who lead that team in the change process.

The physician leaders in the narrative above followed a series of process steps and successfully generated change. The first step was the creation of a sense of urgency. The scenario involving our intern, Dr. P, was not uncommon. The long lead times in placement of tunneled central lines resulted in aggravating and alarming delays in patient care. These delays were responsible for causing the placement of three times as many PICC lines as were actually needed. Deleterious issues surrounding PICC lines were also indentified and included infection, overutilization, and confusion regarding PICC line orders. These problems all stemmed from a lack of standard work; together, they provided the urgent motivation for the change process.

The second step was forging a group that has the power to create change, and that is supported and championed all the way up the chain of command. Equally important is the involvement of the people closest to the process being changed. In both examples, the group is composed of local experts involved in the process being changed.

Once this group is formed, it must create the vision of change and develop a strategic path. That is step three. In the second example above, the vision of the division of pediatric general and thoracic surgery was to reduce the lead time for scheduling tunneled CVCs. The guiding coalition mapped out a strategic plan that included creating a single new line request form, transferring the scheduling of catheter placement to the referring services, identifying and reserving a fixed number of OR blocks for catheter placement scheduling, and developing an easily accessible online calendar.

The fourth step in the process was to communicate the vision of change that has been established. In our case, this was successfully done by examining PICC utilization. A PICC checklist was incorporated in the providers' daily rounds, and this promoted and ensured increased awareness among users of the system. Eventually, a computer-based order set for PICC line requests was created, which served as both an education and communication tool.

Once the desired change is outlined and the vision communicated, the fifth step involved amending the current system to eliminate any barriers to change. The division of pediatric general and thoracic surgery, for example, allowed patients in need of central lines to bypass the typical surgical consult in clinic or in the hospital prior to scheduling the procedure. This systems revision opened the way for achieving the ultimate goal of reducing lead time. Yet the goal of reducing lead time is never-ending; every improvement requires even greater improvement on the journey toward best practices.

Thus, the sixth step encouraged the team to design short-term wins that reassure larger audiences that the change process is, in fact, working. This fuels momentum and keeps the team engaged in the process. For example, after the creation of a line order sheet to request a surgically placed line, lead time was reduced 25 percent over the first year. With additional changes, a 75 percent reduction was achieved the following year (See Figure 5.3).

In addition to building credibility and drawing more people into the process, these short-term wins provide stepping stones for further projects and greater refinement. And, as the sixth step made clear, the short-term gains also act as a springboard for change on a larger scale. For instance, the creation of a sixth vital sign (discussing central line status) in the pediatric intensive care unit (PICU) eventually evolved into a hospital-wide, consensus-based pathway embedded into the daily workflow of all providers.

As more people are brought into the improvement process, they are empowered through involvement. They come to realize that each team member offers something valuable and unique to the change process. Using this bottom-up approach, people who might otherwise not have a chance to provide input become leaders in their group. They gain confidence in their abilities to lead change and, ultimately, to teach it to others. Eventually, a self-perpetuating cycle is created in which processes are improved and new leadership is developed.

This cycle of energetic change—the seventh step—will gain robust momentum, making it nearly impossible to derail. And it is at this point that continuous performance improvement is successfully anchored in the culture of the organization.

Note

1. Darren Migita, Ken Gow, and Jeff Avansino, "Transforming Doctors into Change Agents," *American Academy of Pediatrics* (April 1, 2009): 1155–61. Reproduced with permission from *Pediatrics* 123:1157–61. Copyright © 2009 by the AAP.

Chapter 6

Clinician Engagement: CPI Applied in a Not-So-Touchy-Feely Environment

Bryan King, MD
Director, Psychiatry and Behavioral Medicine
Seattle Children's Hospital

Ruth Benfield, RN, MS, FACHE
Vice President, Medical Psycho-Social Services
Seattle Children's Hospital

Debra Gumbardo, RN, MS, NE-BC
Director, Psychiatry and Behavioral Medicine
Seattle Children's Hospital

It is shocking but true: in some parts of the United States, parents have felt compelled to make the devastating decision to abandon their children in an emergency room in order to access mental healthcare.

The "mental health void," as described by *New York Times* writer Judith Warner, is characterized by a dearth of mental health providers, significant gaps in inpatient and residential capacity, and poor service integration. These factors converge to create a perfect storm in which children suffering from hallucinations, uncontrolled aggression, and suicidal impulses are languishing on waiting lists for services.

That's why, when Nebraska passed a "safe-haven" law to provide an alternative to the rare—but tragic—cases where an infant might be abandoned and sometimes left for dead by an overwhelmed and frightened new parent, officials were surprised to see nearly forty young teenagers, most with serious mental illness, turned over to the state.

The Pacific Northwest is no different than America's Heartland when it comes to the frustration and painful experiences that families are forced to struggle with as their children wait to access mental healthcare. Estimates, based upon a conservative utilization rate of 2.5 per 1,000 youths, yield a current shortage of two hundred psychiatric hospital beds for children in the State of Washington. And, indeed, over the course of the past year in our emergency department at Seattle Children's Hospital, we have had to divert 140 children in need of psychiatric hospitalization to other facilities or situations. The list of children waiting to access outpatient services is longer still.

Obviously, we must find ways to extend our mental health resources to support these families. At the same time, in an environment where there is seemingly an endless to-do list—always another patient or family that could be seen—there is little energy or enthusiasm for focusing on process or systems issues. It's sad, but it's just a given that things are broken.

Early Struggles

To begin to fix this huge problem, our starting point with continuous performance improvement (CPI) was simple: how could we see more patients within our own system—without creating more work for our faculty and clinical staff?

This was easier said than done. The conventional wisdom is that mental health professionals are more receptive than other clinicians to out-of-the-box thinking. But this isn't necessarily the case. And our experience in the psychiatry department at Seattle Children's as we tried to embrace CPI demonstrates this clearly.

The Department of Child Psychiatry and Behavioral Medicine is composed of care providers and support staff at all levels of training across multiple disciplines—including psychiatry, psychology, nursing, and social work. The University of Washington (UW) largely employs the psychologists and psychiatrists, although not exclusively so. Administration of the department occurs within a complex matrix of partnerships between Children's and UW faculty leaders. The bottom line is that this is an inherently difficult environment in which to introduce significant change.

It is even more difficult because the director of the department is a skeptic who is wary of the ways that "pop psychology" repackages or relabels common human experiences to seemingly confer more significance, or to suggest unique expertise. The department director's "psychobabble radar" is thus very well tuned, and his initial exposure to lean transformation, CPI, and the Toyota Production System set off that radar like a screaming siren. As a result, our department was more than happy to explore process improvements, but we had no interest in cloaking our efforts in kaizen, or in referring to waste as "muda."

The big challenge, then, was getting faculty and staff to commit to a methodology that smacks of psychobabble but that, in fact, acknowledges waste in our system and instills a willingness to help eliminate it. The honest truth is that we have yet to fully meet this challenge in our department, and CPI is still a work in progress for us. But we have moved forward, and this is well worth noting and documenting.

An Organization Mandate

Taking a step back: the organization as a whole had previously developed an executive leadership group that included department medical directors and operations administrators who oversee the day-to-day workings of the hospital. The group had addressed multiple issues specifically focused on safety and quality improvement. With the guidance and commitment of a facilitator who was expert in this methodology, as well as leadership from the president of the hospital, the executive group learned together and committed to a mandate for the organization. The top medical and administrative leadership from our department was part of this team and was involved in all the educational efforts and mandates to move forward.

Despite this engagement, however, our department wasn't truly willing to take a leap of faith for CPI. It seemed obvious that operating room (OR) scheduling was rife with waste and unneeded complexity that arose from the demanding schedule of surgery. But the complexity and waste in scheduling a fifty-minute psychology or psychiatry session with a patient were far less apparent to us.

Nonetheless, the senior leaders in our department participated in several additional trainings that exposed them to CPI principles in theory and practice. Indeed, we were among the first to participate in the "Wash Your Hands" practicum, a weeklong "kaizen" or improvement event at a local manufacturing facility that applied lean principles.

In addition, we participated in the first Japan Super Flow trip, which allowed us to immerse ourselves in factories that had been implementing the Toyota Production System for many years. The trip to Japan cemented the real value of this work because we finally saw for ourselves the cumulative outcomes that resulted from years and decades of CPI effort.

But our department leaders still walked away wondering how they would apply these CPI principles to their work and get others on board; we knew we had a long and bumpy road ahead.

"Our Department Is Different"

Some of those bumps were due to the fact that people in our department wanted empirical proof about CPI. And, because most people see fairly significant incompatibilities between the medical and manufacturing cultures, it's critical that academic leaders are out in front in terms of embracing, adopting, and implementing lean methodologies. One of the accelerators in this process—from our experience, at least—was helping faculty leaders become fluent in lean processing principles and giving them the opportunity to work in the lab (i.e., to directly experiment with CPI and observe its potential). These experiences are critical in getting people to authentically advocate change in the face of potent resistance and doubt. The embrace of CPI may have the appearance of a statement of faith, but we found that in our department it had to be anchored in experience and fact.

We also found how important it is to focus, not only on the improvements that lead to a more reliable and consistent product, but also on the impact that this has on the worker's experience. This notion was displayed in an exhibit which chronicled the evolution of the loom at the Toyota Commemorative Museum of Industry and Technology in Nagoya, Japan (See Figure 6.1). Indeed, in thinking about the earliest modifications to the loom—for example, the introduction of a foot pull to separate vertical threads—Toyota recognized the interdependence of the worker and the machine, the artist and his or her creation.

And, after seeing the incremental gains that come from process improvements, we were also led to the inescapable conclusion that "standard work" and "reliable methods" actually free up workers so they can lavish more attention on the art and craft of their jobs. In the case of the loom, the simple addition of the foot pull eliminated some of the worker's burden; in the case of pediatric medicine, it means more focus on patient care.

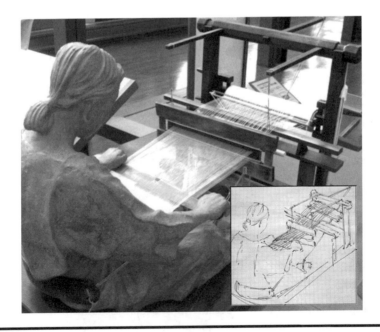

Figure 6.1 Drawing to help see. "Seeing" the evolution of the loom.

After our trip to Japan, we expanded our commitment and included more of our leaders in an effort to offset the perception that we were simply taking a wild leap of faith with CPI. The hospital selected projects that clearly showed we were taking clinicians or staff away from direct patient care or keeping patients from being seen. We then recruited department members to participate in hospital-wide CPI events such as a Rapid Process Improvement Workshop (RPIW) to revise handoff communications. During these events, our staff was exposed to didactic material and had the opportunity to apply CPI principles over the course of a week. These were wonderful opportunities to see how the process worked, and to contribute to the success of areas outside of our own department.

It was helpful that early successes were celebrated throughout the organization, but there were—and remain—challenges in getting the uninitiated in our department to recognize parallels between their work and the improvements in OR scheduling or the labeling of lab specimens. Staff members who were naturally interested and motivated to seek better ways to provide care were intrigued by the successes in other areas. Others continued to believe that "we are different," and that while standard work could be applied to cars and perhaps even the OR, the same did not hold true for us in psychiatry and behavioral medicine.

Creating Some Initial "Wins"

Despite the departmental doubts, we pushed ahead. And point improvement work in centralized scheduling offered us a start as well as key learnings.

We have several outpatient clinics that collectively receive more than 350 referrals each month. The small group of staff members who process these referrals recognized that they were spending more time investigating, correcting, or rerouting referrals than actually scheduling patients to be seen. Our wait list was growing, and we had unfilled capacity among our providers. Consequently, the department's initial CPI event focused on shaping demand and the quality of the referral information received—a daunting task, since it involved changing the behavior of providers outside of our organization. The results of this effort, which reduced appointment lead time by over 50 percent and the number of referral requests returned to providers for additional information by a staggering 95 percent, are shown in Table 6.1.

Departmental Training

With this success under our belts, we ultimately decided that all staff in the department would attend CPI Fundamentals—a full-day course introducing the basics of this philosophy. As we undertook this phase of our CPI journey, it was important that a direct applicability to our psychiatry systems be demonstrated. Having our department leadership, rather than CPI consultants, provide the training helped ensure that this would occur. We also made a strategic effort to have all of our department's staff exposed to CPI as a separate and unified group, rather than

Table 6.1 Psychiatry Clinic Intake Workshop Results

	Pre-Workshop 2006	60-Day Follow-Up	40-Month Follow-Up	% Change
Lead time	77	27	37	–52%
Percentage of referrals returned to provider for additional information	37	2	N/A	–95%

among a group of providers or staff from the hospital at large. In this way, examples and class exercises were able to focus on what was directly meaningful to those in the class—psychiatry and behavioral medicine.

Several challenges that emerged from these initial trainings are worth noting:

- Many providers, and particularly those in academic centers such as ours, had trouble balancing the importance of patient-centric clinical care and success in teaching and research.
- Many clinicians and staff had difficulty accepting the fact that aspects of their work might be seen as "waste" or "non–value added" (See Figure 6.2).

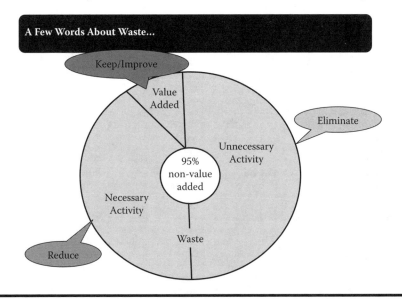

Figure 6.2 Focus on waste versus value-added steps. Results from analyzing value-added steps, non-value-added steps, and waste in a process. Knowing non-value-added steps leads to difficult but necessary conversations with staff.

■ We discovered that CPI is not for those with "thin skins." We urged staff to rise above their own personal interest and investment in keeping the status quo.

■ Many staff members could not accept 50 percent improvement targets; iterative change and improvement over time were not "good enough" for a number of our highly successful colleagues.

These department-focused trainings only went so far to solidify staff commitment to CPI and lean approaches. They did, however, contribute to the use of a common language, which gradually helped many of us get on the same page. It is not uncommon now to hear senior faculty leaders in our department speak about reducing "lead time" for scheduling or "waste" as it relates to searching for equipment or supplies.

Building Momentum

As a result, our neuropsychology service recognized several variables that were contributing to long lead times. Working with one of our quality specialists who had received the foundational CPI training, this group mapped its process from initial visit to discharge and identified several areas of focus. Thereafter, cycle time for test preparation was reduced from 20.4 minutes to 9.2 minutes.

To further extend our knowledge and application of CPI principles, clinical leads and operation managers in our department were invited to participate in the formal weeklong training that was initially offered to hospital leaders. After attending this training, the clinical director of the inpatient psychiatric unit (IPU) commented on the value of seeing the integration of CPI principles in practice. She was later instrumental in implementing reliable methods in the IPU. This ultimately led to a cost savings of over $10,000 per hospital stay (2007–2009), despite an increase in rates during this same time period. (See Table 6.2.) These numbers helped advance CPI within our department.

Table 6.2   Inpatient Psychiatric Unit (IPU) Outcomes Following Implementation of Care Guidelines and Daily "Huddle"

	2007	2008	Annualized 2009	% Change
Length of stay (days)	16.9	13.4	11.4	–33%
Cost per stay	$48,672	$41,808	$37,840	–22%
Patients served	376	473	568	51%

Recognizing Shared Goals

But the fact that professors are in the knowledge business was a plus, too. Most of us choose this scholarly career path to discover and to apply new findings, and to integrate and disseminate these developments so that other lives can be improved. As we found out during our CPI experiences, medicine doesn't have a monopoly on improving people's lives and wanting to make the world a better place. Recognizing these shared goals helped to overcome initial resistance from staff who were apprehensive about looking to manufacturing for solutions in healthcare. For example, we are committed to the notion of "engagement" as a true reflection of how one invests in his or her work. Supporting staff in being able to do their best each day and using people in their fullest capacity is consistent with the concept of eliminating waste associated with over- or underutilizing workers. We also made it clear that staff opinions count and that in the end staff members are the ones who must identify the CPI-based changes that need to take place.

Coming to Grips with Standard Work

Our department continues to wrestle with the idea that CPI means that we must determine a standard approach to care. Standard care means changes, and changes take time to implement; they don't generate benefits or results overnight. We saw this with the use of online order entry or electronic documentation templates. And it cropped up again when we implemented daily "huddles" and team rounding. At first, it appeared that this would require more of our psychiatrists' time. But the exact opposite occurred. Indeed, devoting time to the rounding process reduced the amount of ad hoc questions and requests that came to our attending physicians via phone calls and e-mails.

CPI is science in action. And this registers squarely with our clinicians, who can see that CPI embodies the scientific method of hypothesis generation and testing. Through this thought process, they may come to recognize that by eliminating unnecessary variation with a protocol (or standard work), we can effectively free up more time for psychiatry and behavioral medicine.

Specifically, clinicians understand that once a decision is made to initiate treatment with a particular therapy, the implementation of that decision should be uniform and predictable. This means that a psychiatrist shouldn't need to decide which rating scale to use to monitor change associated with the introduction of a medication, he or she also shouldn't need to calibrate the starting dose of that medicine, and calculating the rate at which the medication is increased should be per protocol and thus becomes unnecessary as well. In the end, all of these potential variations simply divert energy from the most important thing: choosing which medication is most appropriate for a given patient.

We saw the benefits of standard care in other ways, too.

Improving the Quality and Consistency of Inpatient Stays

Our IPU struggled for many years to improve access so that no child who needed a bed would be turned away. A decade ago, admissions of up to 4–6 weeks were the norm and focused primarily on diagnostic evaluation. Managed care companies gradually limited the lengths of stay and challenged inpatient leaders to redefine the role of inpatient care in this changing environment. However, our efforts to improve access by further reducing lengths of stay were unsuccessful. Many argued that the community was not ready to maintain high-acuity patients, given the limited resources. Community programs that touted good results were not readily available in all areas, and parents and providers believed extended stays were valuable. Consequently, the urgent platform for change did not exist, and there was little effort, beyond raising awareness, to support reductions in lengths of stay.

More recently, the inpatient unit redefined its purpose; it now provides behavior stabilization and focused intervention in order to address the immediate precipitants that lead to the need for hospitalization. To improve reliability and quality, the unit developed and implemented guidelines of care for various diagnostic groups and developmental ages. But this strategy alone did not ensure change. A reliable method is only "reliable" when it is consistently utilized. Changes in rounding processes were also adjusted so that rounds were now used to check progress along a pathway to discharge and ensure adherence to clinical guidelines.

While the intent of these guidelines was to improve the quality and consistency of care, an unintended consequence was further reductions in lengths of stay. Indeed, lengths of stay and costs for patients served were reduced by 33 percent and 22 percent, respectively; at the same time, the number of patients served per year nearly doubled.

It is worth noting that simply looking at length of stay, or even suggesting it as a target for improvement year after year, did not yield any traction; but efforts to improve treatment quality and consistency actually impacted both cost and length of stay dramatically.

An Ongoing Journey

Though our didactic experiences were helpful in mobilizing faculty and staff, experience in practice has proven to be the most critical engine for change in our department. Over time, we have learned that identifying relatively small, but significant, opportunities for process improvement helps "pilot" new approaches while making sure we challenge people to do work they are actually capable of performing. And our experiences, both on the IPU and in our neuropsychology service, underscore the fact that the cultural transition to a CPI environment in a medical setting is incremental and iterative.

This evolutionary element of CPI is embodied by Toyota in many ways. When you watch the Toyota assembly line in action after decades of lean processing, for example, you are looking at efficiency and consistency that make error proofing seem like a well-choreographed ballet.

Our department isn't quite at that level yet—it's more like a rugby match. But our trainings have provided an opportunity to reemphasize our goals for CPI, and we're moving the ball downfield. To be sure, we have reiterated our priorities: quality and safety through the use of standard clinical protocols, improving access to care through the elimination of waste, and greater staff engagement.

While we haven't come close to solving the children's mental health void that exists locally and nationally, we believe that CPI gives us the tools to do the most with what we have, and to reach more families than we ever have in the past. And it's now safe to say that CPI is no longer considered "psychobabble" in our department; on the contrary, it's seen as a critical element in our work, and an effective way for us to provide better care for patients.

Chapter 7

Ending the Paper Chase in the Operating Room

Sally E. Rampersad, MB, DCH, FRCA
Director of Quality Improvement, Department of Anesthesiology
Seattle Children's Hospital

Lynn D. Martin, MD, FAAP, FCCM
Director, Anesthesiology and Pain Medicine
Seattle Children's Hospital

Surgery used to be a pretty risky procedure at our hospital. We were fairly disorganized and had no up-front information-gathering process in place, and so we asked the same questions of patients and their families many times before they got into the operating room. If you keep asking over and over, you're bound to get conflicting or incorrect data—and that usually leads to a mistake and an erosion of safety.

To make matters worse, very little of the patient input we received was actually written down in a cogent and systemized way. Everything was uncoordinated, and there were disparate scraps of paper in a host of people's hands.

Thankfully, we were able to harness continuous performance improvement (CPI), which has taken the repetition and disarray out of this process. Now, we're all on the same page—quite literally—and there's no hidden information that could pose a threat to a patient's well-being. In addition, surgeons and circulating nurses now have time to touch and take care of patients, instead of running down data and verifying documentation trails. And, looking forward, this positive experience has begun to prepare us for the advent of electronic medical records, which will take hold in the coming years.

Choosing Where to Start

We decided to attack this problem using a Rapid Process Improvement Workshop (RPIW). After completion of value stream mapping and careful assessment, the documentation RPIW was chosen because it was highly visible to all medical and nursing staff who worked in the operating room (OR) environment, because all parties agreed that the processes for documentation needed updating and improving, and because this CPI event had a high likelihood of producing improvements that staff would appreciate and support.

The OR documentation project fulfilled all of these criteria—and delivered even more. In the end, it improved teamwork and efficiency as well as our working environment. It also eliminated waste in the system that was hindering safety and effective work flow.

As important and fruitful as this CPI project was, however, it's worth noting that it wasn't the highest priority item following the value stream assessment. But our leaders sensed that the operative services culture wasn't ready for the change necessary for other higher priority projects. In addition, there was a strong desire to get this documentation work completed ahead of the proposed implementation of the computerized physician order entry (CPOE) system.

Looking back on the OR documentation project, we view the waste reduction component as being truly critical. Waste reduction can serve as the primary driver for improvements in quality, cost, delivery, and safety—and it's accomplished through engagement of involved staff.

In our particular process endeavor, quality was ensured by having new documents designed by the staff who would use them; indeed, needed items were added and unnecessary or duplicate information (waste) was removed.

Cost savings were realized because the number of documents was reduced from twenty-one to fourteen to eight after CPOE implementation. This cut printing and reordering expenses.

Delivery of care to the patient was facilitated because the improved documentation reduced the search time for needed information and decreased duplication in information, so staff had more hours for direct patient care.

Finally, this project had a strong impact on safety. Preproject assessments demonstrated multiple episodes where duplicated information was not consistent in all locations—for example, home medications and allergies to medication. Less duplication of information directly reduces the potential for dangerous or harmful error.

Waste: Cleverly Disguised as Real Work

Focusing on waste is essential. Anything that consumes resources but adds no value for the patients or their families is classified as non-value-added waste. As is commonly seen in the manufacturing sector, 95–99 percent of the steps are non–value added in a service industry like healthcare.

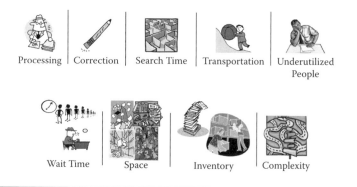

Figure 7.1   Waste comes in many forms. The nine types of waste.

Some steps may be non–value added, but they are still necessary from a regulatory perspective. An example of a regulatory non-value-added step would be the need to document usage of narcotic medications. Figure 7.1 categorizes different types of waste.

Waste comes in many different forms and is carefully disguised as "real work." These types of non-value-added waste include the following:

Processing (redundant and unnecessary steps, excess checking, and overutilization)

Correction (revisions and updates)

Search time (looking for information, people, supplies, and equipment)

Transportation (needless movement of people, materials, and information)

Underutilized people (limited use of mental, physical, and creative abilities)

Wait time (delays and queues)

Space (storage of unneeded inventory and lack of workplace organization)

Inventory (idle information, supplies, and materials)

Complexity (unnecessary product choices, and inefficient or frustrating process boundaries)

All of the different forms of waste were seen in our OR documentation project, especially in processing, complexity, and search time.

In addition to non-value-added waste, two other less commonly recognized categories of waste have been described: unevenness or variations in work processes, and overburdening of staff and/or equipment (See Figure 7.2). For example, the hourly variation in patients flowing into and out of the operating rooms commonly results in peak periods (midday) of demands on staff, equipment, and space.

Traditional quality improvement focuses on enhancing the reliability and quality of the few value-added steps, resulting in small incremental improvements in

Table 7.1 Waste Worksheet

Types of Waste	Observations from Three Actual Walks
Processing: Redundant and unnecessary process steps, excess processing (overutilization), excess checking, and inspection. Excess use of energy of all types.	Information was copied from nursing forms to anesthesia preoperative forms to the anesthesia record. See also "Underutilized people" (below).
Correction: Redo's, fix-ups, returns, markdowns, and managing customer complaints.	Information was not always transcribed correctly from one form to another, resulting in the need for "check steps" to determine which version was correct.
Inventory: Idle finished or in-progress materials, ingredients, supplies, or information.	The total number of forms was reduced from twenty-one to eight, so a smaller amount of storage space is now needed for our inventory.
Wait time: Delays and queues of all types.	The total amount of time needed to complete a preoperative assessment was longer than it needed to be because nursing and anesthesia each had their own questions to ask and did not reliably share the information obtained.
Search time: Time spent looking for information, people, supplies, and equipment.	Information could be in one of several places, resulting in search time for critical information or rework in finding the information again.
Transportation: Multiple handling steps and needless movement of material and information.	See comments under "Processing."
Space: Storage of unneeded items, excess inventory, or the general "mess" that builds up over time. Excess space required due to inefficient process flow.	See comments under "Inventory."

Table 7.1 Waste Worksheet (Continued)

Types of Waste	Observations from Three Actual Walks
Complexity: Complex process flows. Product choices that confuse customers. Organization boundaries that introduce inefficiencies and frustrate customers.	Our families were frustrated that multiple providers asked the same questions. "I already told the nurse that Johnny is allergic to penicillin. Didn't you read his chart?"
Underutilized people: Not utilizing the full mental, creative, and physical abilities of staff. The lack of involvement and participation of all members of the workforce.	Work that could have been done by medical assistants and nurses was done or redone by the anesthesiologist, underutilizing the skills of one group and overburdening another group of workers.

the overall process. But removing waste from the system (unnecessary steps) results in a less complex and more reliable process that can be completed more quickly. Therefore, reducing waste has a far greater impact on increasing the efficiency of a process and, as a result, cutting the costs.

The RPIW Process and Results

Our RPIW process started with a lead time of about six weeks; during this period, we gathered data to establish a benchmark of where things actually stood and determined what we wanted to achieve in the way of waste reduction. The process owners for this event were the nursing director for the OR and the anesthesiology director for the OR. This team defined the boundaries of the project,

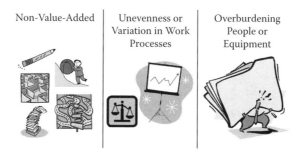

Non-Value-Added | Unevenness or Variation in Work Processes | Overburdening People or Equipment

Figure 7.2 Three categories of waste. Waste hides in ways that can be difficult to detect and measure.

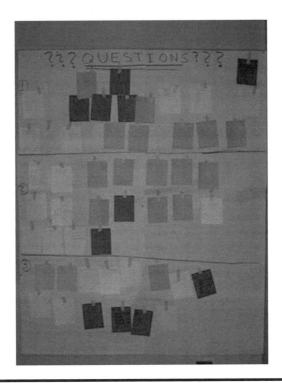

Figure 7.3 Roles. Many processes and services rely on multiple individuals doing their part. Defining the roles involved is an early step in a Rapid Process Improvement Workshop (RPIW).

in-scope and out-of-scope processes, and targeted outcomes for the improvement team. Another important process during this lead time was assembling the team that would work together during the RPIW week. This team building played a major role in the success of the RPIW because key representatives from all areas of operative services were identified by OR leadership and invited to participate in the group; as a result, managers, anesthesiologists, and nursing and support staff were all at the table. This allowed each team member to bring his or her own experience to the group in order to identify the major issues and create solutions that would work for everyone.

An information systems analyst and vendor representative (for the new forms) were also on the team. These individuals helped develop real-time working drafts for new composite forms. A representative from the hospital forms committee was also available to the team and, in the latter stages of the workshop, was able to approve, on the spot, different iterations of the new forms. This meant they could be trialed immediately before the end of the workshop week. And it was also instrumental in making sure that feedback from the OR staff could quickly be incorporated into the final version.

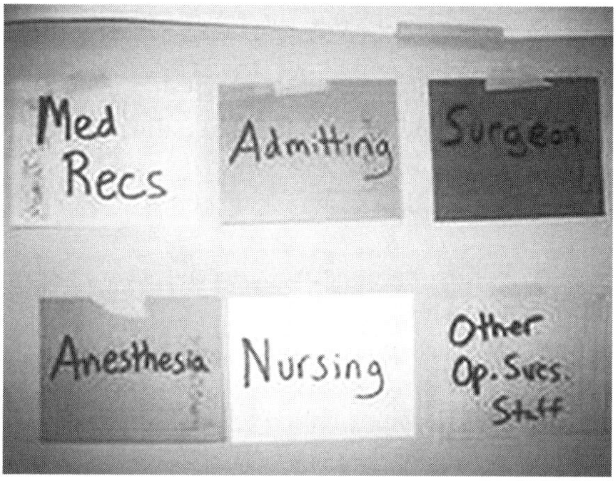

Figure 7.4 Process map. Process maps are used to uncover the discrete steps needed to deliver the outcome. Each role and its contribution are identified by color in the process map.

If this work had been done outside of the RPIW, essential input from all users of the forms would have been lacking, and each new iteration would have taken weeks or even months to approve and print. The result, in this case, would have been significant cost and rework.

We agreed that the ultimate success of our CPI work would be evaluated on four key measures: reduction in the number of forms; reduction in the number of lines of information; reduction in the number of information transfers from one form to another; and staff satisfaction, which served as a proxy for time.

As mentioned above, we succeeded in reducing the number of forms and lines of information (See Table 7.2). And costs were also reduced. The combined cost

Table 7.2 Workshop Results

	Before	*After*	*% Change*
Number of forms	21	14	33
Number of lines	1,001	718	28
Repeated lines	360	40	89
Times forms were repackaged	12	4	66
Number of noncarbon reprint (NCR) forms/number of additional NCR pages	12/33	10/17	17/48

[a] NCR forms are costly and error-prone due to difficulties in reading them.

for the old anesthesia record and charge sheet was $332 per thousand. The new design was $275 per thousand. Overall cost reduction was 14 percent. Since this workshop, the volume of cases has greatly increased through our operating rooms, so the money saved is even greater than this initial estimate.

In terms of staff satisfaction, we decided to use a five-point scale: "lousy," "poor," "okay," "good," and "great." And we also included questions about the following:

■ Effectiveness of information transfer (between specific subprocesses)
■ Support for error-free patient care
■ Ease of finding patient's chart
■ Ease of finding the forms you need
■ Overall effectiveness of documentation tools
■ Frequency of duplication of information

The results of the staff survey after we implemented changes in the OR documentation process were positive. The number of "lousy" and "poor" responses was reduced, and the number of "good" and "great" responses was increased. Specifically:

■ When it came to the information handoff from recovery to the parent, the "lousy" and "poor" responses dropped from 36 percent to 5 percent, and the "good" and "great" responses jumped from 4 percent to 39 percent.
■ In answering whether the new OR documentation supported error-free patient care, "lousy" and "poor" responses from the staff decreased from 37 percent to 14 percent, while "good" and "great" responses increased from 13 percent to 27 percent.
■ Assessing the ease of finding needed forms, the staff's "lousy" and "poor" responses fell from 33 percent to 5 percent, while the "good" and "great" responses more than doubled, from 24 percent to 49 percent.
■ In terms of overall effectiveness of documentation, the "lousy" and "poor" responses slid from 33 percent to 14 percent, and the "good" and "great" responses grew from 24 percent to 41 percent.

Finally, when asked, "How often do you copy information from one form to another?" there was a decrease in "always" responses from 64 percent to 10 percent, and an increase in "seldom" responses from 6 percent to 46 percent.

Even though we made huge progress and tremendous strides in the wake of the RPIW, we realized that there were other changes that needed to be made in order to keep improving the OR documentation process. We recognized, for example, that there was still more waste that we could drive out of the system, and so we deployed the PDCA cycle to achieve further gains (See Figure 7.5).

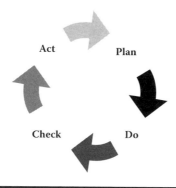

Figure 7.5 Plan, do, check, and act (PDCA) cycle. It's better to get some improvement today than to wait months hoping for perfection. PDCA drives the cycle of continuous improvement.

Culture Change and Process Change Go Hand in Hand

The OR documentation project changed our processes and opinions, but it also drove cultural changes.

Everyone realized that we were duplicating work and adding waste when patients and families were asked multiple times by multiple providers about drug allergies. We also recognized that this increased the possibility of error and the probability of irritating the people we serve.

So, we decided that allergy inquiries should be handled by the admitting RN and documented on the preoperative "boarding pass" (a new combined form that is used by the admitting RN and anesthesia) (See Figure 7.6), and that this information would not be duplicated on the anesthesia record or on a separate pre-anesthesia document (because this no longer existed). This was a big change for anesthesiologists to accept and embrace; and frequent communications as well as leadership commitment were required to help ease the uneasy transition.

Our work on the OR documentation project succeeded because the right people were invited to do it, and because it was well supported by leaders—in nursing, anesthesia, and surgery. It was also well aligned with hospital priorities and the concerns of the workers in the OR.

Just as importantly, throughout the weeklong RPIW, those who would ultimately be affected by the documentation changes were kept "in the loop." We let them know of the proposed changes and the progress of the workshop team, and we offered them opportunities for feedback. To achieve this, "town hall" meetings were held, so that all staff from operative services could review the work of the

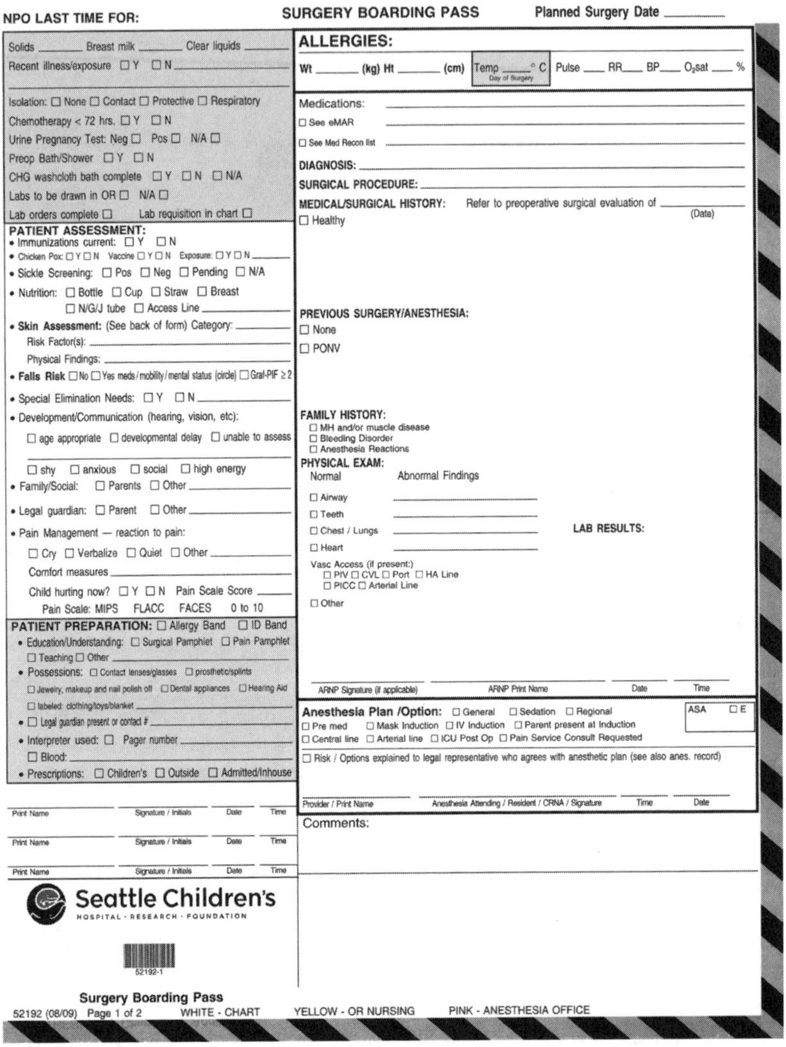

NPO LAST TIME FOR: **SURGERY BOARDING PASS** Planned Surgery Date _____

Solids _____ Breast milk _____ Clear liquids _____

Recent illness/exposure □ Y □ N _____

Isolation: □ None □ Contact □ Protective □ Respiratory

Chemotherapy < 72 hrs. □ Y □ N

Urine Pregnancy Test: Neg □ Pos □ N/A □

Preop Bath/Shower □ Y □ N

CHG washcloth bath complete □ Y □ N □ N/A

Labs to be drawn in OR □ N/A □

Lab orders complete □ Lab requisition in chart □

PATIENT ASSESSMENT:
- Immunizations current: □ Y □ N
  - Chicken Pox: □ Y □ N Vaccine □ Y □ N Exposure: □ Y □ N _____
- Sickle Screening: □ Pos □ Neg □ Pending □ N/A
- Nutrition: □ Bottle □ Cup □ Straw □ Breast
  - □ N/G/J tube □ Access Line _____
- **Skin Assessment:** (See back of form) Category: _____
  - Risk Factor(s): _____
  - Physical Findings: _____
- **Falls Risk** □ No □ Yes meds / mobility / mental status (circle) □ Gral-PIF ≥ 2
- Special Elimination Needs: □ Y □ N _____
- Development/Communication (hearing, vision, etc):
  - □ age appropriate □ developmental delay □ unable to assess
  - □ shy □ anxious □ social □ high energy
- Family/Social: □ Parents □ Other _____
- Legal guardian: □ Parent □ Other _____
- Pain Management — reaction to pain:
  - □ Cry □ Verbalize □ Quiet □ Other _____
  - Comfort measures _____
  - Child hurting now? □ Y □ N Pain Scale Score _____
  - Pain Scale: MIPS FLACC FACES 0 to 10

PATIENT PREPARATION: □ Allergy Band □ ID Band
- Education/Understanding: □ Surgical Pamphlet □ Pain Pamphlet
  - □ Teaching □ Other _____
- Possessions: □ Contact lenses/glasses □ prosthetic/splints
  - □ Jewelry, makeup and nail polish off □ Dental appliances □ Hearing Aid
  - □ labeled clothing/toys/blanket _____
- □ Legal guardian present or contact # _____
- Interpreter used: □ Pager number _____
  - □ Blood: _____
- Prescriptions: □ Children's □ Outside □ Admitted/Inhouse

Print Name | Signature / Initials | Date | Time

Print Name | Signature / Initials | Date | Time

Print Name | Signature / Initials | Date | Time

ALLERGIES:

Wt _____ (kg) Ht _____ (cm) Temp _____ ° C (Day of Surgery) Pulse _____ RR_____ BP_____ O₂sat _____ %

Medications: _____

□ See eMAR

□ See Med Recon list

DIAGNOSIS: _____

SURGICAL PROCEDURE: _____

MEDICAL/SURGICAL HISTORY: Refer to preoperative surgical evaluation of _____ (Date)

□ Healthy

PREVIOUS SURGERY/ANESTHESIA:

□ None

□ PONV

FAMILY HISTORY:
□ MH and/or muscle disease
□ Bleeding Disorder
□ Anesthesia Reactions

PHYSICAL EXAM:
Normal   Abnormal Findings

□ Airway _____
□ Teeth _____
□ Chest / Lungs _____   **LAB RESULTS:**
□ Heart _____
Vasc Access (if present:)
  □ PIV □ CVL □ Port □ HA Line
  □ PICC □ Arterial Line
□ Other

ARNP Signature (if applicable) | ARNP Print Name | Date | Time

Anesthesia Plan /Option: □ General □ Sedation □ Regional   ASA ____ □ E
□ Pre med □ Mask Induction □ IV Induction □ Parent present at Induction
□ Central line □ Arterial line □ ICU Post Op □ Pain Service Consult Requested
□ Risk / Options explained to legal representative who agrees with anesthetic plan (see also anes. record)

Provider / Print Name | Anesthesia Attending / Resident / CRNA / Signature | Time | Date

Comments:

Seattle Children's
HOSPITAL · RESEARCH · FOUNDATION

52192-1

Surgery Boarding Pass
52192 (08/09) Page 1 of 2   WHITE - CHART   YELLOW - OR NURSING   PINK - ANESTHESIA OFFICE

Figure 7.6 Boarding pass. The boarding pass reduced duplication of work (waste), potential for error, and patient and family dissatisfaction due to answering the same question multiple times. Anesthesiologists learned to trust clinicians from other departments—a culture change.

RPIW team and make comments about what they liked and didn't like. We also received lots of suggestions and things to consider.

In addition, the changes were broadcast to all those affected through e-mail and in their respective staff meetings. Those who had served on the RPIW team acted as "champions" and "implementation coaches." Leaders made sure that the workshop team was allowed uninterrupted, paid time during the workshop in order to get this important work completed.

Once the OR documentation work was completed, leaders took back a clear message to their staff that the new processes and new documents were to be used with every patient every time. Old forms were actively removed from inventory. Our leaders modeled this behavior and served as coaches, and everyone learned a new way to work with less waste; but the most gratifying part of this CPI experience is that it resulted in a happier staff and safer care for our patients.

Chapter 8

5S and Demand Flow: Making Room for Continuous Improvement

Charles Hodge
Vice President and Chief Procurement Officer
Seattle Children's Hospital

Devin Prenevost
CPI 5S Program Manager
Seattle Children's Hospital

Imagine you have just built a new healthcare facility. The contractors are gone, the equipment and furniture are in place, and everything is in order. You bring in the supplies and staff, and then open for business.

Now imagine that you revisit this facility one year later. The clean, organized work environment that you left is now ordered chaos. This "lived-in" operation houses cabinets of trial medications, broken equipment, and piles and drawers full of excess and/or obsolete supplies. Random—and often outdated—notifications and other literature cover the desks and walls. There's no standard stocking procedure for the various work areas, so they all look and operate quite differently. Rubbermaid carts have begun to pop up everywhere, as all the built-in storage is filled to capacity. Critical supplies can't be found, so more are ordered, and then hoarded. And the once beautifully organized facility, built to facilitate flow, now supports a hundred different micro or custom operations.

This is an old story that plays out time and again. The once spacious workspace is now cramped and completely inadequate. It is not a visual workspace, so waste grows. Inventory and other resources pile up. Staff members spend more time in motion, searching and managing the "ordered chaos," than they do caring for patients. And continuous performance improvement (CPI) efforts are slowed to a halt, because no one can possibly improve flow in such an inadequate workspace.

We experienced all of this at Seattle Children's Hospital—especially in the operating room (OR). The space the OR occupies in the hospital is not unusual; fourteen operation rooms surround a large-sized sterile core, where critical supplies and equipment are stored to support the service. Over time, the core filled up with excess supplies and equipment that ultimately spilled out into the ORs themselves.

The excess filled the core and surrounding operating rooms until one of the ORs was completely shut down and converted into a storage room. At the time, OR capacity wasn't needed as much as storage capacity, so OR 10 became a default hold for rarely used equipment. Eventually, it would be used to hold all other "What do I do with this stuff?" supplies and equipment. A simple solution really; just shove it in the room and close the door—out of sight, out of mind.

With no process or ownership, OR 10 became a place where undecided or unused supplies and equipment went to die. But not all the supplies and equipment pushed into OR 10 were obsolete. The room also held equipment that was needed on a daily basis. And, as the room filled to capacity, it became increasingly difficult to retrieve the needed equipment from this very expensive "bone yard."

Over the course of just a couple of years, OR 10 was filled to capacity and sacrificed in the name of clutter. Unfortunately, however, demand for operative services at the hospital started growing, and reached 12 percent annually (See Figure 8.1). This created a desperate need for rapid and substantial change.

Nothing gets the attention of senior leadership like a problem that hits the bottom line. It was easy to use OR 10 as a storage facility when the room wasn't needed for patients. But when capacity is strained, and you have a 400-square-foot storage room (costing $4,000 per square foot) holding about $100,000 worth of supplies and equipment, you have a problem.

Indeed, a functioning OR (at capacity) adds nearly $1 million (or 2 percent) to the net profit of an enterprise the size of Seattle Children's. And, about 40 percent of the patients who flow through the OR become inpatients, driving additional revenue. So, with that kind of upside potential, you'd better deal with waste—and in a hurry.

But how? What solution could be implemented to reclaim the wasted OR space and make it more of a profitable revenue producer without adding burden to staff or other areas within the organization?

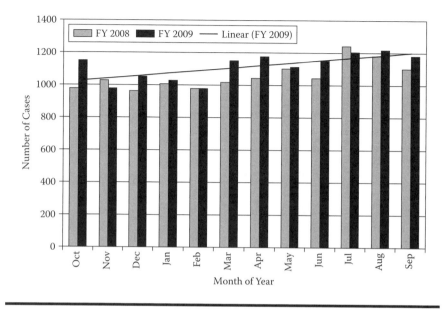

Figure 8.1 OR case volume growth.

The answer we came up with was 5S, a visual system that creates and maintains higher levels of organization, efficiency, and safety. 5S also decreases training and search time while reducing wasted time and resources.

Decades old, 5S was popularized by Japanese manufacturers who in turn learned the principles from Frederick W. Taylor's *Principles of Scientific Management* and the application of similar principles at the Ford Motor Company.[1] The 5S's translated from Japanese are seiri (sort), seiton (simplify), seisō (sweep), seiketsu (standardize), and shitsuke (sustain). Each stage of the 5S process is specifically designed to transform the workplace and set in motion a culture of waste elimination.

The 5S process begins when a team of users defines which items are essential for the functioning of the workspace and which are unnecessary. The items are then *sorted* by necessary versus unnecessary. Unnecessary items are removed from the workspace.

During the *simplify* stage, the team designates optimal point-of-use (POU) locations for the necessary items. The goal in this phase is to place resources (supplies, equipment, documentation, etc.) at the point of most frequent use. This ensures that items are immediately available to users.

Once POU use locations are identified and items are placed, a visual sweep plan is developed. A *sweep* is a visual and physical check to ensure that items have been returned to their designated POU locations. The plan outlines who performs the sweep, and when and how often the sweep will take place.

Next, the team must create *standards* that dictate how the workspace will be used. Standards must sufficiently dictate workspace protocol so that anyone entering the workspace is able to visually ascertain where to locate items and how to use the space.

The last "S"—*sustain*—is where most of leadership's attention is focused in an effort to preserve the gains, as well as shift the culture to the ongoing work of maintaining a visual workplace. In order to sustain the gains of the previous four S's, the team creates a sustainment plan outlining an audit schedule and how to respond to problems, inconsistencies, and nonfunctioning standards.

Auditing is a formal process in which team members evaluate the efficacy of the 5S efforts. A standard audit form is used throughout the organization. An important function of the auditing process is creating a standard to identify, discuss, and manage found issues/opportunities. Once an opportunity has been identified, team members create a plan to immediately address it. The plan is enacted, evaluated, and modified as necessary. The audit and problem-solving processes are continuous, as are all aspects of 5S. All are part of the plan, do, check, and act (PDCA) cycle. Team members constantly evaluate the workspace and standards to ensure that waste is eliminated and time is maximized.

The outcomes of the 5S process include reduction of cost, increased safety, and higher levels of teamwork and accountability. Teams who complete the initial 5S process and diligently maintain their efforts will see a decrease in costs related to employee efficiency. By establishing a visual workplace, in which every item has a specific location, employees will spend less time searching for supplies, equipment, and other critical resources.

During a 5S event in the diagnostic radiology department of Seattle Children's, the 5S team designated locations for their highly used supplies at the POU in the exam rooms instead of having to retrieve these critical materials from a supply room over 150 feet away (significantly reducing the wastes of motion and transportation). This standardization of process and procedures also created an environment of safety and improved patient and staff satisfaction.

In another effort, the building and engineering department used 5S to reduce the waste of search time. The department originally stored all of the hospital plans by rolling them up into a bank of PVC pipes. On average, it took building engineers from fifteen minutes to two hours to find a particular plan (each was unrolled and reviewed until the right one was found). During its 5S event, the team created standards on how to store and catalog plans, and how to discard out-of-date plans. With the new visual system fully in place, building engineers had removed the guesswork, and the average search time dropped to five minutes.

5S efforts have also helped in the area of reducing supply costs at Seattle Children's. The backbone of this effort is to simply standardize the supplies and control the inventory. After a 5S team in the surgical unit determined the appropriate par levels for its POU carts, it discovered that the department was storing over twelve thousand units of excess medical supplies. Discarding unused and expired materials also improved safety in the workplace. During the same surgical unit process, the team discovered that more than 250 of its twelve thousand excess medical supplies had expired and were unfit for use (a serious safety hazard).

The combination of eliminating waste and regulating supply storage also frees up space. Recently, several administrative departments at Seattle Children's combined office spaces. Prior to the move, each department completed 5S events that were focused on common office supplies and storage. After the events, the departments went from 880 square feet of storage space for common office supplies to a total of 160 square feet. This saved the hospital 720 square feet of space and nearly $100,000 in annual supply expense.

Those who participate in 5S events and understand the methodology become the cornerstone of any organization's continuous improvement efforts. In the spirit of PDCA, team members hold each other accountable for established standards and procedures. They use the auditing process to keep the program in check, and they ensure that the new organized culture remains intact. Ultimately, the 5S process empowers employees to work toward a more efficient workspace because it provides them with the tools and frameworks that help identify areas of waste and the means to improve.

Understanding the benefits of previous 5S process events, it was obvious to the OR leaders that these powerful tools would provide the perfect solution to their critical problem. The expected benefits of transforming OR 10 from an expensive storage closet to a revenue-driving OR were also clear. In the end, the new space would provide the hospital with much-needed capacity, support surgical services, or add extra recovery space.

And, the numbers we crunched showed that either way—if the space was used as an operating room or as a recovery room (Phase 1 Recovery)—the net incremental income could be about $1 million (See Table 8.1). Moreover, the newfound space would provide capacity needed by the service for next ten years, and add roughly 2 percent to the net profit of the organization. In addition, critical equipment would be moved closer to the POU—and this would significantly reduce the wastes of search, motion, and transportation for the staff throughout the OR areas.

A successful 5S project in OR 10 would also help embed and establish an ongoing environment of waste control while instilling the team with a deep appreciation of the visual workplace. And, if successful, the project would generate a sense of organizational ownership from all staff.

As mentioned above, the true purpose of 5S is to create a work environment that enables staff members to quickly spot problems. This is especially important in areas where disruption and waste could pose life-threatening situations.

Here's a good example: at Alcatraz Prison, shadow boards (a common 5S tool) for all the knives in the kitchen were created well before 5S became a manufacturing standard to improve safety. With one glance, a guard could tell if a knife was missing and thus posed a significant security concern.

This level of concern is just as high in the operating room. In healthcare, we mask problems by adding inventory and equipment, but this is not conducive to CPI. A robust 5S program, however, brings needed controls without waste. Our

Table 8.1 Comparison Chart as Operating Room (OR) versus Phase I Recovery

Use as OR	
Days per year	250
Cases per day	4
Net income per case	$1,114.78
Incremental net income	**$1,114,775.57**
Use as Phase I Recovery	
Days per year	200
Hours used per day	3
Patients per hour	1.5
Additional cases	900
Contribution per case	$1,114.78
Incremental net income	**$1,003,298.01**

belief was that a success in OR 10 would help us gain consensus to expand 5S efforts into all operating rooms at the hospital. In the process, we would become proficient at waste removal and gain enough momentum to sustain our CPI campaign.

Prior to implementing the 5S process in OR 10, the OR leadership team (the administrative director, two physician leaders, and a nursing leader) had made several unsuccessful attempts to reclaim the space. The reason these attempts failed was the top-down, directive approach (another healthcare norm) employed throughout the effort. The leadership team subsequently decided to implement only parts of the 5S process. This directive was also poorly received by OR staff members, who felt little ownership of the project. As a result, the one piece of the 5S program that they chose to implement was sorting. The result was simply a shifting of unnecessary items from one place to another, and these items were continually moved around based on immediate space needs.

Without a team approach, buy-in from all staffing levels, and support for the entire 5S process (from planning to sustaining), the temporary gains were simply unsustainable. OR staff members routinely found themselves facing the same problem of too much space being dedicated to storing outdated and unused materials. These previous attempts underline the importance of leadership commitment to the entire 5S process and also the importance of staff involvement. To be successful, 5S projects, and CPI efforts generally, must be done *with* staff, not *to* them. A successful 5S program requires organizational focus, absolute commitment, and staff involvement.

With a fresh focus on implementing a long-term solution, the OR leadership team realized the need for this absolute commitment. So, the team now followed the standard process for implementing 5S in order to address its problem—space constraints at the same time as increased demand for service.

Members of the OR leadership team started by developing the appropriate and accepted framework, which would ultimately lead to the project's success. With support from two of the hospital's CPI consultants, OR leadership also performed three primary functions. The first was defining the scope and goals of the event, the second was to teach the basic 5S concepts and methodologies to the team, and the third was to schedule an event to be led by the CPI consultants.

Leadership's first call to action was identifying the project sponsor. Sponsors champion the continuous improvement methodology. Sponsors also retain resources and protect the integrity of the auditing process.

The leadership team then identified the area owner, who would partner with the sponsor to identify process boundaries, clarify event targets, invite event team members, and have the ongoing responsibility for managing the process. To produce optimal results, the area owner ensured that audit measures were in place and monitored. The area owner would also describe the project to the staff, discuss possible changes within the project, and provide constant support for the team and program.

Finally, OR leadership formed a management guidance team (MGT). This team defined the event targets and created the project charter. The team encouraged event participants to implement changes and action plans.

The sponsor and area owner formed a cross-functional team to participate in the OR 10 5S event. Team members were picked for their expertise in the work area as well as their understanding of the supplies and equipment that were stored in OR 10. The team included surgical technicians in addition to members from OR nursing, anesthesia, supply chain management, and environmental services. Each team member was then trained, rallied, and relieved of his or her daily tasks so that 100 percent of the time needed could be dedicated to the project.

Leadership's active role in each step of the process—from being present during observations and tours of the area, to consistent check-ins during the event—created the recipe for our success. In practical terms, this meant that leadership kept removing barriers that allowed us to make progress and perform at our best. And, looking back, if leadership hadn't kept saying that we could accomplish meaningful results in three days, it definitely would have taken us longer to get where we needed to go. The constant—and encouraging—refrain from the top was "It can be done."

Thorough planning, the right resources, tenacious leadership and commitment, and staff involvement—all of these factors produced dramatic and successful results. The space was transformed from a storage closet to a space ready for clinical use. The team was able to remove broken and expired equipment, remove expired medical supplies, and move critical supplies and equipment closer to the clinicians' POU without burdening other work areas or staff.

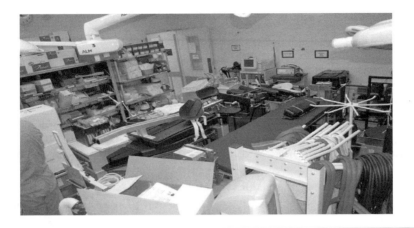

Figure 8.2   OR 10: Pre-5S. Most thought it would take several multiday 5S events to transform this room from a storage room into something more useful.

The bottom line is that this reduced the amount of time clinicians spent searching for and moving items and resources in and out of OR 10. The team also created a reliable method for sustaining the gains made during the three-day event (See Tables 8.2 and 8.3). Finally, the group was able to create ownership and clearly define roles and responsibilities. And, when all was said and done, proud team members claimed ownership of the project, which quickly became a department norm. It was

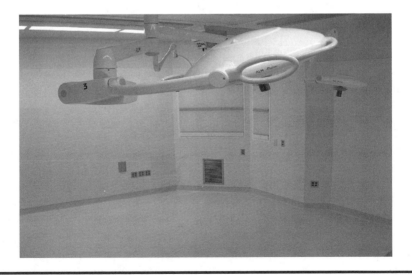

Figure 8.3   OR 10: Post 5S. The OR 10 5S team was able to convert an ad hoc storage room into a space ready for clinical use in three days.

Table 8.2   5S Results

5S Measures	Before	After	Cost Savings
Floor space used (sq. ft.)	0 available for clinical use	400 available for clinical use	$1,600,000
Inventory	> 500 items	0	
Safety and ergonomic improvements	Expired and soiled supplies, and personal injury hazards	Proper and safe storage, preventing injury and infection	
Number of workspaces	0	One or more (depending on clinical use)	> $1 million in annual revenue for clinical use of space!
Travel distance (staff, materials, paper, etc.)	Supplies were inaccessible	Equipment now close to point of care	

Table 8.3   5S Strategy to Sustain and Continuously Improve

What	Who	How Often
Resort (level 4 of sort)	5S team	N/A
Inventory-level check (level 4 of simplify)	5S team	Weekly
Routine discussion plan (level 4 of sustain)	5S team	Monthly
Training other staff (level 2 of sustain)	Team Lead	Every weekly staff meeting for 1 month
Sweep (level 3 of sweep)	Team Lead	Recommended: Daily visual sweeps for first 3 weeks; weekly cleaning and replenishment sweeps
3 times a week thereafter		

obvious to almost everyone that this wasn't just another top-down management whim; this was an empowered team, having fun and making a difference!

We've discussed the financial benefits of the 5S event for OR 10, but what resonates is the 8 percent in overall OR capacity we added through our efforts. That 8 percent increase means that our surgeons can now potentially schedule an additional twenty patients/operations per day.

But the biggest takeaway here is that the 5S event and process helped set the stage for even greater improvements. As we've said, 5S is foundational to all organizational CPI efforts, and a visual workplace enables staff members to see and effectively remove waste—especially consumable supplies (medical, pharmaceutical, office, etc.).

The question, of course, is why most healthcare organizations order and carry excess supplies. The answer, as best we can ascertain, is that they lack supply standards (so they buy a huge variety), they have no storage standards (so they buy more than needed), or they fear running out (so they hoard and, again, buy more than they need). In most healthcare organizations, this leads to a serious problem. Supplies eventually accumulate, and then they tie up much-needed capital in what we call "excess and obsolete" (E&O). To combat accumulated inventory that leads to locked-up capital, a reliable method for supply distribution is needed. And at Seattle Children's, that reliable method is called "demand flow" (DF) (See Table 8.4).

DF is a supply replenishment system that ensures that the right supplies are delivered to the right place, in the right quantity, and at the right time. The primary objective of DF is to reduce the waste inherent in the supply replenishment process. DF starts with a forecast based on actual consumption trends. Each ordering department and work area is studied to determine the volume and velocity of the supplies it consumes. Upon completion of the study, kanbans (a visual signal) are

Table 8.4 Demand Flow

Improved Area and Process	Expected Results Post–Demand Flow Install
Non-value-added process time	Reduced 47,000 hours per year
Storage space in clinical work areas	One-half of current
Storage space in central warehouse	One-quarter of current
Lead time for supplies replenishment	Same to next day
Recycle and waste (associated with supplies)	One-quarter of current
Excess and/or obsolete supplies	Eliminated
Product returns	Eliminated

sized to hold one to five days' (depending on the frequency of delivery) worth of the area's supply requirements. Kanbans are then set in place within the work area (inventory node), where their "turns performance" is continuously managed.

The DF program at Seattle Children's utilizes a "two-bin" kanban system (about 95 percent of the supplies are distributed in bins; items too large for bins are triggered via kanban cards). In most nodes (clinical work areas), the bins are sized to hold one week's supply. Replenishment is triggered when the empty bin is placed in the designated holding area by the person consuming the supply. Materials handlers retrieve the empty bins and return them to the "DF stage" (an area located within the central warehouse). Bins are scanned at the stage area, and this, in turn, signals the primary distribution partner to pick supplies and fill the empty bins. The bins are filled within twenty-four hours of scan, and returned to the originating node.

The DF program at Seattle Children's is unique because it doesn't rely on supplies kept in our central warehouse. Fill orders for the kanbans are sent directly to third-party manufacturers and distributors, which allows the program to scale up (or down) without inventory holding costs. Supplies are also delivered ready to use (most of the packaging is removed prior to delivery). Last, upon issue, the frequency with which the kanban has been filled is recorded. Kanbans that are filled more frequently than expected (hot) are sized up to meet the increased demand. Kanbans that have not been filled over a certain time period (stale) are sized down or removed from the program entirely. This keeps the program aligned with shifting volumes and/or changes in user preferences and technology.

In addition to creating a visual and organized system for supply replenishment that helps eliminate E&O, demand flow also reduces non-value-added process time, as well as storage space in clinical work areas and central warehouses.

Taken together, 5S and DF have helped our hospital eliminate great amounts of waste. But both processes, by their very nature, keep pointing us toward new areas of improvement, where we can reduce even more unnecessary cost. And each time we trim, we're able to deliver better care to our patients, the ones who really matter. That's the beauty of CPI; we're glad it's part of our professional lives.

Note

1. Frederick W. Taylor, *Principles of Scientific Management* (New York: Harper, 1911).

Chapter 9

Developing and Implementing Pull Systems in the Intensive Care Unit

Kristina H. Deeter, MD, FAAP
Fellow, Pediatric Critical Care Medicine
Seattle Children's Hospital

Jerry J. Zimmerman, MD, PhD
Director, Pediatric Critical Care Medicine
Seattle Children's Hospital

Insuring Comfort during Critical Illness: A Question of Balance

In providing care for critically ill children, probably the most common and arguably the most important intervention involves alleviating pain and anxiety. Continuous infusions of analgesic and sedative agents are frequently used in intensive care units (ICUs) as a means to provide a constant level of comfort. This approach has been proven to decrease the discomfort associated with mechanical ventilation, traumatic and surgical wounds, invasive devices, and procedures. Besides this basic humanitarian benefit, analgesics and sedatives also decrease oxygen consumption, modulate intensity of the stress response, foster patient

93

safety in a potentially dangerous ICU environment by reducing risks of falls from the bed and the dislodgement of critical invasive devices, and facilitate bedside nursing care.[1] For children, adequate sedation is particularly critical and based on patients' developmental level and ability to communicate and understand what is happening to them.

On the other hand, continuous infusions of analgesics and sedatives have been identified as independent predictors of longer duration of mechanical ventilation as well as extended ICU and hospital length of stay.[2] Prolonged sedation has also been associated with increased procedures, acquired neuromuscular disorders, delirium, and posttraumatic stress disorder. Patients may become tolerant of sedatives, prompting dose escalation and ultimately resulting in delays in the restoration of normal mental status and drive to breathe, delaying the patient's ability to liberate from the ventilator. Sedation may limit clinicians' conduct of thorough physical examinations. Accordingly, evolving neurological injury may be missed. Excessive and/or prolonged administration of analgesics and sedatives can lead to drug tolerance and even dependency, increasing the risk for serious, even life-threatening withdrawal disease if these medications are discontinued too abruptly.[3] Long-term consequences of analgesics and sedatives on the developing brains of children are largely not understood.

In trying to balance comfort (both pain and anxiety) needs for the individual patient a multitude of variables are operative, and it is easy to swing between oversedation and undersedation, particularly in the absence of a standard approach. Administration of sedative infusions and boluses is highly variable, and historically has been based on individual physician preference and nurses' subjective assessment of pain and anxiety. In general, practice variation based on physician preference has been associated with both poorer outcomes as well as higher costs. Objective scoring systems for pain and anxiety have recently been developed. But even these assessments inherently vary depending on the scoring system used, nursing experience and bias, and even time of day.[4]

Providers strive to keep patients comfortable and pain-free. However, many end up oversedated or receive levels of sedative infusions that later make weaning of ventilator-support complicated and may also result in drug withdrawal issues. Most care providers are comfortable with increasing levels of sedation for patients receiving mechanical ventilation. Conversely, providers have not had as much success decreasing sedative infusions while avoiding signs of drug withdrawal.

Weaning from sedation can take from days to months and may prolong the duration of hospitalization. Children are often sent home on prolonged oral analgesic and sedative medication–weaning protocols that create risks for patient and family safety (e.g., accidental overdose, ingestion by another family member, and the inexperienced ability of the parent to monitor for signs of drug withdrawal).

Due to these and many other concerns about the detrimental effects of continuous sedation, comfort protocols are being developed and trialed worldwide in both adult and pediatric ICUs in an attempt to minimize these complications. Recent randomized trials summarized in peer-reviewed publications have demonstrated that such protocols decrease the length of mechanical ventilation and hospital length of stay.[5,6] This is turn may lead to decreases in other complications such as ventilator-associated pneumonia, ventilator-associated lung injury, hospital-acquired infection, and venous thrombotic disease.

Love, Medicine, and Chaos

Prior to the development of Seattle Children's Hospital's ICU Comfort Protocol, everyone had the right intention, and approaches to analgesia and sedation were based on training, experience, and the personal preference of individuals. No reliable method was in place as a guideline of care. Patients were frequently oversedated, and the need for prolonged sedative weaning utilizing oral methadone and diazepam was common. Many classes of sedatives were being utilized, frequently simultaneously. No controls were placed on drug escalation. Immediacy of patient comfort, with less regard for the subsequent consequences, was the norm. Many felt that our patients were receiving a tremendous amount of analgesic and sedative medication. Survey data relative to analgesia and sedation administration in ICUs internationally have similarly demonstrated wide intrahospital and interhospital variability in clinical practice.[7,8]

Homeostasis as a Pull System

In 1878 the renowned physiologist Claude Bernard noted that "all of the vital mechanisms, varied as they are, have only one object: that of preserving constant the conditions of life in the milieu interieur." Later, this concept was further developed by Walter Cannon and termed "homeostasis."[9] This framework largely provides the rationale for care of critically ill patients, who typically lose their ability to maintain homeostasis. In actuality, the provision of critical care involves iterative plan, do, check, and act (PDCA) cycles; attempting to restore some aspect of homeostasis; and employing continuous titration of various therapies in response to changes in patient status.

Interestingly, this describes a classic pull system that is customer (patient) driven and that responds only when the customer (patient) needs it. Whereas a push system might attempt to force changes in patient status at a time that might increase risk to the patient, a pull system continuously responds to changes in patient status, whether subtle or overt. PDCA cycles define titration of therapy based on feedback

Figure 9.1 Facilitated patient comfort homeostasis utilizing the ICU Comfort Protocol. Critically ill patients experience a variety of pain, anxiety, and stress insults that vary in intensity over time. These "actions" represent the primary inputs affecting patient comfort. The ICU Comfort Protocol is a patient-demand pull system based on continuous quantitative assessment of the patient by the bedside nurse utilizing the ICU Comfort Score, with resultant measured reactions by escalating or weaning various comfort measures, including the titration of infusions of analgesic and sedative medications. This approach to comfort homeostasis is governed by reliable methods for patient comfort assessment and drug administration, and insures that the patient receives adequate but not excessive medications to insure comfort.

of changes in patient status. This logic is widely used in delivery of care in ICUs, and we felt than an ICU Comfort Protocol (a reliable method) could be successfully applied for the administration of analgesics and sedatives.

On the Bus along a Yellow Brick Road

So began an enthusiastic journey of continuous performance improvement (CPI). First, a thorough review of existing Seattle Children's ICU analgesic and sedative practice, diverse as it was, followed by a review of the current evidence provided by the practice of other leading children's hospitals, were conducted. Not surprisingly, successful models of pediatric sedation protocols were almost nonexistent, and there were almost no examples of such protocols that had been thoroughly researched and published. As part of the ICU value stream mapping process, the need for development of an ICU Comfort Protocol was identified as a priority.

With support from hospital administration, a multidisciplinary team was assembled to develop and implement an ICU Comfort Protocol. From the onset, the primary goal was to improve the comfort and safety of critically ill children. It was reasoned that if this overall objective was realized, it seemed logical that decreased overall analgesic and sedative drug use, improved ICU staff satisfaction surrounding the issue of patient comfort, enhanced patient flow through the ICU (realized as shorter duration of mechanical ventilation and ICU stay), and reduced overall cost per ICU patient would also be achievable.

Rain, Mud, and Potholes

In the development of a new protocol for sedation and analgesia for the ICU, the implementation team faced many challenges and obstacles. In pediatric medicine, the patient population ranges from newborn babies with immature nervous systems and metabolism to full-grown young adults and everything in between. Pediatric critical care practitioners notably provide care for a substantial population of children with chronic special healthcare needs. Provision of appropriate analgesia and sedation is especially challenging for these vulnerable children.

Creating a protocol for the administration of medication to such a range of sizes and developmental levels was daunting. It was necessary to think critically about the sedative agents involved, the timing of administration, the peak and duration of effects, the quantitative assessment of appropriate analgesia and sedation, opportunities to minimize drug administration, and the weaning of the medications.

The implementation team sought to identify the most effective and safe sedatives and analgesics that allowed for escalation and weaning while minimizing withdrawal effects. Choosing intravenous agents with dosing that could be easily converted for oral administration was also deemed to be important to decrease hospital length of stay.

The next challenge came in the selection of a sedation scale, as the entire proposed protocol revolved around nursing responses to a patient's "comfort score." A sedation scale provides a target around which the patient's needs are matched with medication administration or withdrawal.

Ideally, a reliable sedation scale

1. reflects the presence and intensity of clinical conditions requiring analgesia or sedation;
2. targets an optimal level of sedation;
3. defines clearly discrete, ideally nonoverlapping, comfort strata;
4. identifies a sufficient number of strata to permit drug titration;
5. exhibits reliability and validity;
6. demonstrates ease of education and implementation; and
7. responds to longitudinal changes in comfort level.

In the current discussion, the sedation scale reflects the "check" step in repetitive PDCA cycles attempting to restore patient comfort homeostasis. While there are many reliable scales available for adults, there are few designed for pediatric care, and certainly no gold standard exists.

To simplify the education process, the implementation team decided to continue to use the same comfort and sedation scale that had been used in the ICU over the past few years. This ICU Comfort Score was developed and validated within the Seattle Children's Hospital ICU, meets most of the criteria for an effective sedation scale, and demonstrates excellent interrater reliability. It should be appreciated that other ICUs have demonstrated success using alternative scales such as the Comfort Scale and Richmond Agitation-Sedation Scale (RASS). Astutely, the team recognized that it was important to not introduce another change into the system, as the other aspects of the protocol represented a significant departure from the status quo.

Another acknowledged challenge in delivering effective and safe sedation for patients receiving mechanical ventilation is providing training and education for all ICU providers. Medical staff caring for these fragile patients would need education regarding the medications being used, anticipated side effects, pharmacokinetics, and the treatment of complications. Teaching would need to include standard doses, peak effect time, and the metabolic elimination of these drugs. Ultimately, such education would improve provider knowledge of and skill in the administration of analgesic or sedative infusion and bolus dosing in the ICU.

All ICU service providers were stakeholders that would need to be involved in the rollout of an ICU Comfort Protocol, as patient safety and work flow would be compromised if different services utilized different protocols. Designing standard work for a common ICU intervention would undoubtedly be beneficial to ICU patients, but convincing anesthesia, surgery, and specialty service colleagues of this assertion was another story. Encouraging participation by these groups was essential to create consensus for and ultimately compliance with an ICU Comfort Protocol.

The Importance of Multidisciplinary Leadership

With clear goals in mind, and recognition of the many challenges to be faced, a multidisciplinary implementation team began work on designing a protocol. Key team members and their respective roles included the following.

Physician Leader

It was important to identify someone from the ICU staff who was respected clinically, had an ICU administrative role, and was knowledgeable about continuous performance improvement. This leader was knowledgeable about ICU sedation practices and helped to shape the ICU Comfort Protocol. Additionally, this person was also involved with ICU strategic planning and facilitated inclusion of the protocol into ongoing ICU CPI work.

A formidable challenge for this role was the development of consensus among physicians, with focus on the importance of relinquishing autonomy (i.e., to the bedside nurse) while simultaneously enthusiastically embracing accountability for the ICU Comfort Protocol team model. The generation of clinically meaningful data would be particularly important for this group of largely skeptical stakeholders. For this transition, the director of critical care medicine served as the physician leader.

Process Owner

Identification of a single person to champion the need for standardization and to be responsible for the process was essential. This person assumed principal ownership for all aspects of development and implementation of the ICU Comfort Protocol. Responsibilities of this individual included conducting individual and team meetings to provide education and promote consensus, overseeing construction and "just do it" PDCA revision of the algorithm, supervising physician and nursing education, and organizing objective data collection to compare effects of the intervention. The process owner was a pediatric critical care medicine fellow.

Clinical Nurse Specialist

An energetic nursing leader was an integral component of the team. She championed the need for the proposed change, and encouraged and educated the nursing staff. The clinical nurse specialist had outstanding bedside, administrative, and people skills that were critical in both development and implementation of the protocol. She was respected by the nursing staff, a characteristic that was instrumental in facilitating change in practice.

This individual managed the grassroots education phase of implementation, oversaw the auditing portion of compliance analysis, and fostered protocol sustainability. A particular challenge for this leadership role included recognition of a differential approach to experienced nurses versus more junior nursing. The former nurses were definitely more suspicious of the process due to lingering nightmares of previous failed "reengineering promises." On the other hand, new graduate nurses viewed ICU Comfort Protocol implementation as another interesting facet of orientation education. The nurse manager employed the "dangling carrot" of empowering bedside nursing practice (essentially independent serial and continuous PDCA cycles) as the key element of the ICU Comfort Protocol.

ICU Pharmacist

Pharmacy staff must be involved in the creation of any clinical protocol that involves the administration of medications. For the ICU Comfort Protocol, the lead pharmacist was instrumental in providing nursing and physician education and information about the sedative medications that were considered for the algorithm and

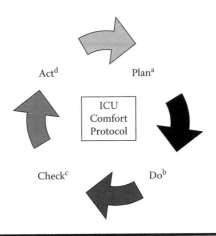

Figure 9.2 Nursing bedside interaction with the ICU Comfort Protocol. In this scheme, the titration of ICU comfort is portrayed as a continuous series of PDCA cycles that characterize delivery of critical care in general. (a) *Planning* involves implementation of the comfort plan derived during daily interdisciplinary rounds. Depending on the patient status, this target may involve anything on a spectrum from very light or no sedation to heavy sedation where the patient exhibits minimal spontaneous movement. This target will usually change over time. (b) *Doing* reflects administration of the prescribed standard concentration analgesic and/or sedative infusion. (c) *Checking* refers to real-time, dynamic bedside nursing assessment of the patient's ICU Comfort Score, based on quantifiable symptoms reflecting status of pain and anxiety. (d) *Acting* characterizes the empowered bedside nurse titrating the analgesic and sedative infusions based on the target comfort goal (a, stated above) and the patient's current status (c, stated above). Because the ICU Comfort Protocol prescribes a scheduled assessment every four hours, the process functions as standard work and not just a reliable method. Protocol forcing function of the scheduled assessments provides the pull in this methodology.

comparing agents routinely used at other institutions. Based on research linking delirium to the use of benzodiazepines, she played an important role in creating a protocol that minimized the use of this class of sedatives. The pharmacy staff became responsible for bedside auditing of compliance and ongoing, real-time education of staff on rounds and at the bedside.

Designing and Marketing the Standard Work Product

After gathering similar protocols from both adult and pediatric institutions and reviewing the existing literature, development of a general framework and theory of what the implementation team considered to be an optimal approach to comfort began. Protocols based primarily on continuous infusions as well as those based solely on bolus medications were both considered. Ultimately, the team concluded that a hybrid of these two approaches would be most effective and created an algorithm in which bolus medication doses were given to achieve a specific acute effect with a low rate of medication infusion provided for background effect. The protocol suggested frequent bolus doses to maximize speed of effect, while the continuous infusions were titrated slowly based on the number of boluses required over a specified time interval to reach a targeted level of comfort.

Morphine was selected as the primary protocol medication due to its well-known safety and efficacy profile among children. As beneficial synergistic effects between opioids and benzodiazepines are well described, the team opted to include a benzodiazepine (lorazepam) as an adjuvant medication for use when comfort was difficult to obtain with morphine alone, thereby allowing individualization within a standard protocol.

Even though surgical patients (admitted following surgery or invasive procedures) and medical patients (admitted for pneumonia or seizures, for example) might have very different sedative and analgesic needs, the team decided to proceed with the development of a single ICU Comfort Protocol. With the benefit of hindsight, this was the obvious correct standard decision.

Education Phase

Educating over two hundred nurses, as well as a multitude of physicians and other care providers interfacing with the ICU over a short period of time, was only possible with thorough preparation and planning. Initially, the team scheduled a month of preparation time, followed by two months of focused education prior to the planned implementation date. Practically, this proved too lofty a goal, as implementation was delayed by almost two months. However, setting a deadline forced focus on the task. A preparation phase consisted of development of in-service sessions, production of laminated bedside cards and posters to place around the ICU, and training of the nursing governance team, a group of influential nurses who are elected by their peers to guide ICU nursing policy. This leadership group was involved in the early development of the protocol (see "Creating Consensus ('Buy-In')," below), and was trained as "super users" to answer common implementation questions.

The clinical nurse specialist and the process owner created a PowerPoint presentation that outlined the need for an ICU Comfort Protocol, reasons for moving forward with protocol implementation, a description and discussion of the actual standard work, and a case-based quiz at the end. Twenty separate sessions were led by the nursing governance team and involved small groups of ten nurses over a one-hour period usually scheduled during their regular shift. Two additional resource nurses were employed during the weeks of training in order to facilitate patient care while bedside nurses received training. A computer-based module was also created in order to provide bedside continuing education training for new staff during their orientation.

In addition to the nursing staff training, a training session was held with the ICU attending staff and fellows. Each month four new residents begin their rotations in the ICU. These individuals ultimately are responsible for transcribing the majority of orders for ICU patients (including ICU Comfort Protocol orders). Understanding that it would be almost impossible to teach the protocol to nearly one hundred residents at one time in one place, a decision instead was made to provide just-in-time training about the protocol during their ICU orientation. They were also provided pocket cards with a figure outlining the algorithm on one side and tips and ordering assistance along with the ICU Comfort Scale printed on the other side.

Creating Consensus ("Buy-In")

Hospital administration agreed that an ICU Comfort Protocol should be implemented, and that it was essential that the ICU attending physicians were engaged and receptive to the protocol. These individuals were met with early in the protocol's development and frequently one-on-one to discuss concerns and suggestions. These ICU physicians were reassured that protocol-driven care (standard work) need not stifle individual decision creativity or clinical judgment. The success in treatment of acute lymphocytic leukemia (ALL) over the last fifty years was provided as a relevant example. In the 1950s, a diagnosis of leukemia in a child was essentially a death sentence; however, due to iterative therapeutic PDCA clinical research cycles and rigorous standardization of care, over 90 percent of children routinely now survive.

Understanding individual case exceptions was emphasized, as this information would inform future adjustment of the protocol. Accordingly, ICU staff were told that they would be able to identify exceptions from the protocol whenever they felt it was clinically necessary, but that the team would be carefully tracking these exceptions. Needless to say, not everyone was happy prior to implementation. However, with patience, listening, addressing concerns, and providing data collected along the way, feelings began to change. Eventually, the protocol took care of itself with its own success as the staunchest opponents soon became allies as they watched the ICU Comfort Protocol work and clinical care improve.

The nursing staff initially felt burdened by the need to learn a new protocol and change their clinical practice. They soon realized that they had gained autonomy within the structure of the protocol and were no longer dependent on calling a physician to obtain orders for analgesic and sedative infusion rate changes to maintain patient comfort. They were provided new tools to deliver analgesia and sedation and were able to take pride in how well they maintained comfort with minimal medication.

The process owner also met with physicians representing medical, anesthesia, and surgical services. By including them prior to protocol implementation, we were able to make them partners in the development of the protocol, thereby increasing buy-in and trust.

A Remarkable Story

Implementation of the ICU Comfort Protocol is a remarkable story (See Figure 9.3). In less than two years, introduction of this standard work has significantly improved patient care and patient flow through the ICU. We have seen a dramatic reduction in overall benzodiazepine use. The team tracked compliance, provided bedside education and feedback on daily rounds, and prospectively gathered data for a human subjects institutional review board–approved study examining the first three months of protocol introduction. By February 2009, initial data and experience were presented and favorably received at a national critical care meeting. By the summer of 2010, a publication comparing the year before and the year after

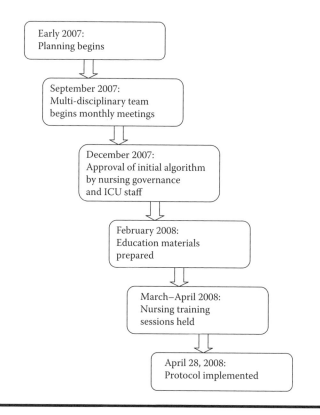

Figure 9.3 ICU Comfort Protocol implementation timeline. The high-level milestones to implement the ICU Comfort Protocol.

protocol implementation was drafted. Data from this study show that the protocol has markedly decreased the duration of both benzodiazepine and morphine infusions[10]. As larger groups of patients are followed over time, statistically significant decreased days of mechanical ventilation and ICU length of stay are also expected.

Most performance improvement experts would identify implementation of the reliable ICU Comfort Protocol method as a continuous performance improvement success. Seattle Children's ICU experienced profound culture change around providing continuous comfort to critically ill children in a little over a year. Patient comfort is now discussed daily on medical rounds and plays a major role in nursing shift sign-outs. Subjective survey results demonstrate that the ICU staff is more satisfied with how analgesia and sedation are provided now as compared to before the change. ICU respiratory therapy staff now conducts daily readiness trials assessing suitability for discontinuation of mechanical ventilation on all relevant patients. Though this routine had been previously attempted without success, it is now part of the daily care of each patient and represents a key aspect of the overall goal to decrease days of mechanical ventilation and length of ICU stay.

Improved communication with anesthesia and surgical colleagues has encouraged continued and expanded use of the protocol with good results. This ongoing attention to the protocol and provision of feedback and support to the ICU staff has helped to maintain the ICU Comfort Protocol. Seattle Children's pharmacy staff remains actively involved on medical rounds tracking levels of sedation and the need for bolus medication dosing, and occasionally surveys for ICU Comfort Protocol compliance.

Online materials and computer-based modules allow new nursing graduates, newly hired care staff, and float pool nurses quick and easy access to protocol training. Seattle Children's electronic feedback system permits any staff member to comment, praise, or challenge sedation practices. All such feedback is immediately reviewed and addressed by the ICU nurse manager, and is utilized to drive iterative PDCA cycles to revise and improve analgesia and sedation practice as appropriate. On the suggestion of the nursing staff, a related protocol designed for nonmechanically ventilated patients has also been successfully adopted.

Other ICU Pull Systems

1. Traditionally, medical rounding once or twice a day is focused on the creation of a daily care plan. This approach results in stuttered patient flow through the ICU, as opposed to an ideal model where continuous bedside rounding would again mimic iterative PDCA cycles and provide more at-the-moment, patient-driven escalation or weaning of therapy in synchrony with the natural course of the illness. In this latter ideal state, rounding becomes an exercise of determining where the patient is positioned relative to an expected natural course trajectory for a given diagnosis or disease. Work in the ICU becomes 24/7/365.

2. A variety of visual cues is now commonplace in ICUs to ensure the adequacy of a myriad of supplies needed to provide critical care. A less utilized tool, a patient status board or trajectory andon, summarizes the state of a number of variables that relate to pull of the patient toward ICU discharge.

These variables might include the absence of hemodynamic instability, the resolution of pulmonary failure, the tolerance of enteral nutrition, the discontinuation of nonessential invasive catheters, the provision of transfer education to the family, the identification of a receiving care team, the composition of transfer orders, the completion of respiratory therapy, and nursing and physician communication with respective ward counterparts.

Each activity is coded as red (not finished), yellow (in progress), or green (completed). This visual tool allows all care providers to assess the dynamics of overall patient flow in the ICU, the trajectory for an individual patient, and what needs to occur next to pull a particular patient toward PICU discharge. Empty ICU rooms are similarly coded as red (dirty), yellow (being cleaned), or green (ready for admission) (See Figure 9.4).

Room	Room Status	Assigned Nurse	Assigned Resident	No Hemodynamic Instability	No Pulmonary Instability	Non-essential Catheters Removed	Discharge Criteria Met	Plan for Ward Analgesia/Anxiolysis	Nutritional Plan in Place	Family Education Complete	Floor Orders in Place	Attending to Attending Signout	Resident Signout	RT Signout	Care Coord/Social Work	Receiving Unit Ready	Date/Time Ready for Discharge	Notes
4134-1	Y	Claire	Frank	G	G	G	G	G	G	G	G	R	Y	G	G	R		
4134-2	Y	Betsy	Susan	G	R	R	R	Y	G	R	R	R	R	R	R	R		
4135	Y	Kelly	Susan	G	G	G	G	G	G	R	G	R	G	G	G	Y		
4136-1	Y	Vanessa	Frank	G	Y	R	R	Y	G	R	R	R	R	G	G	R		
4136-2	Y	Vanessa	Frank	R	R	R	R	R	R	R	R	R	R	R	R	R		
4137	Y	Denise	Elizabeth	G	G	G	G	G	G	G	G	G	G	G	G	G	12/15, 0730	
4138	Y	Annika	Susan	G	G	Y	G	G	G	Y	R	R	G	G	G	Y		
4139	Y	Teaessa	Susan	R	Y	R	R	Y	Y	Y	R	R	R	R	R	R		
4140-1	G																	
4140-2	Y	Claire	Ahmad	Y	R	R	R	R	R	R	R	R	R	R	R	R		
4141	Y	Denise	Elizabeth	G	G	G	G	G	G	G	G	R	G	G	G	G	12/14, 1900	
4142-1	R																	
4142-2	Y	Gloria	Ahmad	G	G	G	R	G	G	R	R	R	R	R	R	R		
4143	Y	Karen	Ahmad	G	Y	R	R	G	G	R	R	R	R	R	R	R		
4144	Y	Gloria	Elizabeth	Y	G	R	R	Y	R	Y	R	R	R	Y	R	R		

Figure 9.4 Trajectory andon summarizing individual and overall patient trajectory in the ICU. This simple visual tool permits rapid assessment of individual as well as total ICU patient status. Specifically, it identifies tasks that need to be completed in order to pull the patient toward ICU discharge. Red: incomplete or unresolved; yellow: in progress or resolving; and green: complete or resolved. In general, more overall red hue indicates higher ICU illness intensity and slower patient flow toward ICU discharge, while more overall green hue indicates lower ICU illness intensity and faster flow toward ICU discharge.

3. Standard work or clinical pathways for individual diseases should identify expected patient trajectories and hence facilitate patient flow. This information delineates specific discharge criteria at the time of admission as well as expected patient status at various times following ICU admission. In addition, the clinical pathway suggests specific interventions as well as laboratory and imaging studies along the way. It is designed to standardize the overall approach to a patient, such that the effect of altering this approach can actually be measured. It is not designed to stifle care provider creativity. Reasons for not following clinical pathway standard work are documented and summarized to iteratively improve the standard work algorithm.

4. A number of critical care standard work and decision support tools that provide adequately explicit algorithms to promote pull therapy to continuously reestablish physiologic and biochemical homeostasis are under investigation. All of these tools employ the concept of iterative PDCA cycles with scheduled serial assessments and actions based on an overriding care plan and results of the assessments.

Although still controversial, a multitude of studies indicate that high blood sugar among critically ill adults and children is associated with increased morbidity and mortality. Ongoing clinical investigations are attempting to define both the benefits and risks of so-called tight glucose control utilizing continuous or scheduled blood glucose measurements linked to titration of a continuous infusion of insulin. In this regard, carefully designed computerized decision support tools have been shown to be superior to simple paper protocols or clinician judgment in terms of achieving a target blood glucose value (accuracy) and reducing variation around this target (precision).

Similar computerized decision support tools have been designed for safe weaning of mechanical ventilation support among patients with acute lung injury, with goals of reducing duration of mechanical ventilation as well as ventilator-associated lung injury. Persistent need for mechanical ventilation represents the most common reason for prolonged ICU length of stay, and achieving both goals would have the effect of pulling the patient toward earlier ICU discharge.

Another common intensive care intervention involves infusion of various vasoactive and cardiotonic drugs to support cardiac output, blood pressure, and organ perfusion. By continuously assessing a variety of input variables such as blood pressure, oxygen saturation of the blood, vascular volume status, and urine output, an algorithm can be derived to provide objective decisions regarding the escalation or weaning of such infusions. The complexity of such tools increases exponentially with the number of input variables.

It is easy to envision how such decision support tools could be implemented in a closed-loop fashion. For example, a device providing continuous monitoring of a patient's blood glucose can provide an electronic signal to a pump controlling an infusion of insulin. Similarly, devices continuously monitoring patients' exhaled carbon dioxide and blood oxygen saturation can provide electronic signaling to a mechanical ventilator to automatically adjust rate or depth of mechanical breaths or oxygen concentration being delivered. In the future, such approaches may not only facilitate patient flow in intensive care units but also allow for built-in error proofing.

Conclusions

The provision of critical care medicine naturally relates to a series of PDCA exercises all inexorably coupled with restoration of a patient's biochemical and physiologic homeostasis. When these cycles are delineated with standard work and longitudinally linked, a natural flow system is realized that pulls the patient toward steady recovery and more timely discharge from the ICU. This chapter discussed how such a system was designed and implemented to provide adequate but not excessive comfort for critically ill children. Similar approaches are being developed and tested to rectify other aberrations from homeostasis during critical illness, and include standard work adequately explicit algorithms for the control of blood glucose, provision of mechanical ventilation, and delivery of vasoactive and cardiotonic drug infusions.

Eventually, an almost unimaginable amount of patient data will be captured from the complete electronic health record. These patient profile data related to specific conditions or diagnoses will be continuously updated to generate a graphical description of patient trajectory. Such systems will provide early identification of patient vulnerable periods per sophisticated programs designed to assess variance from expected trajectory and hence to avoid errors and to facilitate pull of the patient through his or her critical illness experience. Comparison of treatment effects and outcomes across healthcare systems will be possible and will drive iterative improvements in the specific standard work that will lead to precision in expected pulled patient trajectories.

Notes

1. J. R. Jacobs, J. G. Reves, and P. S. A. Glass, "Rationale and Technique for Continuous Infusions in Anesthesia," *International Anesthesiology Clinics* 29 (1991): 23–38.
2. J. P. Kress, A. S. Pohlman, and J. B. Hall, "Sedation and Analgesia in the Intensive Care Unit," *American Journal of Respiratory and Critical Care Medicine* 166 (2002): 1024–28.
3. J. D. Tobias, "Tolerance, Withdrawal, and Physical Dependency after Long-Term Sedation and Analgesia of Children in the Pediatric Intensive Care Unit," *Critical Care Medicine* 28 (2000): 2122–32.

4. E. Ista, M. de Hoog, D. Tibboel, and M. van Dijk, "Implementation of Standard Sedation Management in Pediatric Intensive Care: Effective and Feasible?" *Journal of Clinical Nursing* 18, no. 17 (September 2009): 2511–20.

5. A. D. Brook, T. S. Ahrens, R. Schaiff, et al., "Effect of a Nursing-Implemented Sedation Protocol on the Duration of Mechanical Ventilation," *Critical Care Medicine* 27 (1999): 2609–15.

6. T. D. Girard, J. P. Dress, B. D. Fuchs, J. W. Thaomaon, W. D. Schweickert, B. T. Pun, D. B. Taichman, J. G. Dunn, A. S. Pohlman, P. A. Kinniry, J. C. Jackson, A. E. Canonico, R. W. Light, A. K. Shintani, J. L. Thompson, S. M. Gordon, J. B. Hall, R. S. Dittus, G. R. Bernard, and E. W. Ely, "Efficacy and Safety of a Paired Sedation and Ventilator Weaning Protocol for Mechanically Ventilated Patients in Intensive Care (Awakening and Breathing Controlled Trial): A Randomised Controlled Trial," *Lancet* 371 (2008): 126–34.

7. S. Mehta, L. Burry, S. Fischer, et al., "Canadian Critical Care Trials Group: Canadian Survey of the Use of Sedatives, Analgesic, and Neuromuscular Blocking Agents in Critically Ill Patients," *Critical Care Medicine* 34 (2006): 374–80.

8. M. D. Twite, A. Rashid, J. Zuk, and R. H. Friesen, "Sedation, Analgesia, and Neuromuscular Blockade in the Pediatric Intensive Care Unit: Survey of Fellowship Training Programs," *Pediatric Critical Care Medicine* 5, no. 6 (November 2004): 521–32.

9. W. B. Cannon, "Organization for Physiologic Homeostasis," *Physiological Reviews* 9 (1929): 399–431.

10. Deeter KH, Ridling DA, Linggi G, King MA, Di Gennaro L, Lynn AM, Zimmerman JJ. Introduction of a sedation protocol in a pediatric ICU. Crit Care Med 2008; 36 (Suppl): A181 (Abstract 701). SCCM 38th Critical Care Congress, Nashville, TN, 1/31/2009-2/4/2009.

Chapter 10

Delivering Compassionate Care through Clinical Standard Work on Rounds

Glen Tamura, MD, PhD
Medical Director, Inpatient Medical Units
Seattle Children's Hospital
Associate Professor of Pediatrics
University of Washington School of Medicine

Darren Migita, MD
Pediatric Hospitalist
Seattle Children's Hospital

Inpatient Rounding: Why Are We Doing This?

They arrive at the doors of our hospital afflicted by infection, tumor, and trauma. Often they come to us cradled in the arms of their parents, whose fear of what will occur next is surpassed only by their love for their child. Parents instinctively hope that within the walls of this hospital lie the expertise and medical machinery to cure; and when disease has exceeded their abilities as parents, they entrust that child to us. Yet a hospital remains an unfamiliar landscape replete with a new language, razor-sharp needles, pulsating magnetic resonance imaging (MRI) scanners, and hordes of white-coated personnel scurrying from here to there in a seemingly uninterpretable dance. A child's cure often lies at the end of a course difficult to navigate or endure. Tubes will be placed into their bodies, and difficult-to-pronounce medications will be injected into their bloodstream. We may further ask that radioactive tracer dye is swallowed, that blood be siphoned daily for testing, or that they be made temporarily unconscious for a painful procedure during which multiple sharp objects will be brought to bear.

Adding to the patient and family's challenge is the asymmetry that exists between medical professionals and the patient and family. The gap of knowledge between the two parties is generally wide and apparent. Without a means of communicating about each step of a child's care, a hospital stay can devolve into a frightening experience even absent an awful prognosis. Indeed, the application of medical interventions without proper explanation can appear as torture to the untrained eye. In the end, this series of events may lead to a cure, but if we fail to pause to inform, answer questions, acknowledge fears, explain the unexplained, and listen with the utmost humility, we have erred. The art of medicine is not merely the proper execution of applied science but the application of that science as art. Art in medicine is a combination of knowledge, partnership, compassion, transparency, and action. We seek to bring this art to the bedside for every patient every day by applying the principles of reliable methods and clinical standard work. Our story is about one aspect of clinical standard work, the creation of family-centered daily bedside rounds.

The Inpatient Medicine Service: The Players

The word "teaching" has special meaning at Seattle Children's Hospital. Graduates from medical school who choose a career in pediatrics come to us for an additional three years of intensive training, known as "residency" and these young physicians are known as "residents." Those in their first year are referred to as "interns," and those in their final two years are known as "senior residents." Attending physicians, or "attendings," are those who have completed their residency and have varying amounts of formal specialty training. Attending physicians have ultimate responsibility for all medical decisions and oversee the training of the residents. At SCH, patients on the inpatient medical service are divided among and cared for by three teams. Each team is composed of attendings, senior residents, and interns.

There are other players critical to the care of the patient. The bedside nurses log the greatest number of direct hours at the patient's bedside. They ensure that the plan for the day is executed and report any changes in clinical status to the MDs. Due to their nearly continuous presence at the patient's bedside, they are most likely to be privy to emotions in raw unfiltered form.

Pharmacists also play a critical role. They assess the patients' medications on a daily basis, look for potentially dangerous drug interactions, and, most importantly, ensure that dosages are correct. In short, they ensure that we do not harm our patients with the very drugs intended for cure.

Rounding: Where We've Been

"Rounding" is a long-standing tradition in medicine. Although definitions vary, it can be loosely viewed as a meeting in which the clinical problems of a particular patient are discussed by the care team. Prior to 2003, our system of rounding was highly variable. Each morning, attendings and interns would gather in conference rooms and discuss each patient on their service. Once this was accomplished, the team would then scatter to examine certain, but not all, patients and write the orders of the day. Depending on the day of the week, the preferences of the attending, and, perhaps, the nature of the patients, rounds were different every day. For this and other reasons, this system of rounding was fraught with difficulties.

Due to the day-to-day variability of this system, families and RNs could not reliably predict which members of the care team would meet with them, if any at all. The daily plan formulated in the conference room was created without the input of RNs or family, who often held critical information about a patient's condition. As a result, plans were quite often changed as the day progressed, leading to significant rework and further confusion for the patient and family. Moreover, communication between the key players and patients was not reliable. Plans were often initiated without explanation. One could imagine the dissatisfaction of a parent whose child was whisked off for a computerized tomography (CT) scan without having met with the MDs who ordered the study! Without a deeper understanding of reliable methods and standard work, errors such as these were accepted by the care team as a regrettable part of the norm.

Sir William Osler, who many describe as the founder of modern medicine, pioneered the tradition of teaching in medicine at Johns Hopkins during the late 1800s. He disliked didactics and fervently insisted that physicians in training learned best at the patients' bedside—a principle which holds true to this day. In fact, his hope was that his epitaph would read, "He brought medical students into the wards for teaching." Osler stated, "I desire no other epitaph … than the statement that I taught medical students in the wards, as I regard this as by far the most useful and important work I have been called upon to do." Undoubtedly, rounds at SCH had evolved into something much less patient oriented than Olser envisioned.

Solution: Reliable Method for Rounds

Problems associated with rounds, including serious clinical errors related to poor communication, motivated SCH leaders to find ways to improve the process. SCH had begun to use continuous performance improvement (CPI) tools adapted from the Toyota Production System and had used this methodology on other projects with good success. Clinical and administrative leaders recognized that the complex multidisciplinary rounding process, which was neither capable nor efficient, could be improved using CPI tools. This decision to use CPI tools for this project was a major advancement in the hospital's use of CPI methodology, as it was the first time such a complex clinical and teaching process had been addressed using this approach.

Three process owners led the project: Georgeann Hagland, RN, director of the medical unit; Dr. Sterling Clarren, medical director of the inpatient medical unit; and Dr. Richard Shugerman, residency program director. In addition, one of the pediatric residents, Dr. Maneesh Batra, was also recruited to ensure that the resident perspective was heard and respected. Together, this group designed and planned a Rapid Process Improvement Workshop (RPIW) to fundamentally rework the rounding model. They collected data that the workshop team would use to redesign the rounding process, and recruited team members that included representatives from all the roles on rounds, including attending physicians, resident physicians, floor nurses, and discharge coordinators. The workshop was held over five days.

Prior to attending the RPIW, none of the staff involved had ever been involved in CPI processes, and so the first day was used to introduce and train staff in the fundamental principals of CPI and team dynamics.

The team then moved into a data collection and analysis phase highlighted by a "3 actuals walk." The team was broken into small groups that observed the "actual people" performing the "actual process" in the "actual location." During the 3 actuals walk, they recorded a variety of data, including process steps and the time required for each step. Although the observers were experienced clinicians who had participated in rounds for years, they learned many new things about the process of care. In particular, each observer became aware for the first time of many tasks that the various roles (interns, residents, attending physicians, nurses, care coordinators, et al.) were performing. By taking this broad and comprehensive view of the process, team members gained invaluable insights into the waste created by the current processes. When later describing their observations, there were many moments when team members laughed out loud at processes that were so convoluted with communication so poor that laughter or tears were the only reasonable responses. The team then analyzed the data they had collected with a focus on "value-added" and "non-value-added" steps from the patient's perspective. The team was shocked to find that few of the steps performed in rounds were truly of any value to the patient (see Table 10.1).

The team then brainstormed and designed a fundamentally new rounding process with the specific goals of eliminating 50 percent of the waste, while improving outcomes. The resulting process became and still remains the basic model by which rounds occur at Seattle Children's Hospital.

The most straightforward change was the creation of standard rounding times for each service. Each medical team cares for both general pediatric patients and

Table 10.1   Process Map Step Analysis

Analysis of Steps: Rounding on the Medical Service		Current	New
Analysis based on a 3-year-old male with a lung infection transferred from an outside hospital, with a 3-day length of stay	Number of steps	178	59
	Number of value-added steps	33	26
	Percentage of value-added steps	19%	44%
	Number of queues	23	4
	Number of delays	32	5
	Number of handoffs	17	10

subspecialty patients who are assigned to particular teams. Subspecialists had previously contacted the teams ad hoc, and would expect the team to round whenever they called. Under the new system, each subspecialty was assigned a standard "rounding time."

The new process also redefined the participants on rounds. To the residents and attending physicians who had previously been the sole participants were added the bedside nurse, the discharge planner, and a new role, the "team coordinator." In order to allow the bedside nurse to participate, rounds were moved out of the conference room to the patient's room. It is worth noting that although the team discussed the possibility of including parents on rounds, in the initial rollout of the new system, the bedside nurse was tasked with voicing the concerns of families; families were subsequently included on rounds five months later as part of the plan, do, check, and act (PDCA) process. This fundamental shift in rounds allowed all of the key stakeholders—physicians, trainees, nurses, discharge planners, and patients and their families—to discuss the case and to come to a consensus on the plan. Discharge coordinators had previously spent many hours in the afternoon trying to contact team members to discuss arrangements for discharge, and frequently only identified those needs when the patient was ready to go home. The presence of discharge coordinators on rounds allowed them to communicate with the team much more easily, and to reliably identify home care and other needs and arrange for them to be ready on the day of discharge.

The team coordinator role has ultimately proven to be one of the most successful innovations of this workshop. Team coordinators have certain concrete duties on rounds, including calling nurses to let them know that the team will be arriving soon for rounds, shepherding the team through the most efficient route to see all of the patients, and acting as timekeeper by reminding the team when they need to meet with various subspecialists. In addition, during rounds they are able to identify tasks that do not need to be performed by clinicians, such as arranging primary care provider appointments after discharge, scheduling tests, and obtaining outside records, and complete those tasks, thus eliminating much of the nonclinical work from residents' and nurses' workload. Finally, team coordinators have proven to be a steady influence on rounds, helping to standardize a wide variety of new processes even as residents, interns, and attending staff change from week to week. For example, as part of an RPIW on communication with primary care providers at discharge, the team coordinators were charged with providing house staff with a daily list of patients whose primary care provider needs a discharge call, monitoring whether the discharge call is documented, and updating the list accordingly. Team coordinators have taken pride in this role, and discharge calls are now made on approximately 75 percent of patients, up from less than 50 percent before their involvement.

The sequence of work and content of rounds were also standardized, with specific tasks for all of those present. The primary intern presents the patient's history, and assessment and plan for the day. The bedside nurse and family then ask any questions they have, and provide input. The discharge coordinator then identifies any home care needs. The senior resident provides feedback and refines the plan, and the attending physician speaks last. During this process, the nonpresenting intern enters orders in the computer in real time as decisions are made, and reads them back to the presenting intern at the end of rounds to confirm those orders before submitting them. Finally, the senior resident and/or the attending physician make teaching points for the trainees.

Why Was This So Difficult?

Communication with key stakeholders was critical for successful implementation. Although stakeholders were represented on the team, and those team members were committed to a successful implementation, this alone was not enough. Care was taken to have separate meetings with each stakeholder group, with presentations by the stakeholder representatives. Feedback was elicited, and changes were made to the plan in response to the concerns expressed. After implementation, feedback was elicited from all team members. In retrospect, this communication was well worth the effort.

Perhaps the most difficult challenge in the implementation plan was that many subspecialists were reluctant to commit to attending rounds at scheduled times. Many subspecialists had other responsibilities, such as procedure block time and clinics, that created barriers to their attendance at the assigned times. Implementation required the direct and strong intervention of Dr. Bruder Stapleton, the chair of the Department of Pediatrics, to insure that the required scheduling changes could be made and that the various subspecialty divisions would be held accountable for respecting the assigned rounding times. Without his leadership, implementation would have been impossible.

After the new rounding structure was implemented, it is not surprising given the global nature of the changes that further difficulties were encountered. In particular, the trainees were highly dissatisfied. Although they made a good faith attempt to implement the rounding plan, and several aspects of the plan met with their approval, there were serious consequences of the new rounding process. These problems were related to the smaller teams created in the new system, with only a single senior resident and two interns. These small teams were particularly vulnerable when both interns and senior residents frequently left for various training requirements. With loss of these personnel, these teams frequently became too small to function in the afternoons. In addition, frequently the team was forced to hand off patients to other teams in the afternoon—these cross-cover teams were then required to make important care decisions without the benefit of having been present on rounds.

These very real problems were ultimately addressed approximately two months after the initial implementation, again in the spirit of PDCA. The new rounding process and the scheduled times for rounds were maintained. The smaller teams were paired so that each team now consisted of two senior residents and four interns. This allowed the teams to function more effectively as various personnel left the hospital.

In retrospect, this response to the residents' concerns was much too slow. Enormous dissatisfaction built over the two months before the rounding system was revised, significantly impacting morale among both residents and interns as well as attending physicians and nursing staff. In subsequent process improvement projects, care has been taken to allow for much more rapid responses to concerns after implementation.

Measured Improvements

What effect did this intervention have on our patients? The NRC/Picker survey tool is a seventy-seven-question survey mailed to a randomly selected population of patients post discharge. After implementation of the new rounding process in June 2004, survey responses ($n = 359$) revealed statistically significant results for questions regarding "overall rating of care" and "knew which doctor was in charge" based on chi-squared analysis. For the question "Overall, how would you rate the care your child received in the hospital?" the percentage of "excellent" responses increased from 44 percent (October–December 2003) to 67 percent (October–December 2004). Problem score ratings showed a downward trend (lower is better!) during the equivalent time frame ($p < 0.01$). For the question "Did you know which doctor was in charge of your care in the hospital?" the percentage of "yes" responses increased from 59 percent (October–December 2003) to 82 percent (July–August 2005). Problem score percentages fell from 41 to 19 percent during the same periods ($p < 0.016$). Though not statistically significant, for the question "Did you have confidence and trust in the doctors caring for your child?" the percentage of "yes, always" responses increased from 65 percent (October–December 2003) to 85 percent (July–August 2005). Problem score percentages fell from 34 to 14 percent during the same period.

A process map step analysis also revealed significant improvements. When a typical three-day stay of a medical patient was dissected, clear gains became evident.

The point that data speak powerfully should not be underestimated. Data appeal to our sense of logic, and because they are unemotional by nature, data have the unique ability to repel anecdotal resistance. All members of the design team immediately recognized what these data represented: better patient care. Concepts developed in industry had fused with medicine; manufacturing techniques and the art of medicine had been chimerized, and a new cadre of "true believers" in CPI had been born. Just as Toyota had propelled forward the Lexus brand by combining previously incongruent concepts of luxury and performance, the general medical service at SCH had now fused efficiency and the art of medicine. And the experience of our patients and families benefitted greatly.

Replication and PDCA

The general medical service represents only a portion of all the services at SCH. The logical next step was to attempt to spread these rounding techniques to other services. As of July 2009, the general surgery, hematology/oncology, bone marrow transplant, neurosurgery, orthopedics, cardiology, and cardiac surgery departments and the pediatric intensive care unit have completed RPIW events to operationalize standard rounding techniques. Replication has afforded us the opportunity to refine our reliable method for rounding and continuously improve based on the iterative experiences of the services. We have distilled our standardized elements of rounds into a single, easy-to-digest document which serves as the template for each replication event (see Figure 10.1). Moreover, we have standardized each team member's specific role in the rounding process so that their expertise contributes to the daily plan of care each day for every patient (see Figure 10.2).

For example, the bedside RN brings forth issues relating to barriers to discharge or any "hidden" family concerns that the MD team may not be aware of, pharmacists bring forth issues relating to drug safety, and nutritionists ensure that growth

Elements of Standard Rounds

Seattle Children's
HOSPITAL · RESEARCH · FOUNDATION

Create a work method for the rounding process with components 1-4 below. Demonstrate its reliability with component 5. A reliable method must be consciously developed and documented, always followed – by everyone performing the work, "owned" by someone and basis for improvement.

		Completion
1	**Create a standard rounding schedule (Mon-Sun)**	25% 50% 75% 100%
	Establish a consistent start time	
	Communicate to families when they should expect to see you each day	
	Establish a consistent starting location	
	Track appropriate cycle time/takt time per patient	A
	Round on every patient daily (if not, communicate with family about variation from standard)	A
	Coordinate/sequence the rounds of different services on the same unit to avoid overlap of RN resource	
2	**Create a reliable method for rounding roles and team structure**	25% 50% 75% 100%
	Define and standardize the roles involved in rounding (include role of the interpreter)	
	Define what the team needs to do	
	Assign one role to have ownership of rounds	
	Assign one role to have ownership of whiteboard to update the plan of care	
	Ensure RN is consistently present and an active participant	A
	Ensure overnight care coordination data is presented	
	Introduce team to family by role at the start of rounds	
3	**Standardize whiteboards**	25% 50% 75% 100%
	Ensure there is a whiteboard in every room (per patient)	
	Ensure each whiteboard has four distinct quadrants:	
	Upper left hand corner: Patient name, RN name, room #, etc.	
	Lower left hand corner: Family questions	
	Upper right hand corner: Plan of care (in a way the family can understand)	A
	Lower right hand corner: Discharge criteria (in a way the family can understand)	A
	Ensure whiteboard usage is the same across services	
4	**Involve families in rounds**	25% 50% 75% 100%
	Track % of families participating in rounds, as partners in the care team	A
	If families decline rounds, give them the opportunity to ask questions/provide feedback via other venues	
	Give families an idea of when rounds start and when you expect to arrive to their room	
	Utilize whiteboard with family during rounds:	
	Ensure questions from the lower left hand section have been answered	
	Discuss plan of care with family	A
	Discuss discharge criteria with family	A
	Standardize family communication handouts across services, and seek approval from Family Services	
	If you do not round with family communicate with them about the variation from standard	
5	**Audit rounding process**	25% 50% 75% 100%
	Use standard audit tool	A
	Audit weekly until process is stable	
	Report audit results on standard spreadsheet (used by all services)	
	Task someone who is not involved in rounds to do the audit	
	Ensure process owners attend rounds periodically	

A = Included in Audit Plan   08-20-09

Figure 10.1   Elements of standard rounds template. Each service line deals with specific diagnoses; however, families value consistent, predictable interactions with clinicians, and standardizing rounding between services helps deliver that.

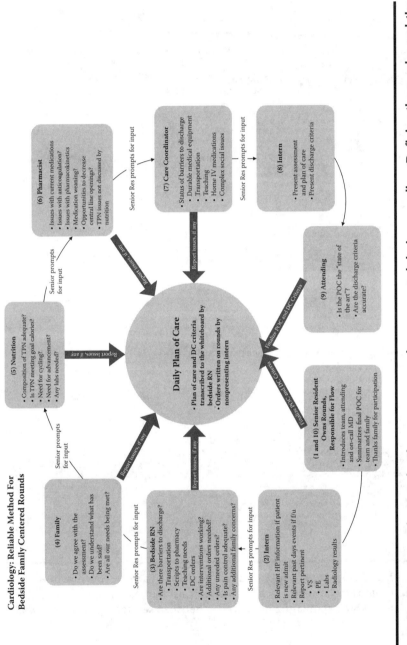

Figure 10.2 Daily plan of care for rounds. There are many roles represented during rounding. Defining those roles and the expectations for them reduces ambiguity, uncertainty, waste, and mistakes.

parameters are appropriate. The family is witness to all of this input from their team, and their understanding of the plan is confirmed on a daily basis. Questions are solicited and fears are allayed to the best of the team's ability. In the end, the product we seek to manufacture is not an automobile, but rather a daily plan of care that is created in partnership, transparent to all, instituted without delay, and executed with compassion—a fusion of art and medicine.

Chapter 11

Developing Standardized Inpatient Care for Patients with Asthma

Edward Carter, MD
Director, Pulmonary Clinical Services
Clinic Chief, Asthma
Seattle Children's Hospital

John Salyer, RRT-NPS, MBA, FAARC
Director, Respiratory Care
Seattle Children's Hospital

Introduction

Imagine that you are at a large children's hospital with well-trained staff who treat more than eight hundred admissions for acute asthma each year but that your hospital does not have a standard approach to the management of asthma. Thus, two patients with acute asthma of similar severity might receive completely different doses, frequencies, and methods of administering medications. For example, one patient with acute asthma could receive 10 mg of albuterol (a bronchodilator medication used to ease breathing) every two hours and remain on this dose and frequency overnight despite clinical improvement because the pediatric resident on call does not have time to reevaluate the patient. Another patient who is receiving 2.5 mg of albuterol every four hours deteriorates but does not have his therapy escalated for similar reasons. There is no standard approach that specifies how to assess the need for and response to bronchodilators, and nurses and respiratory therapists (RTs) are relegated to simply administering the ordered medications. This leads to unwarranted variation in resource consumption and increased hospital length of stay (LOS), with significant cost implications. Thus, two patients with similar asthma exacerbations can have significantly different hospital LOSs, and, conversely, patients with different levels of severity might end up spending the same amount of time in the hospital. Before implementing changes in asthma care using continuous performance improvement (CPI), the length of stay for asthma at our institution was approximately two days (see Table 11.1), which was similar to the national average LOS amongst pediatric tertiary care hospitals. However, by implementing changes through CPI, we standardized our asthma care, which decreased hospital LOS, empowered nurses and RTs by allowing them input into the medication-weaning process, and decreased physician workload.

In this chapter we detail our efforts to improve certain aspects of inpatient care for patients with asthma at Seattle Children's Hospital. This is the story of how we instituted changes and standardized care using CPI methods and tools. We describe how we standardized the management of patients hospitalized with asthma, in large part by systematizing our approach to aerosolized medications.

We considered the following CPI principles extremely important if we were to achieve lasting and significant improvements.

- Frontline nurses, RTs, and physicians would be the foundation of any lasting change.
- Decisions on clinical process design changes would need to be based on the best evidence and driven by data, whenever possible.

Table 11.1 Length of Stay (LOS) and Number of Asthmatic Admissions

Year of Discharge	Mean LOS (days)
Year 1	2.05
Year 2	2.12
Year 3[a]	1.77
Year 4	1.81
Year 5[b]	1.53
Year 6[b]	1.52

[a.] Our asthma clinical practice guidelines were implemented in Year 3.
[b.] Implementation of the conversion from small-volume nebulizers (SVNs) to metered dose inhalers with a valved holding chamber (MDI-VHCs) occurred in the fall of Year 5.

- We could not let the perfect become the enemy of the good. There is always a degree of warranted variation in clinical processes. We approached this project with the realization that we could not achieve complete standardization but that there was significant opportunity for improvement.
- Technology alone would not be the solution to our problems, but it might be an important enabler of improvement.
- If we were to achieve long-term sustained improvement, we would need to employ the plan, do, check, and act (PDCA) cycle. This would require us to develop credible measures of our process (metrics) to review periodically in order to make incremental improvements to the process over time.

Methods

This CPI project consisted of the following:

- Team creation
- Process analysis and literature review
- Protocol development
- Policy and operational changes
- Staff training
- Measurement

Team Creation

To effect change, we knew that we had to start with leadership, both managerial and clinical. However, we sought to avoid a top-heavy decision that would "trickle down" to the employees. Rather, we wanted leadership to provide perspective, be persuasive, identify and bring the right team members together, and help develop the most effective implementation strategies. We realized that sustained long-term improvement in any process was not possible without ongoing engagement from both middle and senior management.

We formed a multidisciplinary team, which included RTs, management and staff nurses, attending physicians, and the pediatric chief resident, to study this process and devise a plan to create more standardized clinical work. We cannot overemphasize the importance of the proper composition of such a team, which included representatives from all of the involved constituents. Organizations are often tempted to have such teams be made up entirely of administration and clinical leadership. However, this can be a serious error because administrative personnel may be disconnected from the complex realities of frontline clinical processes. Since clinical processes have many owners, participants, and constituencies, a representative team is necessary in order to analyze and create acceptable process change. There are clear advantages to involving clinicians early on rather than waiting until the implementation phase. Late involvement of clinicians can lead to unspoken disgruntlement when they realize they were not invited to participate in the fundamental design. Additionally, we were careful to give our team the freedom to explore a wide range of possible solutions and to empower them to implement the changes they had proposed.

Our team soon realized that one of the major problems with our asthma management was relying primarily on the house staff to check on patients and wean interventions, especially aerosolized bronchodilators (e.g., albuterol). The design of their work flow simply did not allow them to see these patients often enough to ensure efficient and timely weaning of aerosolized medications. In addition, we noted that there was significant variation in the methods used for the delivery of albuterol.

Process Analysis and Literature Review

In the spirit of "stealing shamelessly" and being evidence based, we reviewed published reports on asthma protocol development and the different methods of bronchodilator (albuterol) delivery. It was clear that other hospitals had been able to reduce asthma LOS and cost of hospitalization,[1] and we found that the use of standard clinical scoring tools for assessing acute asthma severity was increasing.[2] We also performed an exhaustive review of the literature on the methods of administration of inhaled bronchodilators in children.

We analyzed the data and found that our initial LOS was approximately two days (see Table 11.1) and that 9 percent of inhaled albuterol doses were being delivered by metered dose inhaler with a valved holding chamber (MDI-VHC), while 91 percent were being given by a small-volume nebulizer (SVN) (see Table 11.2). We identified multiple studies that found that delivery of inhaled albuterol by MDI-VHC was as clinically effective as, less time-consuming than, and potentially less costly than delivery by SVN.[3–7] We monitored albuterol administration at our institution by creating a standardized report from our electronic medication administration record. The query could be run on request, and it recorded every dose of albuterol administered, the route of delivery, and the clinician who ordered the medication for any selected period. This list was matched to a list of patients with discharge diagnoses of acute asthma.

Table 11.2 Method of Albuterol Administration among Non–Intensive Care Asthmatic Patients Only

Method of Administration	Year 5[a]	Year 6	Year 7
Metered dose inhaler with a valved holding chamber (MDI–VHC)	9%	67%	79%
Small-volume nebulizer (SVN)	91%	33%	21%

[a] Implementation of the conversion from SVNs to MDI-VHCs occurred in the fall of Year 5.

Protocol Development

Nursing leadership polled bedside nurses to determine how much resistance there would be to the changes in the asthma care model and albuterol delivery systems. It was important not to make top-down decisions but rather ones in which the clinicians (nurses, RTs, and physicians) were able to express their opinions and provide ideas.

The team recognized that there needed to be a standard clinical assessment tool that could be used on all patients. By using such a scoring system, we were confident that our well-trained residents, nurses, and RTs could evaluate patients using the same variables and be more consistent in their clinical decision making. We evaluated various asthma clinical severity scoring tools and chose one that had been developed and tested at our facility and had been found to have good interobserver agreement (see Table 11.3).[8] This was important because it was in keeping with the principle of being evidence based when possible, which helped to align physicians who were hesitant to accept change. While there were some lingering concerns about the validity of the score, we decided that its use was invaluable in creating a standardized framework for clinicians to use in the assessment of patients being treated for acute asthma.

We chose to establish a standardized albuterol-weaning strategy based on the patient's clinical respiratory score. We reviewed the current literature on albuterol dosing and agreed on a starting dose, frequency of administration, and a weaning schedule. The weaning strategy was rendered into a flowsheet-style document that was filled out by the clinical staff (nurses and RTs). The asthma clinical severity score was used to determine how often patients must be assessed and how often they should be treated with albuterol (see Figure 11.1). The nurse or RT could wean the albuterol dose based on the patient's clinical score without requiring a physician order. However, there was an obligation on the part of the nurses and RTs to make sure that the house staff were kept informed of changes in the dose and frequency of albuterol delivery.

We opted to incorporate into our asthma protocol a recommendation that MDI-VHC be the preferred method of administration of albuterol. We believed that there were significant benefits to be gained by administering albuterol by MDI-VHC rather than by SVN. As stated earlier, MDI-VHC has been shown to be as effective as SVN and has some distinct advantages. An SVN treatment typically takes between fifteen and twenty minutes, while an equivalent dosage can be delivered in less than five minutes using an MDI-VHC. In addition, we observed that there was considerable variation in how SVNs were used in our hospital. Some treatments were given by mask and some via "blow-by," which is a highly variable and largely discredited method.[9] We felt that most of this variation would be eliminated by the use of MDI-VHC.

Barriers

As we were developing the protocol for administering and weaning inhaled bronchodilators, we also considered the barriers to implementation.

Table 11.3 The Clinical Asthma Score Used at Seattle Children's Hospital

Variable	0 Points	1 Point	2 Points	3 Points
Respiratory Rate				
< 2 months		≤ 60	61–69	≥ 70
2–12 months		≤ 50	51–59	≥ 60
1–2 years		≤ 40	41–44	≥ 45
2–3 years		≤ 34	35–39	≥ 40
4–5 years		≤ 30	31–35	≥ 36
6–12 years		≤ 26	27–30	≥ 31
> 12 years		≤ 23	24–27	≥ 28
Retractions				
	None	Intercostal	Intercostal and substernal	Intercostal, substernal, and supraclavicular
Wheezing				
	Normal breathing; no wheezing present	End-expiratory wheeze only	Expiratory wheeze only (greater than end-expiratory wheeze)	Inspiratory and expiratory wheeze, diminished breath sounds, or both
Dyspnea				
0–2 years	Normal feeding, vocalizations, and activity	One of the following: difficulty feeding, decreased vocalization, or agitation	Two of the following: difficulty feeding, decreased vocalization, and/or agitation	Stops feeding, no vocalizations, and/or drowsy or confused

Table 11.3   The Clinical Asthma Score Used at Seattle Children's Hospital (Continued)

Variable	0 Points	1 Point	2 Points	3 Points
Dyspnea				
2–4 years	Normal feeding, vocalizations, and play	One of the following: decreased appetite, increased coughing after play, or hyperactivity	Two of the following: decreased appetite, increased coughing after play, and/or hyperactivity	Stops eating or drinking, stops playing, and/or drowsy or confused
≥ 5 years	Counts to 10 in one breath	Counts to 7–9 in one breath	Counts to 4–6 in one breath	Counts to ≤ 3 in one breath

1. There were hundreds of physicians with admission privileges, including hospitalists, community pediatricians, and subspecialists, all of whom prescribed bronchodilators regularly. Most of these physicians had been trained to believe SVNs were more effective than MDI-VHCs in delivering aerosolized medications, and we knew that some of them would be refractory to change and would perceive our efforts as an affront to their clinical autonomy. We needed to find a way to educate our physicians and convince them that unfettered clinical autonomy can result in unwarranted variation in clinical care.

2. Staff turnover among physicians, nurses, and RTs presented problems, particularly among the resident house staff. Even if clinical guidelines were initially successful, it might be difficult to sustain our implemented processes because within a few years the entire house staff and significant portions of the respiratory and nursing staff would have turned over. However, while we realized that this would require ongoing education, we also felt that a successful implementation would serve to change the fundamental culture of this care model and, thus, ingrain the paradigm sufficiently to withstand staff turnover.

3. We needed to teach all the nurses and RTs how to properly use the clinical asthma score and MDI-VHC.

4. We needed to use different venues to reach all the constituents, including classroom instruction, mailed brochures, e-mail, and information posted on the hospital's internal website.

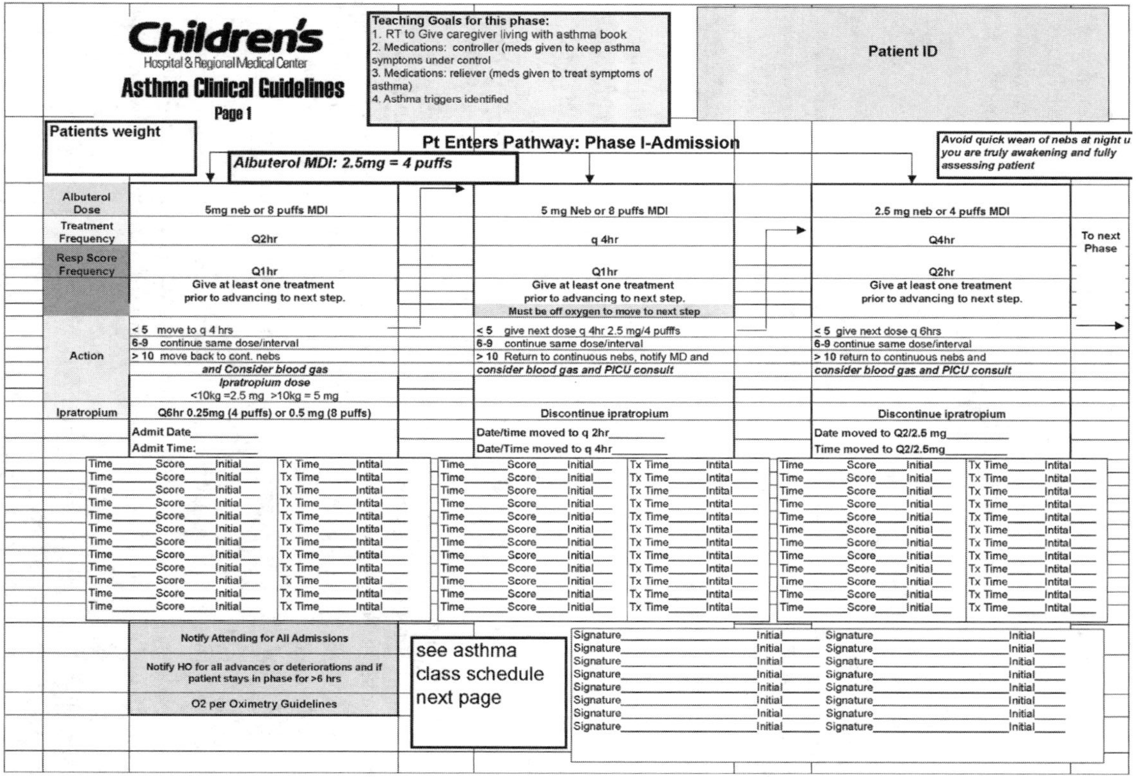

Children's
Hospital & Regional Medical Center
Asthma Clinical Guidelines
Page 1

Patients weight

Teaching Goals for this phase:
1. RT to Give caregiver living with asthma book
2. Medications: controller (meds given to keep asthma symptoms under control
3. Medications: reliever (meds given to treat symptoms of asthma)
4. Asthma triggers identified

Patient ID

Avoid quick wean of nebs at night u you are truly awakening and fully assessing patient

Pt Enters Pathway: Phase I-Admission

Albuterol MDI: 2.5mg = 4 puffs

Albuterol Dose	5mg neb or 8 puffs MDI	5 mg Neb or 8 puffs MDI	2.5 mg neb or 4 puffs MDI
Treatment Frequency	Q2hr	q 4hr	Q4hr → To next Phase
Resp Score Frequency	Q1hr	Q1hr	Q2hr

Give at least one treatment prior to advancing to next step.

Must be off oxygen to move to next step

Give at least one treatment prior to advancing to next step.

Action
< 5 move to q 4 hrs
6-9 continue same dose/interval
> 10 move back to cont. nebs and Consider blood gas

< 5 give next dose q 4hr 2.5 mg/4 puffs
6-9 continue same dose/interval
> 10 Return to continuous nebs, notify MD and consider blood gas and PICU consult

< 5 give next dose q 6hrs
6-9 continue same dose/interval
> 10 return to continuous nebs and consider blood gas and PICU consult

Ipratropium dose
<10kg =2.5 mg >10kg = 5 mg
Q6hr 0.25mg (4 puffs) or 0.5 mg (8 puffs)

Ipratropium
Discontinue Ipratropium
Date/time moved to q 2hr.
Date/Time moved to q 4hr

Discontinue Ipratropium
Date moved to Q2/2.5 mg.
Time moved to Q2/2.5mg

Admit Date:
Admit Time:

Notify Attending for All Admissions

Notify HO for all advances or deteriorations and if patient stays in phase for >6 hrs

O2 per Oximetry Guidelines

see asthma class schedule next page

Figure 11.1 Inpatient asthma clinical guidelines. Standardized albuterol-weaning strategy based on the patient's clinical respiratory score, enabling a nurse or respiratory therapist (RT) to wean an albuterol dose without a physician order.

Policy and Operational Changes

We realized that there were some mistakes that are often made by teams charged with creating process improvements in large, complex clinical systems. We avoided these by ensuring policy concordance with the various policies and procedures previously in place within the hospital and by making the new policies and procedures user friendly and readily available. The bronchodilator policy was extensively revised to include recommending MDI-VHC as the preferred method of delivery of inhaled bronchodilators.

We knew that the process for obtaining necessary supplies had to be smooth and convenient. At the start of our improvement efforts, VHCs could only be obtained from the pharmacy, but as part of the process change they were added to the floor stock of supplies. This may seem like a minor point, but it is important to remember that what seem like small issues can prevent successful implementation.

A standard asthma admission order set was created in our computerized physician order entry program (Cerner CPOE). This was extremely useful in providing consistent care across many different ordering physicians.

The Role of Hospital Leadership

We realized that successful use of CPI required that everyone involved in the process be granted the opportunity to contribute ideas and comments, but we also knew that for us to be successful we needed strong support from the hospital leadership. In addition, successful implementation required a cohesive effort by multiple disciplines. We needed to coordinate the education of nurses, RTs, and physicians in order for them to be on the same page and achieve collective buy-in. This education required a financial investment, which the hospital leadership understood and supported. The hospital leadership further supported this effort by providing information technology support to change order sets, facilitate the use of electronic messages to physicians, and disseminate information via newsletters. They also listened to the concerns and complaints of the physicians who were uncomfortable with the conversion from SVNs to MDI-VHCs.

Staff Training

Implementing this asthma protocol required an intensive education program for the nurses, RTs, attending and community physicians, and house staff. This was accomplished through classroom training, new employee orientation, community physician forums, newsletters, and ongoing bedside education. Our practice model differed from some others in that nurses and RTs shared responsibility for the administration of inhaled bronchodilators. Approximately 65–70 percent of the albuterol treatments were administered by RTs, with the remainder given by nurses.

Before implementation of our changes, there was infrequent use of MDI-VHCs. We decided to train the nurses and RTs together on the use of the asthma clinical severity score, the proper methods of using a MDI-VHC, and the use of the asthma guidelines. In some hospitals, training of RTs and nurses is done separately. However, because our culture has RTs and nurses working closely together, particularly in the care of patients with acute asthma, we opted to train them together. We perceived this as a strength and wanted to leverage this to help ensure success of our proposed practice changes and enhance staff collaboration. We also wanted to ensure that everyone received the same information in order to minimize unwarranted variation in practice execution. Our training included the scientific basis and rationale for why we were implementing these practice changes. This may seem obvious, but our experience and a growing body of literature suggest that not enough time and energy are spent establishing a cognitive framework for changing the behaviors of knowledge workers (e.g., clinicians).[10]

We realized that physician acceptance would be a major barrier to implementing the conversion from SVNs to MDI-VHCs. Many of them were adamant that SVNs were better than MDI-VHCs for albuterol administration, particularly in children. Moreover, we knew that they would push back strongly if they felt "forced" to make a change. Thus, we provided physicians with contact information for the pediatric pulmonologists and RT leadership team so that they could discuss their concerns personally. We also prepared a packet of articles and a statement regarding our rationale for the change, which was sent out to physicians upon request. We believed that the community pediatricians would be the most likely to object to this change because they had less interaction with hospital leadership and were used to making independent decisions. We could not alienate them if we were to be successful. Therefore, we went to great lengths to meet with them and notify them of our planned conversion well before it went into effect.

We relied heavily on the pediatric chief residents to inform the house staff. In addition, we educated the pediatric house staff through meetings, lectures, and ward-based sessions. The Seattle Children's Hospital–based physicians were educated through divisional meetings, e-mail messages, and newsletters.

Throughout the implementation process, we emphasized that this was not a mandate to use MDI-VHCs but rather a strong suggestion based on well-established data. One important tool that we used in our successful implementation was incorporating MDI-VHC albuterol doses into the electronic asthma order set. The order set defaulted to MDI-VHC for albuterol administration, which reminded ordering physicians of the hospital's preference to use MDI-VHCs rather than SVNs. Physicians could still order albuterol via SVN, but they had to go farther into the ordering hierarchy in the computer orders, which required additional mouse clicks.

Measurement Change in Outcomes

After implementation of the asthma clinical guidelines, LOS for children hospitalized with asthma decreased by 21 percent (see Table 11.1). During that same time

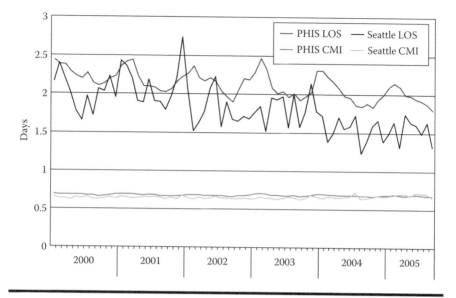

Figure 11.2 Mean length of stay (LOS) among asthmatics per month. LOS and severity of illness for patients with asthma. The Case Mix Index (CMI) is a measure of severity of illness. *Source*: **Data obtained from the Pediatric Health Information System (PHIS) operated by the National Association of Children's Health Institutions.**

period, there was no change in the degree of asthma severity, so we believe the decrease in LOS was due to our change in asthma care (see Figure 11.2).

The proportion of inhaled albuterol treatments administered via MDI-VHC increased from 21 to 79 percent (see Table 11.2). Implementing our changes also resulted in a 21 percent reduction in albuterol administration costs from $12.31 to $10.20 per treatment (see Table 11.4). We have continued to periodically measure these variables, and they have remained fairly constant over the years. We cannot overemphasize the importance of follow-up and repeated measurement of metrics. The plan, do, check, and act cycle is a powerful tool, but sometimes there is an imbalance in the amount of energy and focus applied to various parts of the cycle. Some projects are unsuccessful in the long term because the cycle gets distorted into a plan-plan-plan-plan-do cycle. This results in the majority of time and energy being devoted to planning and implementation and too little time spent on the check and act parts of the cycle. This is due in part to the "What's next?" phenomenon—since we have finished this project, "What's next?" This is caused by thinking projects are mostly finished after the implementation phase. Periodic rechecking of process and outcome measures and incremental adjustments to a process are as important as, if not more important than, the initial planning phase for long-term success.

During the past decade, since the initial implementation of our changes, we have at times experienced "drift" in our asthma care processes, which has been due,

Table 11.4 Cost Analysis of Methods of Albuterol Administration[a]

Method of Albuterol Administration	January–May 2004		January–May 2006	
	Number of Treatments	*Number of Patients*	*Number of Treatments*	*Number of Patients*
Metered dose inhaler with a valved holding chamber (MDI–VHC)	2,474	197	6,178	401
Small-volume nebulizer (SVN)	7,441	714	1,843	295

Device Costs	January–May 2004	January–May 2006
SVN with mask $2.36 each × 3-day length of stay, changing SVN daily = $7.08 × (number of patients)	$5,055	$2,089
Multidose vial $1.94 × (number of patients)	$1,385	$572
MDI canister $2.45 each × (number of patients)	$483	$982
VHC $13.65 × (number of patients)	$2,689	$5,474

Labor Costs[b]	January–May 2004	January–May 2006
MDI-VHC = 13.2 × $0.61 = $8.05 × (number of treatments)	$19,916	$49,733
SVN = 20.4 × $0.61 = $12.44 × (number of treatments)	$92,566	$22,927
Total Albuterol Treatment Costs	**$122,094**	**$81,777**
Total Number of Treatments	9,915	8,021
Total Cost per Treatment	**$12.31**	**$10.20**
% Cost Reduction Compared to First Period		21%

[a] Based on analysis used in J. W. Salyer, R. M. DiBlasi, D. N. Crotwell, C. A. Cowan, and E. R. Carter, "The Conversion to Metered-Dose Inhaler with Valved Holding Chamber to Administer Inhaled Albuterol: A Pediatric Hospital Experience," *Respiratory Care* 53, no. 3 (March 2008): 338–45.

[b] Labor costs are calculated using an average hourly rate of $28 per hour and benefits cost of 30%: ($28.00 x 1.3) / 60 = $0.61 cost per minute.

in part, to turnover of our RTs, nurses, and residents. When this drift has occurred, we have taken measures to correct it, primarily by reeducating staff and making minor changes in our clinical guidelines. In addition, we have routinely reported process and outcome measures to various stakeholders and leaders so that they are aware when there is lack of adherence to our standard care plan. Because we periodically check and recheck our asthma outcome measures, we have been able to promptly identify process drift and take steps to correct it.

Conclusion

This asthma CPI project was implemented successfully and resulted in significant improvements in patient care. In addition, the sustainment of these process improvements has been possible due to effective leadership and the ongoing application of CPI principles. The asthma clinical guidelines, and especially the ability to wean bronchodilator medications without direct physician input, has safely enabled the more rapid and consistent weaning of medications. This, in turn, has decreased hospital LOS and reduced costs. The conversion from SVNs to MDI-VHCs required a paradigm shift from the belief that nebulizers were more effective than MDI-VHCs. Now MDI-VHCs are the accepted mode of albuterol delivery, and it is difficult to remember why we were once so adamant about using SVNs. The conversion to MDI-VHCs has decreased costs while not compromising patient care. Thanks to our CPI-driven process changes, all children with asthma receive similar doses of bronchodilators based on their clinical severity, and medications are weaned, primarily by RTs and nurses, according to a standard clinical scoring system.

Acknowledgments

Many people and departments contributed to this project, including the nursing staff development department, the information technology service, the pharmacy, and the pulmonary medicine division. The nurses, RTs, and physicians who work at the bedside every day at Seattle Children's Hospital are truly the authors of success in the care of our children with asthma.

Notes

1. K. M. McDowell, R. L. Chatburn, T. R. Myers, M. A. O'Riordan, and C. M. Kercsmar, "A Cost-Saving Algorithm for Children Hospitalized for Status Asthmaticus," *Archives of Pediatrics and Adolescent Medicine* 152, no. 10 (October 1998): 977–84.
2. C. S. Kelly, C. L. Andersen, J. P. Pestian, A. D. Wenger, A. B. Finch, G. L. Strope, et al., "Improved Outcomes for hospitalized asthmatic children using a clinical pathway." *Annals of Allergy, Asthma and Immunology* 84 (2000): 509–16.

3. J. A. Castro-Rodriguez and G. J. Rodrigo, "Beta-Agonists through Metered Dose Inhaler with Valved Holding Chamber versus Nebulizer for Acute Exacerbation of Wheezing or Asthma in Children under 5 Years of Age: A Systematic Review with Meta-Analysis," *Journal of Pediatrics* 145, no. 2 (2004): 172–77.
4. C. Cates, A. Bara, J. Crilly, and B. Rowe, "Holding Chambers versus Nebulisers for Beta-Agonist Treatment of Acute Asthma," *Cochrane Database of Systematic Reviews* 3 (2003): CD000052.
5. M. Osmond and B. Diner, "Evidence-Based Emergency Medicine: Nebulizers versus Inhalers with Spacers for Acute Asthma in Pediatrics," *Annals of Emergency Medicine* 43, no. 3 (2004): 413–15.
6. A. Delgado, K. J. Chou, E. J. Silver, and E. F. Crain, "Nebulizers vs. Metered Dose Inhalers with Spacers for Bronchodilator Therapy to Treat Wheezing in Children Aged 2 to 24 Months in a Pediatric Emergency Department," *Archives of Pediatrics and Adolescent Medicine* 157, no. 1 (2003): 76–80.
7. J. W. Salyer, R. M. DiBlasi, D. N. Crotwell, C. A. Cowan, and E. R. Carter, "The Conversion to Metered-Dose Inhaler with Valved Holding Chamber to Administer Inhaled Albuterol: A Pediatric Hospital Experience," *Respiratory Care* 53, no. 3 (March 2008): 338–45.
8. L. L. Liu, M. M. Gallaher, R. L. Davis, C. M. Rutter, T. C. Lewis, and E. K. Marcuse, "Use of a Respiratory Clinical Score among Different Providers," *Pediatric Pulmonology* 37 (2004): 243–48.
9. B. K. Rubin, "Bye-Bye, Blow-By," *Respiratory Care* 52, no. 8 (2007): 981.
10. P. F. Drucker, "Knowledge Worker Productivity," in *Knowledge Management Yearbook 2000–2001*, ed. J. W. Cortada and J. A. Woods (Woburn, MA: Butterworth-Heinemann, 2000).

Chapter 12

Change That Nourishes the Organization: Making the Total Parenteral Nutrition (TPN) Process Safer

Polly Lenssen, MS, RD, CD, FADA

Director, Clinical Nutrition
Co-Chair, Nutrition Subcommittee
Seattle Children's Hospital

Eric Harvey, PharmD, MBA

Pharmacy Quality Manager
Seattle Children's Hospital

David L. Suskind, MD

Co-Chair, Nutrition Subcommittee
Seattle Children's Hospital

Dr. Rich Molteni, the medical director at Seattle Children's Hospital, was meeting with the directors of pharmacy and clinical nutrition in his office one morning.

The discussion centered on a recent event that was both seminal and scary. A toddler had received four times the intended dose of potassium in his bag of total parenteral nutrition (TPN). TPN is the nutrient-rich admixture with over thirty additives that is lifesaving in patients unable to eat or be fed through an intestinal feeding tube.

The child's kidneys were working just fine, and fortunately he was able to maintain his serum potassium level in a safe range. But if the error had occurred in the child with the damaged heart and sluggish kidneys in the next room, the outcome could have been lethal.

Dr. Molteni wanted to know if the dietitians and pharmacists could assume responsibility for TPN order writing. His reasoning was sound: dietitians and pharmacists have the training in nutrition and TPN admixtures, and yet we had medical residents, with no knowledge and no experience, writing these complex medical orders.

This question and proposal were hardly radical. Some hospitals in the community had already sought prescriptive authority for pharmacists to write TPN orders; and our dietitians at Children's Hospital were "ghost writing" orders for the residents and fellows to sign in the neonatal and bone marrow transplant services.

But the conversation with Dr. Molteni ended with the directors of pharmacy and clinical nutrition shaking their heads. Based on the way the hospital was currently structured, and the way it actually worked, they thought it would be impossible to implement TPN order writing by pharmacists and dietitians across twenty services at our academic medical center. They couldn't imagine convincing all the division chiefs and the resident education office to relinquish control of a medical order, or "teaching opportunity." Nor did they have the staff to gather the necessary clinical data to update prescriptions every day.

Several years passed, and numerous reports were published about fatal errors with TPN, especially in children, as well as safe practice standards that were under development.[1-4] And at Seattle Children's, the data were clear: the medication with the highest error rate was TPN.

Encouraged by Dr. Molteni's continuing conviction that we could implement a safer system, the pharmacy and nutrition leadership at our hospital kept emphasizing the high risk with our TPN process in our annual reports to the quality improvement steering committee. So, as the executive leadership at Seattle Children's considered early continuous performance improvement (CPI) projects, improving the TPN process surfaced as an obvious choice.

With executive support and a CPI consultant on board, the project was launched. As expected, the task was enormous. And, using a "value stream improvement" approach to the TPN process, we embarked on what was to become an eighteen-month journey to envision, design, and implement a standard TPN process throughout the hospital.

Today, we are doing much better in this area. We are linked together, and communication and flow are clear and efficient for the most part. But we still have breakdowns, although it's much easier for us to learn and improve because now we have a standard process in place.

Looking back, it's important and instructive to ask how we made this major—and difficult—transition in the TPN process.

It all started with bringing our leadership together in a three-day value stream alignment session. General medicine, nursing, pharmacy, nutrition, home care (where TPN was produced), and administration each attended the session and learned about one-piece flow, error proofing, check steps, queues, and the many types of waste in our processes. They also grasped how these principles from "lean manufacturing" could touch every discipline in the TPN process and help detect errors earlier, before they reached the patient.

The alignment session inspired commitment across the disciplines, which helped sustain the passion and energy for such a large project. The leadership team then met weekly over the next eighteen months to track progress and plan next steps. The team experienced continual recommitment as the methodology naturally broke down "the silos" and dismantled barriers that we faced daily in our work.

Three Rapid Process Improvement Workshops (RPIWs) were planned as weeklong events to design and implement each step in the TPN process: ordering, production, and administration. Baseline data were gathered; in addition to detailed error data on each step of the process, each discipline's satisfaction with the TPN process was measured. Pharmacists experienced intense frustration about the time wasted tracking down residents to clarify and correct TPN orders, and dietitians were equally discouraged to discover prescriptions for too many or too little calories, or inappropriate use of TPN when a feeding tube could have been inserted.

For staffing reasons, the administration RPIW occurred first, fortuitously as it turned out. Administration errors were the greatest in number. These errors included the inadvertent switching of rates for two components—the fat component, which ran at a slow rate, and the dextrose–protein and electrolyte component, which ran at a comparatively faster rate. The risk of an adverse outcome is considerable when electrolytes are not delivered as prescribed, and implementing an error-proofing method was reason enough to participate in this event. Error proofing for this risk included standardizing the labeling and placement of the tubing for the two components to greatly decrease the potential for mix-ups (See Figure 12.1).

Additional mistake proofing implemented as the result of the administration RPIW included matching the TPN label on the bag with the order form, and implementing pharmacy compounding software and an administration checklist.

A major shift also occurred in job assignment, since the process of administration was not standard in the hospital. Previously, the IV team nurse was designated to hang the TPN on the non–intensive care patients; and, after the event, the bedside nurse—regardless of site of care—was accountable for administration (See Figure 12.2).

The RPIW that was viewed as the most challenging—TPN ordering—took place six months into the process. Dr. Molteni believed that accurate calculation of TPN components was an extremely complex skill that was of little interest to most pediatric medical and surgical trainees. And, in most busy nurseries and on many pediatric floors, it's critical that the attending physician provide correct input when

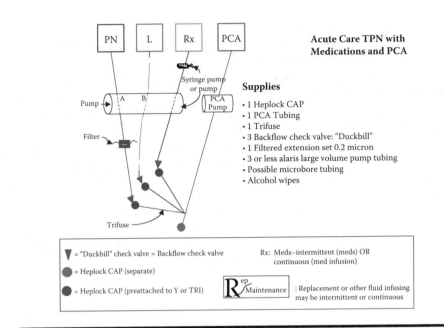

Figure 12.1 Acute care. TPN with medications and patient-controlled analgesia (PCA). A visual used to mistake-proof TPN delivery at the bedside.

Figure 12.2 Order form, checklist, and software. Mistake proofing by validating the three TPN documents needed to deliver TPN.

it comes to the patient's need for TPN; especially important is the articulation of any medical conditions that would dictate unusual preparations or ingredients.

The trick in the RPIW session on TPN ordering was convincing people, especially house staff and their leaders, that this was a "service" to them and their patients, and not a "takeaway" or intrusion on their authority.

The RPIW went well—better than expected—in part because the leadership team populated the management guidance team with senior physician leadership, including the surgical and medical chiefs, and extended invitations to staff pharmacists and dietitians, nurse practitioners, and our chief resident.

When the chief resident spoke, he immediately tore down some of the myths and barriers. He told us it was clear that TPN errors were among the most critical medication errors in the hospital. And, since residents were writing most TPN orders, he felt obligated to join the CPI team that was looking for a solution. He went further by saying that he wanted to not only contribute to designing a system that would minimize TPN ordering errors, but also ensure that resident education in nutrition and pharmaceutical topics wasn't compromised.

After the current state was mapped and all the waste was revealed, the ideal state quickly evolved with little controversy; the model was simple and clear (See Figure 12.3).

Still, there was persistent anxiety about whether resident training was rich enough without practical experience in writing the TPN. Because education is an explicit part of our organization's goals, it was important for some of the project work to develop a system where education was intertwined within the nutrition and TPN process. The model enabled nutrition to become a standard component of daily rounding so that an open discussion between the residents, dietitians, pharmacists, nurses, and attending physicians could take place. Within these discussions, enteral, TPN, and general nutrition education occurred. And, in conjunction with in-house rounds, residents received multiple lectures throughout the year on nutrition and TPN; a process was also set up to accommodate those residents who wanted specific education in writing and ordering TPN.

In the several years since we implemented changes to the TPN process, we have confirmed that skills and competencies in pediatric TPN ordering are not a critical area for pediatricians in their practice. We have worked hard to maintain a practice model that does not undermine the physician leadership—especially in decision making about TPN initiation, termination, and composition—but instead encourages continual dialogue between the physician, the nutritionist, and pharmacists to ensure best care practices for our patients.

Surprisingly, dietitians and pharmacists were a source of resistance when we rolled out the new TPN process model. Some of the pharmacists, for example, worried that the focus on TPN would make the rest of their job less safe. This anxiety dissipated over time as their competence and comfort level increased. For their part, the dietitians welcomed the opportunity to apply their skills, but they felt strong distrust from the pharmacists, who would only sign orders after

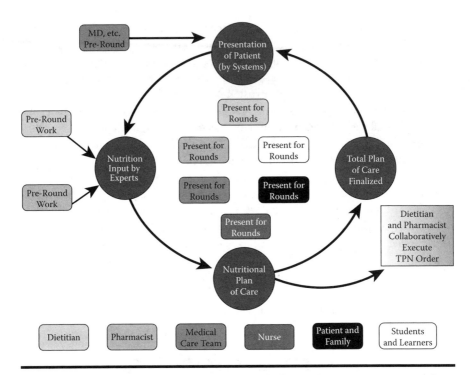

Figure 12.3 TPN ordering process flow. All the patient care team members (pharmacists, dietitians, and the medical team) will be present for TPN decision making seven days per week. That decision making will include initiation, discontinuation, and route. TPN orders will be executed by "TPN order-writing specialists," currently defined as dietitians and pharmacists. A specialist from two separate disciplines is required to execute each order. Over time, others can be credentialed to write TPN orders through a training process.

they personally had a conversation with the physician. These feelings of distrust likewise diminished as staff learned about each other's competence, skill sets, and accountability.

To offset negative feelings and the very real anxieties about change and assuming new responsibilities, we reminded everyone that we did not want to return to the old way in which, on average, one TPN error occurred every day. And we met weekly for problem resolution and education. Some of the questions we raised were as follows: how do we standardize documentation? How do we hand off critical clinical information on weekends? How do you write TPN for a premature infant—if your expertise is in oncology? Our frontline staff members emerged as leaders and piloted the TPN order writing on the weekends, when resource levels within the hospital generally decrease. They also offered up teaching "pearls" about their specialties, and relinquished their "exclusive" expertise in cross-training sessions with their colleagues.

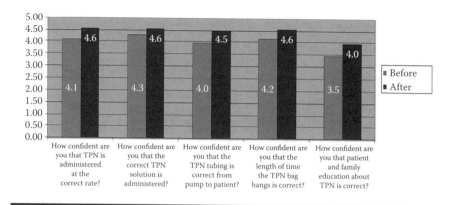

Figure 12.4 Nursing confidence in TPN process. Level of satisfaction among nurses before and after the implementation of the new TPN process.

The huge leadership commitment made at every level in our organization—initiated at the executive level, sustained over the years by midlevel management, and demonstrated in daily work improvements by the direct clinical staff—resulted in a significant cultural transformation. We were no longer willing or able to accept one TPN error a day.

Indeed, nurses, physicians, pharmacists, and dietitians across the board experienced greater satisfaction with the new TPN process (See Figures 12.4 and 12.5). Errors at each step dropped significantly, and this safety improvement rate has been sustained over time (See Figure 12.6).

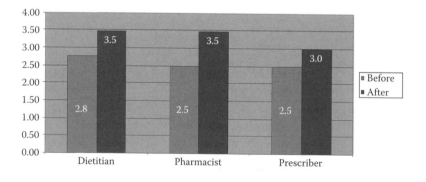

Figure 12.5 Comparative responses for overall level of satisfaction with the TPN process. Levels of satisfaction among various roles in the TPN process before and after the change.

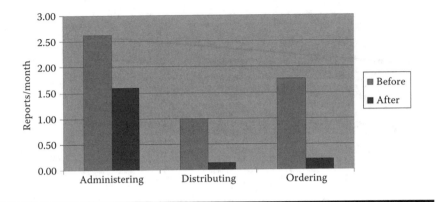

Figure 12.6 TPN incident reports per month reaching patients. Additional evidence validating the effectiveness of the mistake proofing.

Finally, cost avoidance, captured in a retrospective analysis, demonstrates that adding additional labor resources for this major patient safety initiative was a good economic decision (See Table 12.1).

In terms of our third RPIW on TPN production, the leadership team underestimated the length of time it would take to implement the TPN ordering model, and the team ended up cancelling the third workshop because the production side already exhibited strong characteristics of one-piece flow (See Figure 12.7).

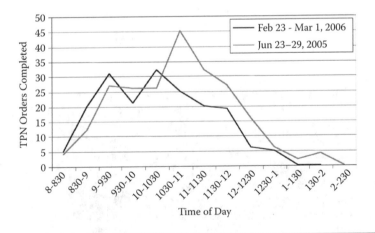

Figure 12.7 TPN order flow. Sustaining one-piece order flow remains difficult but efforts have resulted in reduction of the last minute rush of orders into the pharmacy prior to the noon deadline. Pharmacists can now enter orders without the stress associated with this last minute rush.

Table 12.1   Cost Analysis

	2005 Pre-Implementation	2009 Post-Implementation	Difference
Pharmacist Labor			
Hours spent on TPN	70 hours/week	124 hours/week	54 hours/week
Labor dollars spent on TPN [a]	$236,600/year	$419,120/year	$182,520/year
TPN Utilization			
% of patients receiving ≤ 3 days of TPN	23%	22%	1% (128 orders)
Utilization rate	0.2 TPNs/ inpatient day	0.17 TPNs/ inpatient day	0.03 TPNs/ inpatient day (2,275 orders)
Cost avoided for unnecessary TPN [b]			$300,375/year
Error Avoidance			
TPN errors reaching patients	85/year	51/year	34/year
Cost avoided by reducing errors [c]			$186,422/year
Overall cost impact (−182,520 + 300,375 + 186,422) = $304,277 per year net cost avoidance.			

[a] Estimate $65 per hour as average salary plus benefits during this time frame.
[b] Estimate cost to pharmacy of $125 per order.
[c] Estimate cost per error of $5,483 (based on the most recent adult value and reported in 1999 dollars; most recent pediatric value reported in 2002 is approximately US$11,500).[5,6]

The two workshops we did complete, however, helped us move up the daily delivery of TPN from home care so that we are able to correct the electrolyte and nutritional status of patients one hour earlier.

But the ability to sustain one-piece flow in ordering to meet production and delivery deadlines remains difficult. As the hospital census has increased, and the organization has shifted to standard, family-centered rounding, team discussion has shifted later in the morning and challenged our production system.

The final leadership lesson of the TPN project is that the improvement work is never done. A change in staff behavior across every discipline and multiple sites in such a complex process as TPN requires significant ongoing effort to maintain the initial gains five years post implementation and additional effort to drive the process toward zero errors. Because the organization has embedded CPI into our daily lives and empowered a more horizontal leadership model in which the voice of the frontline staff can influence the process as much as that of the division head, the doubt that we initially experienced in Rich Molteni's office doesn't ever have to get in the way of change again.

Notes

1. Task Force for the Revision of Safe Practices for Parenteral Nutrition: J. Mirtallo, T. Canada, D. Johnson, et al., "Safe Practices for Parenteral Nutrition," *Journal of Parenteral and Enteral Nutrition* 28 (2004): S39–S70.
2. Johns Hopkins Medicine, "JHM Reports Untimely Death of Child Cancer Patient," http://www.hopkinsmedicine.org/Press_releases/2003/12_19_03.html (accessed July 15, 2010).
3. "Two Children Die after Receiving Infected TPN Solutions," *Pharmaceutical Journal* 3 (August 1994): 2.
4. A. Ali, C. Walentik, G. J. Mantych, H. F. Sadiq, W. J. Keenan, and A. Noguchi, "Iatrogenic Acute Hypermagnesemia after Total Parenteral Nutrition Infusion Mimicking Septic Shock Syndrome: Two Case Reports," *Pediatrics* 112, no. 1 pt. 1 (2003): e70–e72.
5. D. L. Kunac, J. Kennedy, N. Austin, et al., "Incidence, Preventability, and Impact of Adverse Drug Events (ADEs) and Potential ADEs in Hospitalized Children in New Zealand: A Prospective Observational Cohort Study," *Paediatric Drugs* 11, no. 2 (2009): 153–60.
6. D. C. Suh, B. S. Woodall, S. K. Shin, et al., "Clinical and Economic Impact of Adverse Drug Reactions in Hospitalized Patients," *Annals of Pharmacotherapy* 34, no. 12 (December 2000): 1373–79.

Chapter 13

Eliminating Mistakes—and Central Line–Associated Bloodstream Infections

Debra Ridling, MS, RN, CCRN
Director, Nursing Quality and Evidence-Based Practice
Seattle Children's Hospital

Howard E. Jeffries, MD, MBA
Medical Director, Continuous Performance Improvement (CPI)
Pediatric Cardiac Intensivist
Seattle Children's Hospital

Danielle Zerr, MD, MPH
Associate Medical Director for Patient Safety—Healthcare Associated Infections
Seattle Children's Hospital

Built-In Quality and Mistake Proofing

Healthcare is complex and dependent upon a combination of people and technology for its delivery. Healthcare providers are human, and they make errors. So, in order to prevent this fundamental flaw from interfering with care, we must move away from a person-oriented view of error to a system-oriented one.[1]

The person-oriented view has dominated healthcare, however; and, as noted in the seminal 1999 report by the Institute of Medicine, *To Err Is Human*, the care we currently provide results in the deaths of 50,000–100,000 people in the United

States each year.[2] To prevent these needless deaths, it is necessary to transition to a system-oriented approach; in addition, we must embrace the principle espoused by pioneering error researcher James Reason, who said, "We cannot change the human condition, but we can change the condition under which humans work."[1]

The continuous performance improvement (CPI) principles that we have embraced at Seattle Children's Hospital (SCH) is a systems-oriented approach that includes two core concepts: built-in quality and mistake proofing.

A key concept that is fundamental to this discussion is the notion of an error versus a defect. An error is made by an individual conducting a specific task. Once the flawed result of this task is passed down the line, to either the next team member or even the patient, it then becomes a defect.

One can better understand the distinction between errors and defects through the use of a quality ladder. A quality system that performs from level 1 to 3 is checking for defects, because the error has been passed down the line. In a level-4 system, the error is detected by the individual who made the error, and in level 5, the error is prevented. In lower quality systems, it may be difficult to determine the etiology for the defect, because it may have occurred many steps before its discovery; in these cases, the potential for patient harm is great.

Mistake proofing is a concept that helps us detect and prevent mistakes. If mistakes can be detected rapidly, then—similarly—they can be corrected rapidly. For example, gauze sponges used during surgery in the operating room have radioopaque components that make them visible on a radiograph.[3] While this does not prevent an error from occurring, it will likely help detect the error early and mitigate its severity. There are numerous treatments that can prevent errors; these can be viewed in a hierarchy from low to high. The progression from low to high treatments usually correlates with an increase in the levels of quality. As we employ mistake proofing, it is difficult to achieve level-5 quality for all processes, but a process can be made safer through the introduction of a higher level treatment. Indeed,

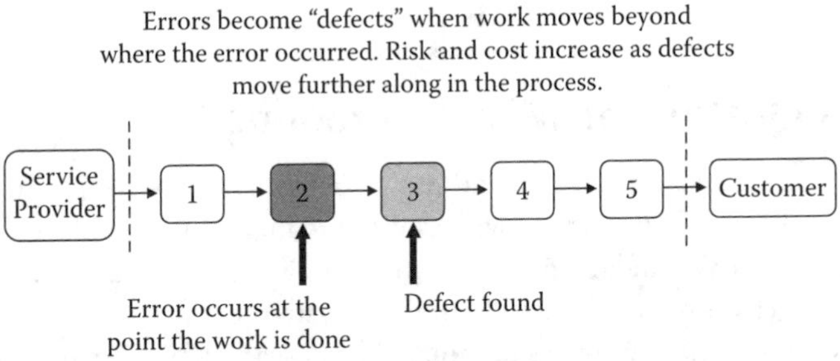

Figure 13.1 Error versus defect. Errors become "defects" when work moves beyond where the error occurred. Risk and cost increase as defects move further along in the process.

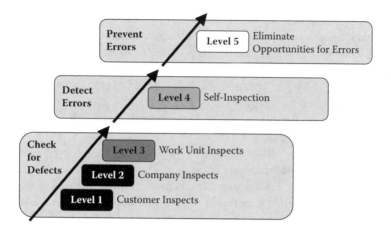

Figure 13.2   Levels of quality system. Five levels of quality: 1 is the lowest level and 5 is the highest level.

particular actions in mistake proofing may be considered on a continuum—from weaker to intermediate to stronger.

For example, moving from employing education (weak treatment) to making operating room staff aware of the need to double-check the patient's ID badge by incorporating a standard checklist that requires a signature (intermediate treatment) represents movement to a stronger intervention, and may prevent errors from being passed along.

Built-in quality combines mistake proofing with the concept of "stop the line," which has been adapted from the manufacturing shop floor. If an error is detected, the line stops until the error is found and a correction is made—regardless of if the error is found by a human or by a machine.

The ability to introduce the concept of "stop the line" requires significant leadership buy-in. This approach also requires a culture that understands the importance of error detection and prevention, despite the impact on short-term inconveniences, such as time delays.

Mistake proofing and the concept of "stop the line" were both extremely helpful, even integral, as we tried to reduce and ultimately eliminate central line–associated bloodstream infections (CLABSIs) at SCH.

Background

Infections have historically been viewed as an unavoidable consequence of critical care medicine. Critically ill patients experience organ failure and are often immune compromised. They routinely require extreme measures and invasive devices, such as central venous lines (catheters), to support them during their hospitalization. These approaches may further suppress the immune system or bypass natural barriers to infection (skin, etc.) and have been shown in well-designed studies to increase risk of infection. As a result, infection was seen as a necessary cost of these lifesaving measures.

Overcoming this belief system was a major challenge as we launched our efforts to cut the number of catheter-associated bloodstream infections. We worked with staff to acknowledge the risk factors and recognize that our usual approaches may not be effective in preventing CLABSIs in select patients; as a result, we had to "think outside the box" about alternative approaches and strategies. This represented a change in thinking among many.

Our early work on CLABSI reduction focused on the practices defined as effective through well-designed scientific studies—randomized controlled trials whenever possible; one of the most effective practices was the use of maximal barrier precautions for catheter placement.[4] This approach allowed us to recognize the extreme inherent risk of infection in many of our patients, but it also gave us a rationale for performing practices that we know reduce the risk of this undesired outcome.

The shift in viewpoint and culture was further facilitated by our previous successes. For instance, when we reduced surgical site infections in an extremely high-risk neonatal and pediatric cardiac surgery population, it proved that what we do makes a difference even in (or, perhaps, especially in) the most vulnerable patients. Surgical site infections were occurring at very high rates in our patients who had cardiac surgery and then experienced delayed closure of their sternum. These were patients who many felt were destined to develop infections.

In order to explore the problem, we organized a full-day multidisciplinary retreat and scrutinized every detail of the care of patients undergoing cardiac surgery.

Several practice changes came out of that important meeting, and subsequent implementation led to a drop in infections that exceeded 50 percent. This result showed that we can make a difference in the outcomes of patients who are at extreme risk for infection. And the success of this effort was foundational in approaching CLABSI work, since many of the same participants from the surgical site infection work group were included in the CLABSI efforts.

Case Description

The initial focus of our CLABSI work was in our intensive care unit (ICU), a thirty-one-bed tertiary care unit that accepts referrals from four states and can be occupied on any given day by newborns or twenty-one year olds. Approximately 40 percent of the patients were postoperative from cardiac surgery. Other patients included those who were post neurosurgery, solid organ transplantation, or bone marrow transplantation as well as those with oncological diagnoses, septic shock, or renal failure, and those requiring extracorporeal membrane (ECMO).

Culture of Safety

Safety culture is an important consideration in any project requiring broad and continual changes in procedures and practices performed by individual staff members. And many experts believe that a safety culture can lead to improved patient outcomes.[5] The Institute of Medicine goes so far as to say that lives can be saved in organizations that exhibit safe cultures, and it suggests that systems, processes, and environments—not individuals—are to blame for most needless mistakes.[6]

CLABSIs were not specifically mentioned in this report, but we now know that these infections contribute a significant risk to patients in terms of morbidity, mortality, and cost. In fact, deaths attributed to CLABSIs are currently considered sentinel events in some states, and often require public reporting.

A safe culture is a culture in which staff members at all levels, including administrators, recognize that the work they do is risky and error prone; it's a culture in which people are absolutely committed to patient safety in all they do; and it's a culture in which errors are openly reported, and dealt with immediately, in a collaborative, no-blame manner so all staff can learn and grow.

We believe that understanding the safety culture is critical for the success of any new change that will require staff members to do things differently. For example, it may be easier to institute change related to the quality of care in a unit where the safety culture is very high rather than in a unit where the safety culture is low.

The safety culture in our ICU was measured by the Safety Attitude Questionnaire (SAQ),[7] as part of the National Association of Children's Hospital and Related Institutions (NACHRI) collaborative, whose aim was to eliminate CLABSIs. We deployed the survey in 2006 and repeated it in 2008. The SAQ is a validated tool promoted by the Agency for Health Care Research and Quality (AHRQ).[8] More than 90 percent of the nursing, physician, and other ICU-based staff participated in the survey, so we believe our results were reflective of our culture.

We reviewed all results as part of routine leadership of our unit; but, when we zeroed in on eliminating CLABSIs, we focused on the aggregate response from nurses and physicians in the categories of collaboration, teamwork, and safety. In analyzing the data, we found that we were one of the top performers within the comparative cohort, and that we had "elite" status in some areas of the safety culture.

Based on our assessment, we felt that our unit was well positioned to participate in this initiative, and we didn't have concerns about staff buy-in. This allowed us to focus more on approaches to care and interventions.

Setting the Goal

The ICU had been working on preventing CLABSIs for several years before a formal hospital goal was set.

This effort involved participation in a Children's Healthcare Corporation of America (CHCA) project to reduce CLABSIs.[9]

Figure 13.3 5S central line cart. An orderly central line cart containing only the items necessary for central line placement.

A core element of that project made certain that central lines were inserted according to the Centers for Disease Control (CDC) guidelines. Indeed, the ICU standardized insertion included the use of maximal barrier precautions with every central line placement and the use of chlorhexidine gluconate (CHG) for skin preparation. And, as part of the insertion project, the ICU staff completed a 5S (sort, simplify, sweep, standardize, and sustain) project of the central line carts. This included standardizing the carts across all ICUs, organizing the drawers in a logical manner so they followed work flow, making all products visible, and eliminating supplies not required for central line placement. This resulted in an environment that made it easy for staff to do the right thing; in the process, it also facilitated the restocking and maintenance of the cart over time.

As we began to focus more on the prevention of CLABSIs, data were made visible to all care providers on run charts and posters that indicated the number of days since the last infection, as well as our CLABSI rate. This information was also posted on websites, sent out by e-mail, and displayed on the units for all staff to see (See Figure 13.4). ICU leadership began including CLABSI rates and prevention strategies on the agenda of staff meetings and various committees. As a result, we kept the problem and reduction goal visible—at front and center—for everyone.

Our hospital leadership—as well as the ICU-based leadership—began to make CLABSI elimination a priority in the fall of 2006, after the CHCA collaborative ended. Hospital leadership set a 2007 goal of reducing CLABSIs across the institution to 5 CLABSIs per 1,000 line days. The formalization of the goal focused significant

Figure 13.4 Days since last infection. Creating awareness and CLABSI vigilance required constant communication through multiple communication channels.

attention, and every department in the hospital became engaged—not just ICU and leadership staff. This was very important, because as the ICU moved forward in its work and began identifying new products and supplies that were needed, collaboration and cooperation with departments outside the ICU were very much required. Financial incentives were also set, so that all midlevel and senior leadership would be rewarded with bonus money at the end of the year—if CLABSI goals were met.

At the same time that our entire hospital began focusing on CLABSIs, our ICU joined the NACHRI CLABSI collaborative. An organization of children's hospitals with 213 members in the United States and around the world, NACHRI developed a focused program, and acted as the facilitator and project manager for a group of member hospitals so they could work on reducing—and eventually eliminating—CLABSIs in their ICUs. NACHRI provided staff, infrastructure, clinical experts, and expertise in leading change. And twenty-seven member hospitals, which included twenty-nine pediatric ICUs, joined the effort to work collaboratively toward ending CLABSIs in their individual units.

The NACHRI project included clinical bundles for insertion and maintenance of central lines (See Tables 13.1 and 13.2). Just as important were the education, resources, and tools that were provided to facilitate quality improvement activities. Specifically, each face-to-face learning session offered lectures on subjects such as sustainability, small-test change, and safety culture. These in-person learning events provided practical tips and advice that helped each individual unit work toward its goals. The sessions also allowed ample time for member hospitals to collaborate and support each other in their improvement efforts.

Table 13.1 National Association of Children's Hospital and Related Institutions (NACHRI) Insertion Bundle

1. Hand washing before procedure
2. Hat, sterile gown, sterile gloves, and full sterile barrier to cover entire bed
3. Chlorhexidine gluconate (CHG) scrub at insertion site for all children ≥ 2 months (some institutions elected to utilize CHG for infants < 2 months old)
• 30-second scrub; 30–60-second air dry
• 2 minutes for groin and 30–60-second air dry
4. No iodine skin prep—no iodine ointment at insertion site
5. Prepackaged or filled insertion cart, tray, or box
6. Insertion checklist (staff empowerment to stop nonemergent procedure if not following sterile insertion practice)
7. Polyurethane or Teflon catheters only
8. Insertion training for all providers (slides, video, etc.)

Table 13.2 NACHRI Maintenance Bundle

1. Daily assessment of line necessity
2. Hand hygiene before line care
3. Catheter site care
a. Chlorhexidine gluconate (CHG) scrub at insertion site for all children ≥ 2 months (some institutions utilized CHG for infants < 2 months old)
• 30-second scrub; 30–60-second air dry
• 2 minutes for groin; 30–60-second air dry
b. No iodine ointment.
c. Change clear dressing every 7 days unless soiled, dampened, or loosened (Centers for Disease Control [CDC] recommended)
d. Change gauze dressings every 2 days unless soiled, dampened, or loosened (CDC recommended)
e. Prepackaged dressing change kit (each unit to define package contents).
4. Catheter hub, cap, and tubing care
a. Replace administration sets, including add-on devices, no more frequently than every 72 hours, unless soiled or suspected to be infected
b. Replace tubing used to administer blood, blood products, or lipids within 24 hours of initiating infusion (CDC recommended)
c. Change caps no more often than every 72 hours, but should be replaced when administration set is changed (CDC recommended); if exposed to blood transfusion, then change within 24 hours
d. Prepackaged cap change kit, cart, or central location (elements local institutionally designated)
5. Parenteral and fluid administration
a. Complete all lipid containing fluid administration within 24 hours of initiating infusion
6. Antiseptic scrub for line entry
a. Indicated for all line entries including medical administration, lab draw, tubing change, discontinuation of infusion, continuous renal replacement therapy (CRRT), extracorporeal membrane oxygenation (ECMO), etc.

b. Institutional practice for alcohol versus CHG
     • Alcohol: 15-second scrub and 15-second dry
     • CHG: 30-second scrub and 30-second dry

The collaboration required rigorous auditing with performance feedback. A key element of this was transparency of process (insertion and maintenance bundle) compliance, as well as outcomes (CLABSI rate), by each individual unit and in aggregate. The interaction was open, and each hospital agreed to identify its units and share results, which were distributed monthly to all participants and made available on the NACHRI website for all members to view. The most helpful part of this was that hospitals were able to review peer institutions' results and identify institutions they thought were most similar to their own for further collaboration and networking.

Although the primary aim of the collaboration was to eliminate CLABSIs in pediatric ICUs, the first-year goal was to decrease the CLABSI rate by half of the baseline. The baseline aggregate rate was 5.4, so the Year 1 target was 2.7.

Defining the Team

In order to undertake the NACHRI work, an ICU team was formed. The team was co-led by the ICU clinical nurse specialist and the ICU medical director of quality; and participants included an ICU fellow, a staff nurse, infection preventionists, the medical director of infection prevention, and others. Neonatal ICU staff members were also involved, because of their close proximity to the ICU, as well as their shared patients and staff.

The group met monthly and followed a standardized agenda for discussion. Key topics included line utilization; audit results for compliance of insertion and maintenance bundles; current rates of infection—both at the unit level and compared to the NACHRI collaborative; and a comprehensive review of every infection, utilizing a template for mini–root cause analysis (mini-RCA), with identification of any causes for follow-up (See Figure 13.5).

When issues related to audit data or findings from individual RCAs were identified, follow-up plans were then developed. The plans utilized CPI principles, such as multiple plan, do, check, and act (PDCA) cycles. For example, when infections were recognized within one week of line placement, the evaluation included a more careful consideration of insertion practices, a review to make sure that staff members were trained and competent, and a check-in to be certain they had the proper materials needed to perform the procedure correctly.

At one point, it was noted that the majority of line infections were occurring within a 2–3-day period after the patient had undergone a surgical procedure off the unit, so focus was directed to those areas. The team deployed resources to the operative departments to observe insertion and maintenance practices, making recommendations for changes that would better align with the standard bundles. In addition, the team considered other factors, such as the order in which multiple procedures should take place in the context of central line placement. Eventually, departments outside the ICU adapted the insertion and maintenance bundles.

Catheter-Related Bloodstream Infection Cause Analysis Sheet

Patient:
Infection date:
Unit/Service:
Postoperative: ☐ Yes ☐ No

MR#:
Diagnosis:
Open Chest: ☐ Yes ☐ No

Type of line: ☐ PICC ☐ CVL n PA n Arterial line ☐ HD
Location(s): ☐ Femoral ☐ Subclavian ☐ IJ ☐ Transthoracic ☐ Arm ☐ Leg ☐ Scalp
Where line placed: ☐ ER ☐ PICU ☐ OR ☐ IR ☐ Floor ☐ outside hospital
Date of placement: D/C: ☐ No ☐ Yes – date_____

Type of line: ☐ PICC ☐ CVL ☐ PA ☐ Arterial line ☐ HD
Location(s): ☐ Femoral ☐ Subclavian ☐ IJ ☐ Transthoracic ☐ Arm ☐ Leg ☐ Scalp
Where line placed: ☐ ER ☐ PICU ☐ OR n IR ☐ Floor ☐ outside hospital
Date of placement: D/C: ☐ No ☐ Yes – date_____

Type of line: ☐ PICC ☐ CVL ☐ PA ☐ Arterial line ☐ HD
Location(s): ☐ Femoral ☐ Subclavian ☐ IJ ☐ Transthoracic ☐ Arm ☐ Leg ☐ Scalp
Where line placed: ☐ ER ☐ PICU ☐ OR ☐ IR ☐ Floor ☐ outside hospital
Date of placement: D/C: ☐ No ☐ Yes – date_____

Type of line: ☐ PICC ☐ CVL ☐ PA ☐ Arterial line ☐ HD
Location(s): ☐ Femoral ☐ Subclavian ☐ IJ ☐ Transthoracic ☐ Arm ☐ Leg ☐ Scalp
Where line placed: ☐ ER ☐ PICU ☐ OR ☐ IR ☐ Floor ☐ outside hospital
Date of placement: D/C: ☐ No ☐ Yes – date_____

Intermittent medications (3 days prior to line infection)

Day 3 prior:	☐ < 10 meds	☐ 10-30 meds	☐ > 30 meds
Day 2 prior:	☐ < 10 meds	☐ 10-30 meds	☐ > 30 meds
Day 1 prior:	☐ < 10 meds	☐ 10-30 meds	☐ > 30 meds
Day of infection:	☐ < 10 meds	☐ 10-30 meds	☐ > 30 meds

Lab frequency (3 days prior to line infection)

Day 3 prior:	☐ none	☐ < 1/day	☐ 1 per day	☐ 2-5x/day	☐ 5-10x/day	☐ > 10x/day
Day 2 prior:	☐ none	☐ < 1/day	☐ 1 per day	☐ 2-5x/day	☐ 5-1 Ox/day	☐ > 10x/day
Day 1 prior:	☐ none	☐ < 1/day	☐ 1 per day	☐ 2-5x/day	☐ 5-1 Ox/day	☐ > 10x/day
Infection day:	☐ none	☐ < 1/day	☐ 1 per day	☐ 2-5x/day	☐ 5-1 Ox/day	☐ > 10x/day

If no arterial line, how are labs obtained: ☐ from CVL ☐ from PICC ☐ from stick

Trips outside of ICU in last week prior to infection(date and location):
Trip 1: Date_____ Location: ☐ Radiology ☐ OR n IR ☐ Cath Lab ☐ OSH
Trip 2: Date_____ Location: ☐ Radiology ☐ OR n IR ☐ Cath Lab ☐ OSH

Figure 13.5 Template for root cause analysis. A central line–associated bloodstream infection (CLABSI) cause analysis sheet for conducting root cause analysis of an infection. Pertinent data and conditions are collected in one place.

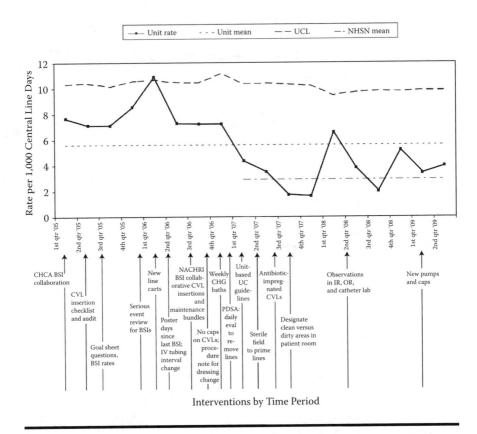

Figure 13.6 CLABSI annotated control chart. The use of a control chart was used to validate that changes made resulted in statistically significant outcomes.

Numerous additional projects took place over the course of several years, and all of them had the same goal—reducing CLABSIs (See Figure 13.6).

This group also undertook more complex projects; one example was the implementation of antibiotic (AB)–impregnated central lines throughout the hospital. The group first reviewed the literature and then talked with peer institutions about the benefits and risks of using such catheters. Once this was understood, assuring collaboration was the issue, as this project required coordination and cooperation from many areas of the hospital, including purchasing, central supply, the cardiac catheterization lab, multiple physician groups, and pharmacists. But the logistics of bringing in a new product, handling potential adverse reactions, and training staff members in how to place new central lines were all managed by the ICU CLABSI team.

A subgroup was also formed to evaluate the risk of thrombosis, which might have been associated with the use of these catheters, because of concerns voiced by at least one peer institution. An analysis was designed to identify patients with catheter-related thrombosis before and after implementation of the

AB-impregnated catheters. We found a similar risk of thromboses between the AB-impregnated catheters and the original catheters. We acknowledge that we did not evaluate this question with the gold standard methodology of research—a prospective, randomized controlled clinical trial—but we believe our quality improvement evaluation was sufficient to answer the question; we also relied on the fact that other peer pediatric institutions had utilized the catheters for some years without difficulty.

Other projects were also scoped out of the findings from the mini-RCAs, such as the need for an improved alcohol prep pad, the use of prophylactic antifungals, and criteria for short-term versus long-term dialysis catheter use.

Changes over Time and Raising the Bar

Reduction of CLABSIs as a hospital goal has continued for three subsequent years, and the specific target goal has been reset annually. The first-year goal was 5 CLABSIs per 1,000 line days, and we achieved a rate of 3.7. The second-year goal was to maintain that rate with a stretch goal to further reduce it. The second-year results were just under 3.7 (or 3.4, taking into account new CDC definitions). Thus, the third-year goal was—once again—to maintain the lowered rate with a stretch goal to further reduce it.

As senior leadership removed barriers, a hospital-wide steering committee was formed to focus on CLABSI prevention throughout the organization. Senior leadership invited members of the committee; and the group included physician and nurse representatives from critical care, medicine, oncology, anesthesia, surgery, radiology, vascular access, infection prevention, as well as other departments. The steering committee was formed so that CLABSI reduction would remain a priority; the committee also provided a forum for cross-department collaboration. Indeed, each department was responsible for presenting key findings from the RCA of CLABSIs in its individual unit. The steering committee provided ideas and suggestions, and it also looked for areas that could benefit from a change in practice or a new level of standardization across units. A guiding principle of this steering committee was to ensure standard practice across all settings.

Mistake Proofing

Mistake proofing and the PDCA cycle—integral to infection prevention strategies—have played an important role in our CLABSI reduction work. While the infection prevention philosophy at Seattle Children's has embraced PDCA in practical terms for decades, we haven't always been conscious of the fact or deliberate in its application. Being conscious and deliberate promotes greater scrutiny of each step as well as a deeper appreciation of mistake proofing.

The "check" component of the PDCA cycle has always been the strength of the infection prevention process. And infection prevention as a discipline has been a leader in the use of standardized definitions and auditing methodologies. But if the "plan" and "do" phases don't incorporate mistake proofing, the interpretability of the data and appropriateness of the subsequent "plan" phases are questionable. If an intervention is truly mistake proof, the ability to draw inferences from resulting data, in terms of whether the intervention "worked" or not, is greatly improved; just as importantly, the data may then be used to drive next steps with greater assurance. The hierarchy of mistake proofing provides us with a clear way of understanding the relative strength of the improvements that were introduced to reduce the incidence of bloodstream infections.

One of the strongest treatments included the introduction of antibiotic-impregnated catheters. To ensure that the AB-impregnated catheters were reliably inserted, we removed all other catheters from the hospital. We reserved an emergency supply of catheters in the central supply department, in case of drug allergy to the coating on the AB-impregnated catheters; but in three years of use, these emergency catheters were never required.

Another strong intervention was the development and application of 5S for the procedure cart, specifically for catheter insertion. The cart was organized by staff members involved in catheter placement, and is now a required element for all insertions. This helps staff follow the proper procedures, since all required equipment is available at the bedside.

Similar to the development and application of 5S for the procedure cart was the creation of a custom, prepackaged kit manufactured specifically for catheter dressing changes. The kit included all elements required for a dressing change, including written instructions for the procedure; once again, this helps staff follow proper procedures by making all equipment readily available at the bedside.

There were numerous weaker and intermediate interventions employed in this process as well—for example, the use of a checklist to be completed by staff involved in the line placement, training, revised policies, and the acquisition of new supplies.

As outlined above, we introduced mini-RCA investigations in our CLABSI work. The initial approach included a retrospective chart review; it also notified providers who had cared for a patient within the past seven days by e-mail if a CLABSI had materialized; the e-mail communication asked if there had been any breaches of practice or procedure, or if there were any suggested reasons for the infection.

Recently, we've added a bedside RCA to be completed within three days of identification of a CLABSI; but we strongly prefer that the RCA be completed on the same day that a CLABSI is identified. This practice involves going to the patient's bedside; huddling with the care providers; and asking for any insight, observations, or areas of concern that might have contributed to the CLABSI. Family members participate in this huddle as an equal partner in care.

Leadership oversight and participation were crucial in engaging providers and getting them to identify practice changes. Our initial attempts with bedside RCAs were met with some resistance, primarily from the direct care staff. They were concerned that a family might be frightened or lose confidence in its care team if suboptimal care or breaches in standard processes were identified.

This response was surprising—particularly in the context of an ICU with a high safety culture score. To allay any fears, nursing leadership met with the bedside nurse prior to the RCA to explain the context and the blame-free nature of this event. These RCAs have proven to be very beneficial, and they have provided us with additional ideas and opportunities to improve our process. In addition, the process has led to specific plans for individual patients while educating family members about the risk of CLABSIs and the protective strategies that can be employed to minimize this risk. This bedside huddle is now practiced across almost all units.

In conclusion, we still haven't achieved a CLABSI rate of zero; but we are trying to understand the root causes of these infections and target those causes with changes in our approaches. We also acknowledge that we don't currently have the tools to eliminate CLABSI events for certain patients who are at extreme risk; yet we are determined to understand these risk factors, and we are committed to the right interventions as appropriate.

In looking back, five key concepts have been important in our CLABSI reduction efforts: continuous quality improvement principles, continual iterative work toward improvement, the collaboration of multidisciplinary teams, the involvement of families, and the visible support of the executive level of administration.

We still have a long way to go on our journey, but it's clear that we've made major strides in eliminating mistakes—and catheter-associated bloodstream infections in our hospital.

Notes

1. J. Reason, "Human Error: Models and Management," *British Medical Journal* 320 (2000): 768–70.
2. Institute of Medicine, *To Err Is Human: Building a Safer Health System* (Washington, D.C.: National Academy Press, 1999).
3. J. R. Grout, "Mistake Proofing: Changing Designs to Reduce Error," *Quality and Safety in Health Care* 15, suppl. I (2006): i44–i49.
4. Centers for Disease Control (CDC), "Guidelines for the Prevention of Intravascular Catheter-Related Infections," 2002, http://www.cdc.gov (accessed July 27, 2010).
5. M. L. Render and L. Hirschhorn, "An Irreplaceable Safety Culture," *Critical Care Clinics* 21 (2006): 31–41.
6. Institute of Medicine, [Home page], 2009, http://www.iom.edu (accessed July 27, 2010).
7. J. B. Sexton, R. L. Helmreich, T. B. Neilands, K. Rowan, K. Vella, J. Boyden, et al., "The Safety Attitudes Questionnaire: Psychometric Properties, Benchmarking Data, and Emerging Research," *BMC Health Services Research* 6 (2006): 44.

8. Agency for Healthcare Research and Quality (AHRQ), [Home page], 2009, http://www.ahrq.gov (accessed July 27, 2010).
9. H. E. Jeffries, W. Mason, M. Brewer, K. L. Oakes, E. I. Muñoz, and W. Gornick, et al. "Prevention of Central Venous Catheter-Associated Bloodstream Infections in Pediatric Intensive Care Units: A Performance Improvement Collaborative," *Infection Control and Hospital Epidemiology* 30, no. 7 (2009): 645–51.

Chapter 14

Balancing the Line in Outpatient Pharmacy

Steven D. Wanaka, RPh
Director of Pharmacy
Seattle Children's Hospital

Barb Marquardt, RPh
Outpatient Pharmacy Operations Manager
Seattle Children's Hospital

Imagine you are a charge nurse in the emergency room (ER) trying to get a patient admitted to a bed in the hospital. You make multiple calls and find out that beds will be available "as soon as we can get the patient discharged." Meanwhile, the ER waiting room is filling up with worried parents and sick children. All exam rooms in the ER are occupied by patients currently being cared for, waiting for test results, or waiting for admission to a hospital bed. For you, it's "another day in the ER," but you know that for the children and parents coming to you for help, the situation is at best stressful and at worst unsafe. So you keep making phone calls, hoping that your calls will "speed things up."

Now imagine that you are a nurse in the hospital. You know the ER is full, so you have been trying your best to "expedite" the discharge of patients on your floor. Your patients with physician discharge orders are ready to go, except they have not received their discharge medications from the hospital's pharmacy. The best you can do is to continue to call the hospital's outpatient pharmacy, where discharge orders are filled, hoping that your call will "speed things up."

Further imagine that you are in the outpatient pharmacy filling the discharge prescriptions. Most of the workload for discharge medications came to you in a "bolus" between 10 a.m. and noon. Some of the orders are complicated, containing more than ten medications. You are working as fast as you can, but the phone keeps ringing!

This was the situation that Seattle Children's Hospital found itself in when they launched a discharge medication turnaround time initiative in 2005. To be fair, medications were only one of the many causes of discharge delays. Nonetheless, the outpatient pharmacy took the challenge seriously and began work on how to remove medications as a "constraint" in the discharge process.

When the discharge medication process improvement work started, the first logical question was "Who are the customers of the outpatient pharmacy?" Customers were identified as the following:

1. Inpatients who are going home from the hospital
2. Postoperative day surgery patients
3. Patients seen in ambulatory clinics
4. Emergency department patients

Pharmacy leadership and staff were concerned about prioritizing prescriptions for inpatient medicine patients at the expense of other patients. If pharmacy focused only on decreasing the turnaround time for inpatient medicine discharge prescriptions, the turnaround time for other patients might increase. After pharmacy leadership explained their concern to the continuous performance improvement (CPI) consultants and inpatient medicine group, all agreed that the focus of the work should be to decrease medication turnaround time for all patients.

During the assessment and planning phase of the work, the team determined that a Rapid Process Improvement Workshop (RPIW) on "outpatient pharmacy flow" was needed. This workshop would require close collaboration between the medical service and pharmacy, so a medical unit physician and the lead outpatient pharmacist were assigned as co–process owners. While it is usually best to assign one process owner to a project, in this case the collaboration between co-owners was a key to success. The co-owners shared information about their respective work flows and facilitated improvement opportunities across the system.

In preparation for and during the RPIW, the workshop team observed current processes and documented their findings. Observers stood in the pharmacy, timed each step of the process, and tracked the movement of people, information, and materials. The observers included pharmacy and nonpharmacy staff. Initially, the pharmacy staff found it difficult to conduct their usual work when people with clipboards and stopwatches watched their every move. For many, this was the first time their work had ever been timed or their footsteps charted. Pharmacy leaders, sensing uneasiness from the staff, took time to introduce the observers to the staff, explain their role in the project, and answer questions. Today you will find that

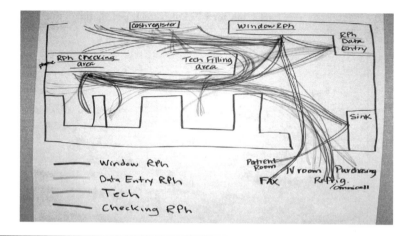

Figure 14.1 Spaghetti diagram. Mapping the "as is" process and the roles supporting it. Although using this form was uncomfortable for the staff at first, this led the way for defining variability in the process.

observations are commonplace in the pharmacy and being observed is part of the job. The results of observations are shown in Figure 14.1.

Once observations were complete, a work balance form was created (See Figure 14.2). The data showed that the pharmacy staff was meeting an average cycle time that was less than the required takt time (rate of customer demand) and that the workloads for the three members of the outpatient "assembly line" were only slightly off balance. At first glance, this made it appear that the pharmacy must be meeting customer demand. However, this was very far from the truth. The average cycle time did not reflect the reality of the wide-ranging variability in the time to perform each step. For example, the step done by the checking pharmacist could take anywhere from 42 seconds to 24 minutes. Whenever a step in the process exceeded the average, queues and backups would develop in the workflow, causing delays and lack of predictability. The work balance form, which shows the takt time, average cycle time, and range of cycle times, was an especially helpful illustration of the need to achieve improved work balance between the three people working on the line: the order entry pharmacist, the fill tech, and the checking pharmacist.

The work balance chart emphasized the need for input from the RPIW team members and all outpatient pharmacy staff on ways to get the cycle time of each job at or below the required takt time. While gaining input from staff was critical for engagement and obtaining the best results, pharmacy managers grappled with the challenge of communicating with staff and obtaining their input while they were actively working on the line. Interruptions could lead to errors, jeopardize patient safety, and cause delays, but the production line needed to continue while the process improvement team did its work. Leaders and staff agreed that communication should occur with the least disruption of the process and maximal input from all

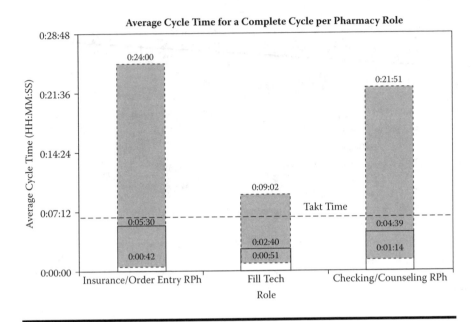

Figure 14.2 Work balance form. The mean cycle time is shown by the solid line. The gray shaded areas show the range in cycle times for each step of the operation.

participants. The group decided to communicate through frequent, brief meetings (< 10 minutes); e-mail messages; and flyers posted in the pharmacy.

The team found that the spaghetti diagram was useful in quickly revealing work flow problems and in stimulating ideas to balance the work. The form showed that staff members traveled away from the pharmacy work area because they did not have the tools and materials they needed in their area. The RPIW team achieved quick wins by placing a fax machine and refrigerator in the outpatient pharmacy area. These two small improvements eliminated wasted time and travel and, maybe more importantly, engaged the pharmacy staff, who saw immediate benefits from the RPIW. One reason for the checking pharmacist's wide-ranging cycle time was the need to leave the outpatient pharmacy area to deliver take-home medications to inpatients being discharged. A delivery could add more than twenty minutes to the cycle time. Since a previous RPIW in 1999, feedback from families about the medication deliveries was generally positive, and the pharmacy staff had long thought the providers, nurses, and families viewed it as a value-added service. By 2005, however, it was clear that families and hospital staff valued timely completion of prescriptions over delivery to the patient's room. The data showed that the checking pharmacist's step was highly variable, and the team realized that variation could be eliminated if the pharmacist stayed in the pharmacy instead of making deliveries to patient rooms. The RPIW team members and the management guidance team decided to eliminate the deliveries in favor of a balanced work flow and more predictable turnaround time.

During the RPIW, the workshop leader introduced the concept of a service promise. The RPIW team calculated a takt time of six minutes, balanced the steps in the prescription-filling work flow, and reduced the variability of cycle times. They decided that the improvements should enable the staff to fill prescription orders of up to five medications per patient within thirty minutes of receipt in the pharmacy. This assumed that orders sent to the pharmacy did not require rework; orders with errors would be returned to the originating patient care unit for correction. These order sets were named "speed scripts." Order sets of more than five prescriptions would take longer, and these order sets were named "complex orders." No turnaround time was defined for complex orders, but the team determined that the pharmacy would have time to work on these larger orders in the afternoon. The RPIW team publicized the thirty-minute service promise and asked nurses not to call the pharmacy to ask if prescriptions were ready until thirty minutes had passed since sending them to the pharmacy.

Many improvements were made during the RPIW, and it was viewed as a success. While the work fell short of meeting the thirty-minute service promise, the average turnaround time decreased by 40 percent (from eighty-nine minutes pre-RPIW to fifty-one minutes 120 days post RPIW).

While 40 percent improvement is impressive, lean thinking in the organization led to the conclusion that this "wasn't good enough" and medications were still a cause for discharge delay. This conclusion led the pharmacy team into another period of analysis of the current situation and further improvements.

It became clear to pharmacy leadership and staff that there had to be a better way than working in a strict "first in first out" system where the pharmacy worked on orders as they were received. The pharmacy needed to know when medications were needed, and to insure that work was completed by that time. It didn't matter if the turnaround time for a medication was twenty-four hours as long as it was ready when the patient needed it. Pharmacy leaders discussed the concept with pharmacy staff members and asked them to give suggestions for improvement. Based on staff input, the team decided to develop a prescription-scheduling system. The system was based on the concept of "heijunka," or load leveling. The staff created a scheduling board which enabled them to schedule completion times for prescriptions in 5–10-minute intervals. The intervals reflected the current cycle times to fill prescriptions. The heijunka board helped level the workload in the pharmacy, and it enabled staff and pharmacy leaders to visually determine if the line was running behind or ahead of schedule. The staff has worked together to continuously make incremental improvements to the scheduling system, and it is still in use three years later.

Perhaps the biggest measure of success is that the phone in the outpatient pharmacy is no longer ringing off the hook because nurses can now count on predictable, timely delivery of discharge medications.

During the outpatient pharmacy's CPI journey, pharmacy leaders and staff have learned many valuable lessons. First, eliminating barriers to effective communication with frontline staff is key to achieving engagement and sustainable results. Second, the people who do the work provide the best ideas for improvement. And, last, while much can be achieved in a five-day rapid improvement workshop, using the plan, do, check, and act (PDCA) process to continue to improve after the RPIW event is critical. CPI truly is a never-ending journey with successes and failures along the way.

Chapter 15

Making the Right Call: The Everett Clinic Registration to Cash Value Stream

Janeen Lambert, CPC, CPC-H, CHC
Associate Administrator of Regulatory Compliance, Chief Compliance Officer
Everett Clinic

Iwalani Paquette
Director of Business Services
Everett Clinic

The lean transformation of the Everett Clinic business services unit began in November 2005. There was great anticipation among the participants, leadership, staff, and consultants; and surrounding staff members were anxious, excited, and curious. We didn't see it then, but in the wake of this experience, no situation, task, or process has ever been quite the same again.

We started with the registration to cash value stream. Once complete, this value stream would span the life of a patient request for service through payment. Over the next four years, the team would improve lead time, remove waste, create flow, and combine work teams to incrementally meet many of the value stream stretch goals (See Table 15.1). The anticipated annual savings of $2–3 million would be realized, and

Table 15.1 Event Summary for the Value Stream from Registration to Cash at the Everett Clinic

	Team Topic	Measurements of Results	Before	After	Change
1	Registration to cash value stream mapping	Total touch time	712 minutes	141 minutes	80%
		Total flow time (including claim time)	64,000 minutes	238 minutes	99.6%
		Total distance traveled	2,074 feet	1,672 feet	19.4%
2	Lean metrics	First pass yield	13.5%	53%	4× improvement

the total resource reduction would climb to an unprecedented thirty full-time equivalents (FTEs) within business services. Administration promised that those engaged in lean work would not lose employment, though their jobs would change. This FTE reduction would be achieved solely from the natural attrition of staff due to moves, job changes, and retirement.

SIDEBAR 15.1

Payback: Assuming 50 percent of the resources in this value stream are dedicated to this work, an 80 percent reduction in touch time. Based on numbers from the accounting department, this will translate into between $2.25 million and $4.5 million in annual savings. In addition, at 6 percent cost of money, an additional one-time savings of $1.0 million will be realized due to higher turns.

- Completed current-state and future-state maps.
- Performed gap analysis for action plans and used a possible, implement, challenge, or kill (PICK) chart to rank "Just Do Its," projects, and events.
- Prioritized events and assigned ownership to all open items.
- Calculated all lean metrics and converted them to business metrics; achieved significant opportunities for labor savings and quality improvement.

Lessons learned by participants:

- Hard to let go of the "ugly."
- Struggling to see the steps.
- A lot behind the scenes.
- We see many opportunities.
- Empowered to make change!

The targets that have been achieved provide compelling evidence of what a novice team can do with lean tools, proper coaching, and administrative support. And, during a time of healthcare crisis and reform, this may well prove to be a key method for taking significant costs out of healthcare by raising the bar on overall customer service and quality.

Mapping the Value Stream

Staff began by learning about the tools that they would be using and the fundamentals of lean transformation. As the mapping process progressed, the participants were amazed that such a simple process like using "sticky" notes to map out the work could be so revealing.

The picture that was initially painted of work flow was not pretty. The way the business unit had always done things—and done them well—was clearly not the best way, and the value stream "map" led the participants to this stark and honest conclusion.

There was no arm twisting, no one-person idea; there was just a map leading us through the current process and helping us to envision better outcomes. Our goal was to create a new way of doing things that was much simpler; and we wanted a process that would move continuously and encourage staff members to work together seamlessly in providing value to our customers.

One of the challenges of improvement work is how to best communicate with, and involve, those who are part of the larger work group but not present in the room during the improvement process. Not surprisingly, it can be quite confusing for these people.

Choices need to be made by leadership when anxiety surfaces; there is a more passive approach, which allows staff members to work through their discomfort on their own, or the active approach, which draws people in. Our business office leadership recognized the potential for resistance and understood that the future success of this process required action. As a result, communications were made constantly through e-mail, informal meetings, and casual walking around to let staff know what was happening.

Team staff members were also invited to the improvement events to share their experiences, expertise, and observations about the work they performed and the process changes being considered, and to offer suggestions and give input.

Updates were posted throughout work areas, and team members, as well as clinic leadership, could monitor progress or participate in a daily huddle.

Management used a positive tone to remind staff that everyone would benefit from the findings. Keeping false rumors from circulating was a priority, especially because process change and the new improvement system being introduced were of interest to staff clinic-wide. Rumors were not unexpected; business services was one of the first units to put this new "lean process" to the test, and a number of people expressed the belief that this was just another fad that someone had read about and now wanted to try for a few months. These naysayers thought the whole notion of "lean" would die a quiet death rather than take hold as an emerging new trend.

It became evident, as the initial weeklong session progressed, that this first mapping was just the beginning of what would become the Everett Clinic business services improvement process (See Figure 15.1).

Figure 15.1 Team value stream mapping process. The Everett Clinic's initial registration to cash value stream. Participants map the value stream from patient request for service to payment to improve lead time, remove waste, create flow, and combine work teams in pursuit of an anticipated $2–3 million in annual savings.

The first "aha moment" from the group was in discovering how the simple task of mapping could provide us with such a clear picture of what we were doing, and just how difficult we had made the process for our customers—the patients.

After this recognition, we realized—once again—just how critical communication and reassurance were to implementing change. There were many questions, and much anxiety and fear, as a sense of what we were doing became increasingly clear. Daily communications, in the form of dashboards and "just do-its," were a must; and we had to advise the larger group outside the room as progress was made and findings were uncovered during the initial event.

People are the most important element of a lean transformation; if you are able to reach people, you will succeed in driving change.

Engaging Your People

Preparing staff members for a process improvement event includes educating them about lean terms and tools, and providing them with the opportunity to learn through exercises and experiential training. Staff buy-in is a must, and the old saying "It takes a village" is applicable here. Without staff buy-in, an improvement system cannot succeed.

It's also important to remember that the event transformation and the transformation of people occur at different times. By the end of the initial event, staff members are believers; after a week passes, however, the belief begins to fade, given the day-to-day bog-down of work. Staff will slowly begin to slide back to the "old ways," and you have to work on auditing the new standard work to catch the subtle shift.

The principle of improving the work flow for the customer is positive and non-threatening, and it produces results that inspire. Indeed, staff members found the tools and scientific data gathering clear-cut and easy to use; and once they learned more, it was obvious that improvement would result in a reduction of rework. New process designs, most specifically using a work cell approach, meant the elimination of steps and, as a result, less work for them.

Still, while they were acutely aware of the fact that the new process supported the Everett Clinic's guiding principles—"Doing what is right for each patient"; "Providing an enriching and supportive workplace"; and "Our team focuses on value: service, quality, and cost"—the reality of change was harsh.

To be sure, change is hard; but change that eliminates the very work someone is performing is very frightening, even if the work itself is not satisfying or does not add value. This is where process change becomes personal.

To sustain change in any organization, leadership needs to be present for the people who count on them for direction, guidance, and security. A strong communication feed must occur. Strong staff retention and reeducation programs must be in place. Staff members need to be reminded constantly that the process is about improvement, and not a reduction in team members. This is a very challenging message to communicate.

At first, there were the nonbelievers, who knew that jobs would change, and that work would be eliminated as defects were fixed. This type of awareness anxiety can create resistance. The Everett Clinic has always been a supportive workplace where our employees are valued and open communication is encouraged. And the Everett Clinic leadership reiterated throughout the value stream work that no one would lose employment, although jobs would change. It was very rewarding to see the clinic live up to that promise, and the staff savings to date have been accomplished without any layoffs.

Work Cell Design

The first opportunity for rapid change came when the initial Registration to Cash event was rolled out in March 2006. The goal was to establish flow for incoming calls and to resolve issues in a timely manner. Two separate departments came together to brainstorm this problem. They made breakthrough progress when two front-level staff members asked, "Why can't phone people from both insurance and customer service answer patient calls?" This idea would require a team approach that engaged two different areas and two different managers.

Quite frankly, this idea may have been more difficult for the managers to fathom than it was for the staff members who suggested it. But from that revolutionary idea came the mapping of a single flow process for incoming patient calls. The team came prepared to announce to its peers the following morning that we would be wiring all insurance and customer service phones so that they would be able to answer calls as a collective unit.

Despite the fears of peer reprisal, the team members successfully implemented the beginnings of a work cell design that would bring together nearly every skill needed to answer patient questions in a single call. This work trial would begin to eliminate the long-standing tradition of specialization in the Everett Clinic business services unit.

The goal of this one-phone program was to reduce waste, the average speed to answer phones, handoffs, and processing time for patient billing and insurance inquiries. And the results were strong. We doubled the number of staff answering calls by combining the insurance phone staff with customer services. We eliminated the phone menu so that patients spoke with a live person. And we cross-trained insurance and customer service staff members to answer any question (See Table 15.2).

In the wake of this success, we began to see just how important the leadership connection is in the lean process. The Everett Clinic business services staff had a relationship of trust with immediate area leadership. Staff members spoke often and openly about their fears of change and work elimination. The trust for the Everett Clinic business services unit only grew stronger as the various process improvement events continued; all that had been explained and promised became reality.

Table 15.2 Business Office Event Results in a Scorecard

	Business Office Phones Scorecard		
	Pre–March 2006	*March 2007*	*Results*
Phone speed to answer	1:21	0:17	–1:04
Handoff turned around	85 hours	1 hour	–84 hours
Same-day resolution	93%	99%	+06%
Days Revenue Outstanding	42.62	38.99	–3.63
Hours of operation	9:00 a.m. to 4:00 p.m.	7:00 a.m. to 8:00 p.m.	+6 hours
Business office FTEs	113.34	102.86	–10.48

Today's Work Today

The second improvement phase saved seven FTEs' worth of staff hours. Leadership and the team decided to use these hours to unburden their leads so they could mentor; the rest of the hours helped create a float group that could work in other areas of business services as needed. As people left the organization to take other positions or retire, these float staff members were moved into permanent positions.

The purpose of this second phase of improvement was to understand work flow throughout customer services and account services and to staff flexibly by hourly demand. To achieve this goal, we redesigned the physical work space, combining account services and customer services. This allowed the merged staff to meet fluctuating demand and answer all questions in an efficient and informed way.

A new mantra was created during this event: "Today's Work Today." And we fulfilled the spirit of the slogan by meeting the demand of work on a daily basis through flexible staffing resources.

After working on the phone processes, we next turned to the cash collection process. The cash collection process included staff from two separate departments located on two different floors—3 FTEs from business services and 2.5 FTEs from accounting. Our goal was to decrease turnaround time, increase efficiencies in workflow, and reduce cycle time through replicating our previous experience by creating a work cell to potentially unite a new team and generate synergy. Management was quick to realize that this change would create a different set of anxieties; it also required a physical move and a different reporting structure.

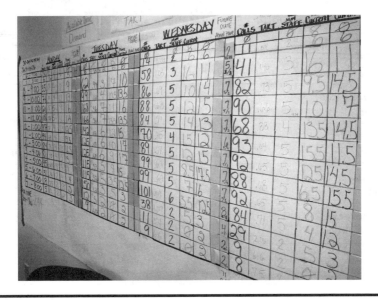

Figure 15.2 Charting of call volumes by day and hour. The hourly call counts were tracked and charted for a few months. Cross-trained staff were assigned hours in the call center to meet the demand. By "flexing" staff on a daily basis, call demand was met with fewer FTEs.

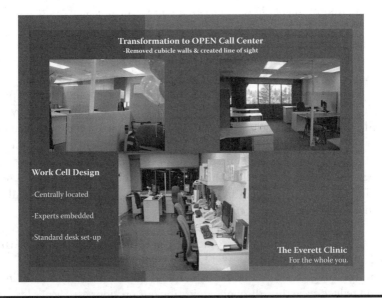

Figure 15.3 Transformation process to an open call center. An open call center created many advantages, chief among them being co-located staff leading to synergy, camaraderie, and easy access to each other and their leads.

Table 15.3 Summary of the Cash Collection Event Work

Cash Collection Process					Location:The Everett Clinic (October 8–13, 2006)	
Team Topic		*Measurements of Results*	*Before*	*After*	*% Improvement*	*Comments*
Business office cash collection processes	1	Cash bag processing time	7:46	2:30	68%	Minutes
	2	Transfer of unused cash bags	30	0	100%	Bags transferred daily
	3	Achieve same-day turnaround on incoming funds	$48,731	TBD	100%	Expect $0 cash left at end of day
	4	FTEs	4.65	3.65	22%	FTE reduction through attrition

Aim: Decrease turnaround time and increase efficiency in payment room workflow, resulting in reduced cycle time.

Knowing the importance of communication, a meeting was organized with the accounting staff to provide an opportunity for those feeling the most ill at ease to share their concerns. The group was open and honest and presented a list of twenty concerns that included everything from the space it would occupy to the unknown of a new management. As the meeting progressed and the team members worked through each item, some of the worries dissipated. This meeting set an example of true commitment to staff, and was a turning point that made this a more successful event for all. Discussing the changes helped reiterate the value that the organization placed on each individual's contribution to the process and provided a forum that validated each person's opinions.

This was a big win for us, too. We were able to streamline the work so that only deposit monies were routed to business services, and there was now a one-way exchange of deposit—no more cash bag return. In addition, errors on balancing were now reported to reception daily (See Table 15.3).

We decided to move into the insurance area after this.

The Value of Standard Work

Further improvement opportunities awaited us when a diverse group from insurance, accounting, reception, and customer service assembled to examine the process for working unpaid insurance claims. Unfortunately, with a variety of carriers and a multitude of rules, staff members were skeptical about the possibility of establishing any standard work for this ever-changing process. But after observing and mapping a wide variety of ways that staff did the same work, the team came up with a standard process. Experienced and new staff could easily follow this guideline and end up with effective results.

The basic vision was to have standard daily one-touch resolution and standard work for processing all claims. We fulfilled this vision by changing the schedules for staff members so they aligned with those of the insurance carriers; we implemented daily huddles for good news and target setting; we created a toolbox for access to basic appeal guidelines; we made sure the claims in the worklist were worked on as they were assigned; and we saw to it that claims were no longer sorted by denial or carrier type—there was now one queue for all staff to pull from daily. The event results were favorable, as showed by the scorecard in Table 15.4.

Six months later, the work list claim count had dropped from thirty-four thousand to seventeen thousand claims. Improvement continues for us in this area; and our staff members recognize and report opportunities for up-front claim issue resolution that will further reduce the need for manual intervention and work queues.

Table 15.4   Insurance Worklist Event Results in a Scorecard

Worklist Event (May 2008)	Pre-Event (February–May 2008)	June 2008	90 Days Post Event (May–July 2008)
Staff satisfaction	67% positive	Goal: 75%	78% positive
Productivity (worklist claims per FTE)	170 per week per FTE	385 per week per FTE	299 per week per FTE
Days revenue outstanding	42.42	43.61	40.22
% weekly worklist claims complete	25%	100%	100% of weekly worklist claims
Touches per claim—rework	6.5	Goal: 3.5	

The Role of Leaders

Lean improvement from a human workforce perspective is much like any behavioral modification, and it requires constant focus and attention. It's imperative that leaders make themselves available, communicate at every level, and coach through obstacles and setbacks. Leaders must always share improvements using understandable data that are made visible with dashboards, messages, rewards, and constant encouragement.

Four years after starting the lean initiative, the Everett Clinic business services staff is better able to adapt to any industry change. Many people in our organization are still finding ways to improve their processes to better meet the work demand of our customers. And defective processes can now be redesigned by the people doing the work; they use their own ingenuity and tools that have become part of our Everett Clinic Improvement System.

We have learned many things about change, but perhaps the most important lesson of the last four years has been that lean transformation efforts are most powerful when they are deployed by frontline staff everyday in the workplace, not just "imagined" in a conference room. This lesson, combined with the knowledge that our managers, administrators, and CEO stand behind us as we transform our culture and our work methods, will continue to drive our success as we move forward.

Chapter 16

Working Hard to Improve Work Flow in the Lab

Bobbi J. Kochevar, MBA, CLS
Children's Hospitals and Clinics of Minnesota

Mark D. Schumann, CLS
Children's Hospitals and Clinics of Minnesota

We were laboring under considerable stress, and our employees felt it. Absorbing 5 percent increases in volume year after year, for five years, had created chaos and taken its toll. You could feel it in the labs. We felt that our only alternative, in spite of a constrained financial climate, was to seek permission from our hospital administration to add staff in the lab.

Today, after adopting, embracing, and implementing lean principles, we live in a very different work world—it's almost peaceful. You walk in at 9 a.m., and everybody and everything are moving along at a smooth pace, even though we're just as busy and volume is still growing.

When we look back on this transformation, we realize that if we had kept on using traditional methods to improve operations and customer and staff satisfaction at Children's Hospitals and Clinics of Minnesota, we never would have gotten where we are today. Faced with rising customer demands, steadily increasing workload, staff fatigue, and job dissatisfaction, the old ways would have taken us down an organizational dead end. Conventional tools like retention bonuses, pay-for-performance increases, modified work schedules, shifting job duties, and team-building exercises would have simply served as temporary band-aids for deep-rooted and complex underlying issues.

And those underlying issues were serious.

Demands for laboratory testing at our hospital had grown more than 10 percent for two consecutive years. All indicators were pointing toward continued growth in testing volumes. But turnaround times for critical laboratory tests were not meeting customer expectations. And volume surges appeared to be random and unpredictable, draining resources and putting quality at risk. Between surges in demand for lab services, we had significant periods of underutilized capacity. Work levels were not equally balanced between lab departments, and we had limited capability and willingness of staff to assist in neighboring departments.

At a national level, an increasingly dramatic decline in the supply of laboratory professionals was putting a strain on the majority of hospital labs. Compounding the shortage, according to the National Accrediting Agency for Clinical Laboratory Sciences, over the last ten years the number of academic programs educating and training these individuals has declined approximately 30 percent. Competition for new graduates was becoming fierce locally, and healthcare facilities were "stealing" employees from each other to meet their basic staffing needs. It was not unusual for vacated positions to remain open for more than six months.

As a result, our lab was consistently operating with fewer staff than we needed, and staff were constantly being asked to work extra shifts to fill holes in the schedule. Use of overtime climbed to over eight thousand hours per year (6.5 percent of total hours) as a means of patching an average of fifteen schedule vacancies each week. Lab managers were frequently required to abandon their management tasks to fill staffing holes and respond to surges in demand. To make matters worse, our staff productivity level was only average, at the 50th percentile compared to national benchmarks for children's hospitals.

Staff fatigue and dissatisfaction levels were very high. Nearly 70 percent of those responding to an employee survey indicated dissatisfaction with their workload, only 19 percent felt encouraged to participate in decision making, and merely 23 percent would recommend the laboratory as a place to work.

Despite low satisfaction and high workload demands experienced by staff, physician satisfaction with our laboratory services remained relatively strong. The largest areas of concern expressed by physicians were related to test ordering, report formatting, and clinic and emergency department result turnaround times.

But we still stood on the brink of organizational meltdown, and had to fix the problems somehow and someway.

Our Journey Begins

Our laboratory's journey and introduction to lean principles as a means of improving operational performance and driving out waste began in 2005. Lab leaders had attended a presentation by a well-respected local hospital laboratory that had utilized lean to transform its operations. The story sounded all too familiar: growing demands for services, the need to maximize efficiency and improve productivity, and dissatisfied staff.

This presentation described impressive success stories: 50 percent improvement in core testing productivity; test result turnaround times cut in half; expenses reduced by 28 percent; and a significant decrease in physical space needs—all by simply reconfiguring testing equipment and eliminating waste. That sounded too good to be true.

We were very interested, so we invited an external consultant specializing in utilizing lean in laboratory settings to present its methodology, timelines, and typical costs. After a short review of lab operations, the consultant shared the vision of creating a work cell of high-volume automated testing equipment to maximize efficiency and productivity. The concept of single-piece flow was introduced as a means of improving turnaround times and quality versus the batch processing that existed at that time. The consultant recommended an eight-week project plan for implementation, requiring roughly eight full-time, dedicated laboratory staff members for the duration of the project. The consultant also projected a budget of roughly $250,000 for construction and consultant fees.

Though laboratory leadership remained interested in lean after the consultant's presentation, great debate ensued. How could the lab free up eight full-time staff for eight weeks when staffing was already extremely tight? Would the project costs be approved when hospital leaders had limited knowledge of lean and very limited appetite for additional expenses? Did we, as a leadership team, have the ability to support the cultural transformation it would take to become a "lean lab"?

Rather than push forward with the consultant, some of us in the lab decided that we should "jump right in" and "just do it." We began studying lean concepts, sending more people to visit the outside lab, and even began drawing up future-state designs. Some of us felt ready to adopt change. Some of us, however, needed more time to process the proposed changes and truly understand the impact on staff. So an obvious dichotomy developed: those wanting to jump right in and do it, and those saying, "Not so fast!"

Coincidentally, senior leaders in the hospital had just been introduced to lean concepts through a consulting firm with implementation experience within pediatric healthcare facilities nationally. Children's administration engaged this consulting firm, and, while the details had not been finalized, this engagement set the stage for the laboratory's transformation and the pioneering of lean within our organization. At this point, we were confident that we would have organizational support for our lean efforts.

What followed were a few weeks of assessment and planning, in partnership with the consulting team. We developed an implementation plan that targeted areas of highest need of flow improvement, waste reduction, work balance, and visual controls. Knowing that nearly 80 percent of all testing in the lab was performed by five highly automated instruments, the concept of developing an automated core work cell began to take shape.

The Work Begins

We understood the monumental effort in front of us and decided to begin the transformation at a smaller scale with a Rapid Process Improvement Workshop (RPIW) and 5S (sort, simplify, sweep, standardize, and sustain) event. Helping staff understand lean concepts by having a few smaller projects under the team's belt prior to such a significant transformation could help with buy-in, support, and the ultimate engagement of the lab employees. To set the stage even further, we made a commitment that staff positions would not be eliminated as a result of the lean initiatives.

The RPIW and 5S events focused on specimen collection and processing to drive flow improvements, eliminate waste, and standardize work. The team was tasked with standardizing blood collection trays, supply management, and specimen processing during two weeklong events. Before the event, every blood collection tray was different. Staff members each had their favorite tray with their own supplies. Equipment was stored inefficiently, with months of excess inventory scattered throughout the lab.

A team of nine staff members from all areas of the lab convened to make the change. Collection tray supplies and equipment were standardized. The specimen-processing area was modified to enhance specimen flow and standardize the work being performed. The main centrifuge used to process specimens was relocated closer to where specimens arrived in the laboratory to minimize travel distance of the staff and the physical specimens.

Immediately following these events, it became quite evident that implementing lean was not going to be as easy as it seemed at the beginning. Our immediate successes were soon hindered by staff hiding their own "personalized collection trays" under desks, excess inventory ordered (by someone on the RPIW team), concerns from left-handed staff working in a right-handed-designed processing area, and a failure to communicate the new locations for supplies.

Soon, it became obvious that careful planning for sustaining gains was just as critical as planning the event, and it was crucial that we, as leaders, remained very involved.

Preparing for Major Transformation

Taking the knowledge gained from the successes and failures of our initial events, we were gaining confidence in the power of lean principles to drive major change within our operation. Staff still had very mixed levels of support, fear, anxiety, and, for some, refusal to change. As leaders, however, we were aligned and ready for change as the laboratory began planning the implementation of a core work cell consisting of the most highly utilized and primarily automated instruments.

During the initial weeks of planning, data elements were collected to determine testing volumes for each instrument, time of specimen collection and arrival in the lab, time for test result completion, staffing assignments, and existing productivity levels. Staff measured how long each instrument took to complete a test. Staff was also engaged in documenting the existing state of lab operations. Spaghetti maps were created, mapping the paths of both specimens and staff (See Figure 16.1).

The spaghetti-mapping exercise, documenting flow within the existing state, quickly confirmed the belief that a significant amount of waste (long travel

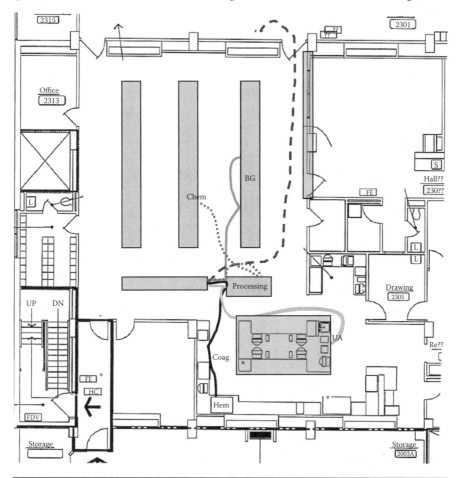

Figure 16.1   Spaghetti map of path of specimens and staff. The "as is" configuration provided visual confirmation of the waste in the process and was the first step in creating a baseline to measure improvement.

distances, and multiple areas where inventory is stored or can collect) within the lab was attributed to the physical configuration of the facilities. The lab was filled with monuments (pieces of large equipment, work surfaces, and physical structures that cannot be easily moved), which obstructed specimen and staff workflow. Work surfaces were laboratory grade, mounted to long, permanent chases. The chases contained the electrical supply, data feeds, source water, and drainage lines to support testing equipment. This tied large, automated equipment to a very specific, inflexible physical location. The chases also contained medical gases, forced air, and suction no longer needed to support modern lab equipment.

Armed with a high-level design vision, the laboratory convened project teams to design the new physical layout recommendation. The following principles were utilized to guide the teams' efforts:

- Develop two work cells: one cell containing automated, high-volume equipment, and one cell containing manual, nonautomated, lower volume testing.
- Minimize monuments.
- Design flexible solutions to enable easy reconfiguration.
- Optimize specimen and staff flow.
- Design inventory control and replenishment systems.
- Improve ergonomics.

Team members were carefully selected to include medical leadership, supervisors, technical staff, support staff, equipment vendors, and external customers. Lab staff was also strategically selected to include those already supportive of lean principles and those resistant to the change. Demonstrating the value added to the daily work of staff quickly converted the "nonbelievers" in the group. Involving those fearful and/or resistant to the proposed changes proved to be an important strategy, as these individuals were able to communicate with, and "bring along," many coworkers with similar feelings.

The teams brainstormed multiple design options on paper. Testing the multiple options against the design principles quickly eliminated many of the designs from consideration. Spaghetti mapping the flow of specimens and staff through the remaining design options ultimately pointed to the final optimal configuration (See Figure 16.2).

Other than the pneumatic tube station used to deliver specimens into the laboratory, monuments were essentially eliminated or minimized. Chases supporting equipment, electrical supply, data feeds, and water supplies were replaced with height-adjustable tables with lockable wheels. Electrical and data elements were provided in a ceiling panel grid, which could be easily reconfigured. Water feeds and drain lines were connected via flexible conduit, allowing flexibility in the location of large automated equipment needing water supply.

Testing equipment was arranged in a U-shaped configuration to optimize the flow of specimens and minimize staff travel distances. The highest volume instruments

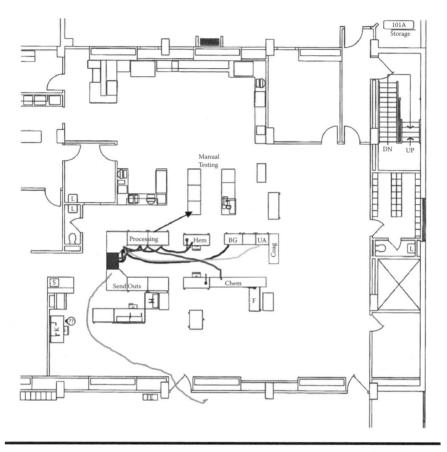

Figure 16.2 Spaghetti map of final optimal configuration. The new configuration changed not only the physical layout and flow, but also roles, work responsibilities, and culture.

were located in closest proximity to the specimen receipt and specimen-processing areas. This configuration, while optimal for flow, quickly revealed a daunting operational issue. The lab, which had operated as six distinct organizational departments, was being transformed into four departments (three unchanged and three blended into one core operation). It would be not only the blending of equipment and staff but also, more significantly, a blending of personalities and cultures.

A significant number of lab technicians had already been cross-trained to work in all of the departments that were now becoming blended; but there remained a significant number of staff with many years of experience and service within our lab who were now going to be asked to work differently, relearn their jobs, and take on additional responsibilities. This proved to be a colossal hurdle. As with any change, there were those who accepted the challenge, those who resisted the challenge, and those who refused to participate.

With design elements formalized and basic operational flow requirements understood, the process of gaining staff acceptance to the new design and training staff to work differently within the new space needed to begin.

Changing Mind-Sets about Batch Processing

Traditional processing in a clinical laboratory consists of work being pushed through the system in batches. A typical day consists of a large number of staff being dispatched in the morning to address the large demand for phlebotomy services. Very little testing is performed during this time because a majority of the staff isn't present in the lab. Upon returning to the laboratory several hours later, the arduous process of receiving, centrifuging, and aliquoting the samples begins.

This batching mentality results in lead times that are extremely long, there is an enormous amount of work in progress, and the work is actually "pushed" through the system rather than "pulled." There is little knowledge of what is happening throughout the value stream, and an imbalanced amount of work is placed upon staff. Surprisingly, even with its limitations and negative outcomes, most staff intuitively accepted batch processing. One theory behind this thinking may be the human desire to feel productive or to feel a sense of achievement. By completing work in batches, the eyes see large amounts of work being completed. Contrast that to single-piece flow, where one unit of work is being completed at a time. The mind is tricked into believing the body is somehow less productive when smaller quantities of work are being produced. There seems to be a disconnect in understanding that more work is actually getting done by using single-piece flow.

In order to challenge the batch-processing mind-set, laboratory staff was put through a simulation exercise on flow. This exercise allowed staff to play a role in a manufacturing assembly line for paper airplanes. The frontline workers were chosen, along with managers, timekeepers, and, of course, the customer. The initial reactions of staff revealed an uncertainty as to how the assembly of paper airplanes had anything to do with their work in the lab. Some were thrilled to revert back to their childhood days and willingly took their seat in the makeshift assembly line. Others had no idea how to make the necessary folds and cautiously took their places. After a quick lesson on paper airplanes 101, the staff was in place.

In the first simulation, staff are placed throughout a couple rooms and given a particular step to perform. They are told that the work will flow through in batches, meaning that work will not move to the next step unless there are five completed in the batch. The time began as the activity started, and it then ran for ten minutes. Staff seated at the workstations downstream in the process essentially sat doing nothing, waiting for work to arrive.

Soon, the deluge of batched work arrived, making it hard to keep up. "Management" circulated along the assembly line, watching the backlogs at various stations and encouraging staff to pick up the pace. The customer was cued to reject anything that was less than perfect, and to change the color preference half way through the simulation.

After time was called, there was an immediate sigh of relief from the "workers." When asked how they felt during the simulation, many said that they felt stressed, frustrated, and rushed. They noted how difficult it was to have no idea when to expect the work, and were surprised to learn how backed up some stations were. When the customer changed color preferences, there was no flexibility in the system, so many of the airplanes did not meet the customer's needs and were wasted. The amount of work in progress was counted, as well as the number of completed airplanes compared to the number of satisfactorily completed airplanes. Not surprisingly, the amount of work in progress was very high and quality suffered.

To a person, the "airplane factory" operators realized that the lab operated in very much the same manner: batches and queues, long lead times, with lab staff feeling rushed and frustrated.

Next, the group was asked to sit in line formation in one room. Each member was then instructed to pass completed work to the next station only when the workstation was able to accept the work using the concepts of "pull" and single-piece flow. The timer was started once more as the second simulation took place. Once again, the customer was assessing quality and prepared to change color preferences midway through the simulation.

After ten minutes, the overall feelings of the workers were assessed. This time, the staff felt calmer, more in control, and better informed. When the customer changed color preferences, the changes were easily incorporated. The total amount of work in progress was drastically decreased, and quality had improved substantially. The staff noted that an added benefit of the single-piece system using "pull" was that it was readily apparent when there was a backlog at certain workstations. This ability to easily see the location of the backlogs would later help us "balance" the workload in the automated work cell.

This simple exercise helped many of the staff begin to understand why their intuitive thinking that "batching is better" is not true. While the airplane simulation was not a "cure-all" to the batch-processing mind-set, the exercise went a long way in opening up everyone's thinking about how the automated cell would operate.

Challenges with Load Leveling

In addition to the design of the automated cell, there were many other lean principles that we found we could apply in the lab. One of those was "load leveling."

Due to the volume of blood gases from both lab-collected and nurse-collected specimens, the blood gas instrumentation was a rate-limiting factor in throughput.

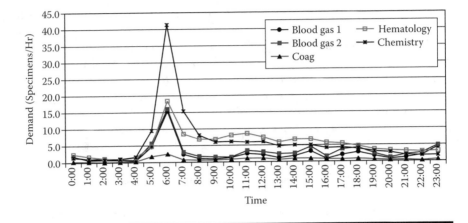

Figure 16.3 Core cell demand by time of day. Using data to find underutilized capacity of the instrumentation and level demand.

Using "nonlean" thinking, we had considered adding additional equipment to cover our peak demand. Our analysis, however, revealed that other than the 5:00–9:00 a.m. time frame, there was actually underutilized instrument capacity (See Figure 16.3). Therefore, we decided to look for opportunities to level the demand peaks by moving our intensive care unit tests to earlier in the day.

Leveling the demand proved to be successful in improving turnaround times by 16–21 percent (See Table 16.1). Many people were impressed and surprised by the immediate impact on operations. It appeared to be a huge success—for both the laboratory and the customers. But not everyone was pleased.

In one particular intensive care unit (ICU), the night shift providers placed lab orders, and the results were available for the day shift providers. With the implementation of single-piece flow, lab results were becoming available before the day

Table 16.1 Turnaround Time (TAT) Data

Analyte	2006 Average TAT (minutes)	2008 Average TAT (minutes)	% Change
ABG	16.6	13.3	20
VBG	17.6	14.0	20
CBG	16.8	13.3	21
PR7	34.0	28.2	17
CBC	57.5	48.0	16
PT	46.5	38.2	18

shift providers arrived. This resulted in some very upset providers, who did not feel comfortable changing care plans, based on the earlier arrival of lab results, that had been judiciously set by the day shift providers. We were asked to "slow down the production line." Rather than choose this option, the timing of the blood draws was adjusted to accommodate the providers' needs while retaining the advantages of the level loading with reduced lead times.

Implementing Standard Work

Implementing standard work proved to be our greatest challenge. The first obstacle was defining the standard way a given task would be performed. There were almost as many opinions as there was staff. Therefore, it was important to allow data to provide the answers. Nothing can be improved if it is not measurable. Our laboratory needed to first understand the current work being done in order to then standardize it. The simple act of watching the current work opened many eyes. Even the long-term, seasoned employees were doing things differently from each other. Time studies were performed to obtain baseline data of the current state. The act of timing staff made some people extremely uncomfortable. And it likely led to falsely decreased times as staff members speeded up their work because they knew they were being timed. Some staff took it personally, and requested that they not be timed. And it soon became apparent that staff members preferred to be timed by fellow coworkers, rather than by the leadership team. In making this simple change, staff members were able to relax, and the data were quickly collected.

After consulting with the technical experts of each section in the laboratory, conducting numerous time studies to gain efficiency without compromising quality, and discussing the pros and cons of the standard work with frontline staff, standard work was determined for the processing cell and the automated cell. As mentioned previously, that was merely the first obstacle.

The biggest change from the current state, which required the biggest staff adjustment, resulted from defining and implementing standard work in the automated cell. The old layout was separated by wasted space, and the ratio of staff to instrument was 1:1. One staff member was responsible for everything related to the instrument (maintenance, calibrations, quality control, and all troubleshooting). In the new layout, all of the automated instruments were now configured in an oval with a staff-to-instrument ratio of 1:6. One staff member was responsible for analyzing and resulting the samples. All other tasks were assigned to other staff. This allowed the auto cell operator to remain focused on throughput. Leadership was on site and readily available to support the staff and coach them on the new operations.

On one particular morning shortly after implementation, a part-time staff member was assigned to the auto cell. Coping with change when it affects every aspect of daily work is stressful for all involved. This stress is typically magnified for part-time staff members, who may miss out on crucial communication or feel they weren't involved in the decision-making process. For these individuals, the idea of running six instruments, when the week before the expectation was to run only one, proved to be too much.

The part-time staff member who was assigned to the auto cell initially positioned herself at one instrument and said that it was unfair to make her run all of the instruments when there were other staff members available. Attempts by leadership to explain the changes and the benefits of the reassigned work fell on deaf ears. The employee left the auto cell, removed her lab coat, and quit on the spot. While this type of response is rare and extreme, it shows the enormous impact that these changes can have on individuals, and the extent to which some people will go in order to avoid the change.

Extending the Gains with the Daily Management System

Our laboratory has been on the lean journey for nearly five years. Setting up an effective daily management system (DMS) is one of the keys to sustaining the gains. Since the most critical time to prevent slipping back into the "old way" is immediately after implementation, we committed to performing daily audits of the new operations. In addition, the laboratory information systems (LIS) personnel built turnaround time reports that generated the information daily. The data from these reports and audits—along with critical information about staffing, instrumentation, and announcements affecting lab operations—were shared at daily staff huddles.

As we began implementing daily management, it became immediately apparent that the focus of our lab supervision was technical, rather than operational. In order to support the staff "in the trenches," we decided to create a position for an operations supervisor on both the day and evening shifts. This position provides coaching, auditing, and daily oversight of operations. Staff hours remained budget neutral as the positions were filled with internal staff.

Today, the DMS is no longer viewed as something "extra," but rather as a part of the daily operations. The daily huddles have eliminated the need for staff meetings that used to take place once a month. These infrequent staff meetings contained outdated information and lasted over an hour, compared to the daily huddles that contained real-time information and lasted for ten minutes. The time that leadership typically spent "putting out fires" was drastically reduced because the daily huddles allowed the staff to ask questions or provide comments about the workflow and have their concerns addressed before they escalated into bigger problems. In addition, this daily face-to-face interaction with leadership has improved morale and built trust.

As part of our DMS, a process improvement committee (PIC) was established to lead the improvements to standard work. The PIC consists of frontline staff representing all shifts and all areas of the laboratory. The committee serves as a decision-making body and approves or denies the submitted requests. All requests not only state what the problem is but also must come up with a proposed solution. If the committee believes the proposal is worth considering, the individual submitting the request is made the leader of the experiment. Involving frontline staff as often as possible goes a long way toward promoting buy-in.

The Journey Continues

Our lean journey has been filled with lessons in leadership, culture, change, and project management. While the transformation continues, signs of the positive impact that lean can have on improving operations have become considerable.

Within one year of implementation, for example, lab leadership no longer felt the strong need to request additional personnel support despite continued annual growth in testing volume. The dependency on overtime to fill open shifts has declined by 25 percent in two years. Productivity in the lab has improved by 5 percent, saving the organization nearly $200,000 annually in labor expense. Even more compelling is the staff's improved perception of their workload. As one staff member puts it, "When I look at our auto cell operating at capacity, I'm amazed at what one person can do. That area is the most satisfying to me. We have greatly increased capacity without a great deal of stress on the operator."

As with life, the operational transformation at Children's Hospitals and Clinics of Minnesota is more about the journey than the destination. For every step that we take forward, we learn and continuously improve our approach. For example, when we initially implemented the auto cell, a staff member noted, "We totally dropped the ball with off-shifts and weekends. There should have been someone present on the evening and night shifts to see that the lean principles were followed and there was a good understanding of what the plan was. The weekends still fall back to our old practices."

As we proceed with this journey, it is critical that staff members continue to be actively engaged. So far, our process improvement committee has received over one hundred requests from frontline staff members to make spot improvements; sixty-seven of those requests have been implemented. We are well on our way as the laboratory continues to sustain the gains with its DMS in place. A few staff members have been lost along the way, but the buy-in of staff continues to climb and the journey continues.

Chapter 17

Rapid Changeover in the Operating Room

Sean H. Flack, MBChB, FCA

Associate Clinical Director, Anesthesiology and Pain Medicine
Seattle Children's Hospital

Lynn D. Martin, MD, FAAP, FCCM

Director, Anesthesiology and Pain Medicine
Seattle Children's Hospital

Healthcare processes require completion of a number of tasks in the delivery of care to patients. Sometimes, these tasks, or steps, directly involve the patient, but many times they are indirectly related and must be completed before or after direct patient care activities. While the patient might expect these tasks to occur, if we asked patients to pay for them, they would probably refuse. Patients come to us for procedures; that's what they think they are paying for.

Many of these indirect steps, though not "value added" for the patient, are necessary to prepare for the next patient. This preparatory work for the next patient encounter is defined as turnaround time or "changeover" steps. From the patient's perspective, these tasks are non-value-added steps (waste) in a process. Worse still, these steps are frequently completed serially, in one-at-a-time fashion; as a result, the total duration of this period of non-value-added activity is often longer than necessary. Examples of unnecessary steps can be seen with each clinic visit, radiology procedure, laboratory run, patient admission, or operating room (OR) procedure.

Time spent on non-value-added changeover tasks reduces the availability of critical resources (e.g., the clinic room, hospital bed, diagnostic equipment, or operating room). Reductions in changeover times will reduce waiting for both patients and staff, lower operating costs, and yield a better return on capital investment because institutional capacity is increased.

"Lean" manufacturing companies have focused for many years on reducing changeover times. Toyota, for example, has reduced the time required to change large body panel–forming presses from hours to minutes. In car-racing competitions, NASCAR crews are able to routinely change four car wheels in less than ten seconds.

Our efforts to improve our patient's experience while achieving significant reduction in room turnover times in the OR will be the focus of this chapter.

Starting with the Patient Experience

Imagine that you are the parent of a child about to undergo surgery. What are your fears? Most likely, pain after surgery will be at, or near, the top of your list. Unfortunately, the reality is that pain management after surgery is often poorly managed. This may surprise you. After all, aren't the doctors and nurses trained and skilled in the assessment and prevention of pain?

The reality, however, is that children frequently endure quite significant amounts of pain after surgery. There are many reasons for this, but two important reasons are an underappreciation of the amount of pain the surgery will cause, and a wish to avoid the many side effects of pain medicines such as nausea, vomiting, itching, bleeding, and excessive sedation.

Recognizing that this is a major problem, the anesthesiologists at Seattle Children's Hospital (SCH) routinely use procedures known as "nerve blocks" to reduce, and even eliminate, the need for traditional pain medications. These procedures help the children wake without pain and consequently help speed their recovery and discharge home. The reasons why these blocks are not more widely used are twofold: first, they require the acquisition of advanced skills not taught to many trainee anesthesiologists; and, second, these procedures are usually performed once the child is anesthetized in the operating room and, consequently, can delay the start of surgery, thereby extending the amount of time needed in the OR or reducing the amount of operating time available to surgeons. These delays might not be well received by either a busy surgeon with a heavy caseload or a hospital administrator looking to maximize operating room efficiency.

Leading Change, Encountering Tension

How, then, did the anesthesiologists convince their surgical and administrative colleagues to support the use of nerve blocks? Three words: passion, patience, and persistence. And two more: "rapid changeover." It required the passion of a leader who was absolutely convinced that this was the right thing to do for his patients. It took patience in recruiting skilled anesthesiologists who could offer these techniques. It took perseverance in not giving in to the stumbling blocks and boulders that occur with the introduction of any new process. And it required an approach, "rapid changeover," that was capable of eliminating the stumbling blocks and boulders from this process.

SIDEBAR 17.1

The day before Dr. Lynn Martin planned to drop out of his anesthesia residency program at Johns Hopkins University, he arrived in the OR to find that his first case of the morning was a boy who had been seriously burned and was receiving a series of skin grafts.

During surgical preparation, Martin suggested to the attending anesthesiologist that, in addition to general anesthesia, the child receive regional anesthesia to block nerve sensation in the area of the painful graft. The attending anesthesiologist agreed.

Hours later, Martin accompanied the boy back to his room. When his mother saw her son sitting in bed contentedly holding a balloon, she burst into tears. Fearing that he had done something wrong, Martin went to comfort her and find out why she was so upset. To his surprise, the mother told Martin that this was the happiest she had seen her child since his admission to the hospital several weeks before.

In that moment, Martin realized the power of regional anesthesia to help children begin their recovery without the stress of postoperative pain. The event not only cemented Martin's career in anesthesia but also continues to inform his leadership in the field.

Dr. Martin believed in regional anesthesia and had a deep conviction that nerve blocks were the optimal way to treat pain after surgery. This is the critical first step. Without passion from the leaders, it is impossible to sustain the work of continuous performance improvement (CPI). But one physician can't take care of every patient, or perform every nerve block. Therefore, Dr. Martin sought and recruited faculty that were skilled in these techniques. Importantly, he recruited a physician recognized as a world authority on regional anesthesia in children to spearhead the project. He assembled a team that supported his vision and could deliver the results he was after.

Next, the use of regional blocks was introduced gradually and incrementally. Simple blocks that took little time to perform were introduced first. Skills were honed, and surgeons were acclimated to the use of nerve blocks. Incrementally, more complex blocks, which required more time to place, were introduced. This is when things got interesting, and tensions between anesthesiologists and some surgeons surfaced. The causes were twofold: success rates and operating room delays.

Surgeons complained that too many of the blocks didn't work well and that the anesthesiologists were taking too long to perform blocks. These concerns—while seemingly disparate—were closely related. Anesthesiologists needed time to perform their blocks correctly and carefully without feeling rushed. However, they were well aware of the surgeons' concerns regarding delays, and so they were performing the blocks in a hurried manner or resorting to quicker, but less effective, techniques. The results were suboptimal pain relief for the patients, longer anesthesia and OR times, and considerable tension between physician colleagues.

This illustrates the importance of the plan, do, check, and act (PDCA) process. A great idea, once implemented, is unlikely to succeed without a rigorous and frequent audit of what is and isn't working. And something had to be done to rescue the vision for pain-free recoveries.

CPI Methods and the Realities of Change

With hospital support, Dr. Martin led a two-day CPI event focusing on the nerve block process and how to improve success rates while also reducing OR times. As with all our CPI events, the team included members from all affected disciplines. In this case, this meant representation from anesthesia, surgery, pharmacy, nursing, and engineering. The outcome was the creation of an external setup process akin to strategies to reduce changeover times employed by companies such as Toyota and Boeing.

Shigeo Shingo, who worked with Toyota to reduce the changeover time of its large stamping presses, first described the external setup process. Located on production lines, these presses were necessarily turned off for the duration of any changeover process. Shingo recognized that a great deal of the changeover process could be completed by the workers in advance, so that once the press was turned off, it could be retooled and ready for use again far more quickly than before.

In a similar fashion, rather than anesthetizing a child and placing the nerve block in the operating room after completion of the preceding case, a procedure room within the operating room suite was modified and equipped so that a child could be anesthetized and "blocked" while the preceding case was still underway. Additionally, the team mapped the steps, and standardized the roles and communication required to accomplish the new process.

As with all CPI projects, data were critical in designing the process and determining whether the work was ultimately successful. Primary outcomes for this project included the creation of standards (reliable methods), the reduction in nonoperative (nonop) time, and significant institutional cost savings. "Nonoperative time" refers to the time between cases when the surgeon is not operating (the time between completing the first patient's surgery and starting surgery on the next patient) and can be considered a form of waste. There will always be some nonoperative time, but the value of external setup is that it reduces this non-value-added portion of the process.

If we look at data from six patients, summarized in Table 17.1, we can see that our team's targets were admirably met. Indeed, the median nonoperative time was reduced from seventy-four minutes to thirty-seven minutes.

If quality improvement were simple, that would be the end of the story: problems are identified, solutions are implemented, and things run smoothly thereafter. In reality, this work is seldom easy and never finished. Despite the measurable successes of this project, bumps in the road inevitably emerged. This is predictable with any new process or venture, and is often compared with lowering the level of a hitherto smooth-flowing river. As the water level is lowered, hidden boulders break above the surface, creating ripples, currents, and even rapids.

Through PDCA, the team found that block room usage had deteriorated over time. The process surrounding its use was complicated, requiring multiple communication steps and considerable perseverance on the part of the anesthesiologist. Also, the room was seldom in a state ready for immediate use because no process had been established for ensuring its daily preparation. Consequently, an anesthesiologist with a shared interest in the project's success was asked to take charge of the block room and lead a fresh effort to maximize its use.

More difficult to address, however, were ongoing tensions between anesthesiologists and some surgeons, which threatened to severely limit the use of nerve blocks at SCH. Although most surgeons had come to appreciate the benefits of nerve blocks for their patients, a minority continued to perceive blocks as high-risk, low-reward procedures. Anesthesiologists also felt that their blocks were being unfairly targeted as the source of some postoperative complications. Once again, strong and resilient leadership was required so that we could persist in establishing nerve blocks as an integral part of anesthesia practice at SCH.

At this point, Dr. Martin took advantage of his close and collegial relationship with surgical leaders to help enlist their support. This led to the development of two groups: an oversight team composed of leaders from anesthesia and surgery that provided guidance and set the tone for collegial interactions, and a working group that used CPI tools to improve all aspects of the nerve block process.

The results? In 2009, regional blocks were used for 2,220 of 18,771 OR cases (11.8 percent). Random manual data collection after the implementation of the block room showed a reduction in nonop time from an average of seventy-four minutes to thirty-seven minutes (a 50 percent reduction). And in follow-up data collection (*n* = 10), nonop time was thirty-six minutes for that sample (sustained improvement).

This case study demonstrates the central role that leadership plays in ensuring that great ideas get translated into established practice. Leaders provide the critical momentum to persist with CPI when challenges inevitably arise. They understand that this work is challenging and takes time. Tenacity is required with colleagues and coworkers who resist change, and patience is needed when

Table 17.1   Focused Event Results

Process Measures	Current Day 1	Trial Process Vision	60-Day Follow-Up
Number of steps	19	14	16
Number of value-added steps	4	7	7
% of value-added steps	21%	50%	44%
Lead time	93 minutes	Scheduled: 75 minutes	Scheduled: 75 minutes
Number of handoffs	3	3	4
Number of checking steps	8	4	4
Number of queues	6	3	2
5S level	1	1	2.8
Staff travel distance	1,000 steps	300 steps	300 steps (↓66%)
Information and equipment travel distance	200 steps	50 steps	50 steps (↓75%)
Theme Measures	Workshop Day 1	New Process Vision	60-Day Follow-Up
Quality	0 reliable methods		5 reliable methods
Cost			206 × $36.88 = $7,597.28
Delivery	Median nonop time: 74 minutes	Median nonop time: 67 minutes (↓9%)	Median nonop time: 37 minutes (↓50%)

initial efforts fail. And data are critical in demonstrating the benefits achieved by CPI work.

Addressing Long Turnovers in Otolaryngology

Over 60 percent of our surgical patients each day present for ambulatory surgery, meaning that they are admitted and discharged on the same day as their surgical procedures. The majority of ambulatory cases come for surgeries (ear tubes, adenoidectomy, tonsillectomy, etc.) by our otolaryngology (oto) staff. However, in studying our processes, we realized that only about 4.5 hours of the ten hours available each day in our oto rooms were being used by the surgeons to perform procedures. Each of the 10–12 cases completed daily included approximately thirty minutes of turnover time. Thus, over half of the available surgery time was actually used turning over the OR. The long turnovers allowed fewer patients into our ORs each day, creating a backlog of cases for our surgeons. As the backlog and associated wait time for the patients and families grew, the OR value stream leaders resolved to focus on reducing long turnover times for ambulatory oto cases. Our hope was to take these learnings from oto and replicate them for all other ambulatory cases in the OR.

A multidisciplinary team of anesthesiologists, surgeons, nurses, technicians, and other support staff was pulled together to focus on changeovers for ambulatory oto surgeries. Targets the team hoped to achieve through the development of standards in the turnover process included a 50 percent reduction in turnover time, an increase in operative time, and a reduction in the time between patients' clinic visits and their surgical procedures.

The first task in changeover improvement is to observe the changeover process and record each step, the roles completing the step, the distance traveled for each role, the time required for each role, and any variations in the completion of the steps. Next, each step must be reviewed to see if it is an internal or external changeover step. Internal steps are tasks that can only be completed while the resource in question is not in use. For example, cleaning the OR floor can only occur when the patient and instrument tables are cleared. External steps are those that can be completed while the resource is in use (e.g., preparation of the instrument trays for the next case). With this more complete understanding and documentation of the changeover process, the team is then ready to begin the improvement process (See Figure 17.1).

Having first 5S'ed the work area, the team began by converting internal steps to external steps whenever possible. For example, surgical case trays now routinely included anesthesia supplies added prior to the case and brought to the anesthesia workspace to shorten anesthesia preparation time. Next, the team focused on the

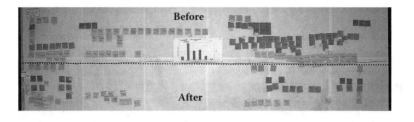

Figure 17.1 Process map before and after. The after model reflects Hirano's rules for rapid changeover in his *JIT Implementation Manual*. These seven rules include (1) begin and end with 5S; (2) change internal tasks to external tasks, then improve the remaining internal tasks; (3) anything that can't be easily moved is the enemy; (4) if you use your hands, make sure you do not use your feet; (5) don't reply on special fine-tuning skills; (6) standards are standards—they are not flexible; and (7) standardize all changeover operations. *Source*: Hiroyuki Hirano, *JIT Implementation Manual: The Complete Guide to Just-in-Time Manufacturing*, 2nd ed., 6 vols. (Florence, KY: Productivity Press, 2009).

remaining internal steps and time required (cycle time) for each role and identified possible areas for improvement.

One major change was the conversion from serial family interactions by the circulating nurse followed by the anesthesiologist, to a single simultaneous encounter with the patient and family. This change eliminated duplication in communication with the patients and families and led to a significant increase in parental perceptions of effective teamwork.

Our observations also clearly documented significant differences in the number of tasks and cycle time by role. Our takt time for room turns was 14.5 minutes. Three of the six roles had cycle times in excess of the takt time, and the anesthesiologists had a cycle time twice as long as the takt time. Through teamwork and experimentation, tasks were balanced among other providers and staff in order to spread the total workload as evenly as possible and meet the takt time. It is important to note that tasks were shifted from the anesthesiologists to the circulating nurse and surgery and support technicians. In addition, the role of anesthesia technician was completely eliminated; this allowed reallocation of this role to support more complex inpatient surgeries. These changes reduced the maximal cycle time by 37 percent to 18.5 minutes (short of the takt time of 14.5 minutes). This represented good progress, with more incremental improvement to come (See Figure 17.2).

At the end of the workshop week, this team had successfully developed a new turnover process in the oto ORs using iterative improvements via experimentation in the actual workplace.

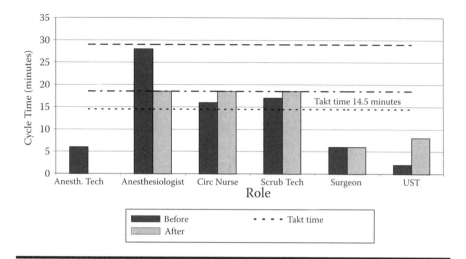

Figure 17.2 Work balance before and after. Rebalancing the workload among staff resulted in a reduction in cycle times. New working relationships among the various roles involved were key.

The new process was significantly more efficient and radically different from our prior practice. Improvements noted from Day 1 (baseline) to the end of the workshop included a 47 percent reduction in steps, a 62 percent reduction in travel distance and handoffs, and a 59 percent reduction in turnover time (see Table 17.2). The key learning from this effort was the building of the team concept with shared roles across typical boundaries, as well as effective communication.

As with all change efforts, one of the most significant challenges is the ability to sustain the changes in the system. And not all of the changes implemented in this effort were sustained. The reliable methods for each role had evolved, but they were no longer being strictly followed by everyone. And turnover times were longer, but they were still significantly shorter than what was seen on the first day of the workshop. The shorter turnover times did produce shorter total lead times (time from admit to discharge) and improved access to the operating suites (reduction in the surgery lead time from clinic to OR from fifty to thirty-four days). But the process was unique in many of its steps, and this made it very challenging to replicate for nonambulatory surgeries. This was particularly difficult in our hybrid or combined ambulatory and inpatient surgery suite.

Despite the slippage in desired outcomes, the leadership team was still pleased with overall reductions in turnover and lead times. Furthermore, the learnings

Table 17.2 Process Data

Process Measures	Baseline	Day 5	% Change	Day 60	% Change
Number of steps	108	57	−47%	57	−47%
Number of value-added steps	6	6	0%	6	0%
% of value-added steps	6%	11%	+50%	11%	+50%
Lead time (minutes):					
Turnover	45	18.5	−59%	27	−40%
Total (admit to discharge)	236	171	−27%	182	−23%
Number of handoffs	8	3	−62%	3	−62%
Number of checking steps	10	3	−70%	3	−70%
Staff travel distance (feet)	4,202	1,560	−62%	1,560	−62%
Theme Measures	Baseline	Day 5	% Change	Day 60	% Change
Quality (reliable method)	0	5	100%	Not available	Not available
Delivery (number of days from clinic to OR)	50.2	50.2	0%	34.3	−32%

from this event were helpful, because they provided very useful experience for the development and opening of our dedicated ambulatory surgery center. In fact, many of the processes designed in this workshop will be incorporated into our new "ambulatory-only" process in our new facility.

Chapter 18

CPI in Basic and Clinical Research

Stephanie S. Axelrod

CPI Fellow
Administrative Director, Research CPI and CPI Consulting
Seattle Children's Research Institute

F. Bruder Stapleton, MD

Senior Vice President and Chief Academic Officer
Seattle Children's Hospital
Chairman, Department of Pediatrics
University of Washington

James Hendricks, PhD

President
Seattle Children's Research Institute

The last decade has been marked by rapid advances in technology that have transformed the conduct of biomedical research and accelerated the pace of scientific discovery. These advances have been fueled largely by funding from the National Institutes of Health (NIH). After doubling between 1998 and 2003, the NIH budget has stagnated in recent years. The current economic crisis further threatens the NIH budget, and with it the pace of scientific discovery. Rather than implementing cost reduction strategies aimed solely at weathering the current storm, it is time for research institutions to adopt a long-term, sustainable approach to cost control.

Our belief—and early experiences—tell us that, when applied rigorously and throughout the research enterprise, continuous performance improvement (CPI) can have a dramatic effect on productivity, cost, and quality. And, because the scientific method is embedded in the tools and techniques of CPI, it is particularly amenable to research.

The leadership of Seattle Children's Research Institute (SCRI) recognized that creating a lean culture would require a strong commitment from investigators. To secure that commitment, it was decided to focus initial efforts on maximizing value and eliminating waste in core processes (value streams) in which the investigator was considered the "customer." This initial focus on supporting business lines included institutional review board (IRB) approvals, animal care services, and other core services.

It is important to note that achieving this initial CPI focus wasn't easy or simple. When hospital and medical leaders from Seattle Children's Hospital (SCH) first heard that they would be learning how to apply improvement methods adapted from a car manufacturer to their clinical realm, skepticism filled the air. "How can we possibly learn anything from an automobile manufacturer?" exclaimed one faculty leader. "We don't make cars—we treat sick children!"

Imagine, then, the amusement of our physician leaders as they viewed a poster on display in a conference room at the Boeing airplane plant in Renton, Washington. They chuckled when they read that the chief complaint of Boeing executives as they began applying lean methods was "What can we possibly learn from a car manufacturer?—We make planes!"

The faculty investigators at SCRI had the same concerns as their clinical colleagues. Indeed, they demanded to know how they could apply improvement methods from a hospital setting into their laboratories. And they felt there were no commonalities. This was understandable, of course. Everybody feels that way at first. For our researchers, trial and error is their work de rigueur, raising questions about the applicability of CPI. And yet the business of research fosters entrepreneurs who have already been applying the scientific method to their work, providing a natural link to the CPI approach.

The scientific spirit spurs investigators to explore better ways of doing their work. They don't doubt the need for improvement, especially in light of their changing world and the economic downturn. In spite of recent stimulus money grants, no one disputes the declining trend of NIH funding, the increased competition for those dollars, and the declining overhead recovery from which our research center directors must fund their direct expenses. Another motivating factor is the high cost of technology. Staying current with the latest technological advances is challenging, even during the most lucrative of financial climates. And, finally, the high price of labor and materials continues to cause investigators to wonder if there are ways to cut costs without compromising quality.

Enter CPI.

In 2006, Seattle Children's Research Institute was one of the first research institutions to adapt the Toyota Production System to a research enterprise. Using CPI principles and tools, SCRI first tackled the challenge of reducing delays in the institutional review board process. The IRB is charged with reviewing and approving research involving human participants. Our IRB is composed of scientists, physicians, nurses, pharmacists, and community members who review research proposals against ethical and regulatory standards. A five-day Rapid Process Improvement Workshop (RPIW) was conducted with the goal of reducing the amount of time required to process an IRB application. Measured as turnaround time (TAT), this time was eighty-six days for a full IRB review.

The analysis and planning for the event involved mapping the process, including how and when delays occurred, how valuable (from the customer's perspective) each step was, and what steps could be eliminated as "waste." When mapping the IRB process, it was determined that the checkpoints were the major cause of delay; and, after process mapping, twenty-two steps from the original fifty-seven were removed from the process, leaving a total of thirty-five steps. The workshop involved IRB staff, investigators, the IRB chairman, and an IRB manager from a partner organization. Thanks to the workshop, the TAT for full-review applications dropped from eighty-six days to 46.5 days. By 2009, the TAT had climbed back up to fifty-three days, but it was still significantly below the eighty-six-day TAT at the start of the CPI event three years before.

Another improvement resulting from the IRB CPI efforts involved placing a visibility board in the IRB office. This visibility board detailed the days in process for each application. If an application exceeded the target approval time for each checkpoint in the process, it triggered a formal troubleshooting review. Using this method of making improvements visible to all was very well received and remains an important component of maintaining and auditing IRB TAT.

Recognizing continuous performance improvement means continuous improvement; in 2010, our Human Subjects Protection workshop further streamlined the IRB process. This event focused on the document review process used by the administrative team charged with supporting the IRB, and the results were impressive. The workshop team reduced the number of steps from 102 to 66, a 35 percent reduction. In addition, the team identified and eliminated six highly variable steps. Importantly, research leaders embraced the philosophy that the patient, and not the investigator, is the customer. By focusing the team on patients and families as the customers, all team members (investigators, nurses, research associates, and lawyers) could clearly see and more readily agree about non-value-added activity, and were equally invested in the outcome.

As the workshop participants tackled this challenge, they held true to the IRB's core purpose of protecting patients as research subjects while incorporating feedback from researchers and research staff in order to support them in their work. The team focused on making the application process easier for researchers and their teams. One important result of the workshop involved offering presubmittal consultation for investigators in order to reduce the amount of communication and clarification that take place after an application is submitted. The team also created templates and simplified the application itself.

According to Kelly Schloredt, PhD, a researcher who participated in the workshop team, "We examined the criteria for approving studies and thought hard about how to make sure the application really focuses on exactly what the IRB needs to know. We eliminated redundancies in the application and included more information that will guide investigators through the process."

Another significant CPI effort was an SCRI workshop designed to improve patient flow in the Pediatric Clinical Research Center (PCRC). The PCRC is available to all investigators conducting clinical research studies at Seattle Children's Hospital. This multidisciplinary facility provides a clinical setting for the conduct of clinical research encompassing a broad spectrum of human pathophysiology and disease.

PCRC resources include the following:

- Facilities within SCH's Ambulatory Care Building, including a laboratory, eight dedicated outpatient exam rooms, one sleep study room, a secured medication room, drop-in computer workstations, a patient interview room, and a conference room.
- Nursing expertise: PCRC nurses provide services that include monitoring patients, performing infusions of investigational agents, processing lab specimens, performing a variety of medical tests, and administering questionnaires, interviews, and surveys.
- An array of medical equipment and supplies.

The PCRC is currently supporting 174 clinical studies with investigators from all across Seattle Children's Hospital. On any given day, the PCRC nurses prepare for eight or more different studies that require many different setups and supplies. In addition, there are numerous researchers and staff from different disciplines who come to the unit to work with the participants on studies that range from behavioral observations to blood draws to chemotherapy.

When the workshop team took a step back to look at their process, they immediately realized that variation in staffing and setups for research visits ultimately caused patients and families to wait anywhere from six to forty-two minutes before everything was in place for a research activity to start.

Among many improvements to the process, the team consolidated and reorganized the location of study materials and supplies (reducing staff travel distance from 265 to 152 feet), created a new visual system to help manage patient flow, and assigned responsibility for rooming patients to one role. The result? Wait time fell to a median of five minutes from a median of twenty-one minutes.

"I was reluctant to use CPI at first, but the approach is incredibly important for the research institute," explained Dr. Bonnie Ramsey, director of the Center for Clinical and Translational Research (CCTR). "We always talk about putting the patient and family first in a clinical setting, and we must also think about it when families consent to participate in research. This workshop, which focused on PCRC patient intake, was a very important first CPI step for clinical research and CCTR."

Recently, CPI principles and tools were also used to reduce the time it takes to begin industry-sponsored clinical trials. A team of research staff and faculty were brought together for a five-day workshop focused on streamlining the processes for initiating clinical trial agreements and final approvals obtained after agreements were reached. During the assessment phase of the project, the team found that the median time for intake and postnegotiation approvals totaled seventy-six days (in addition to the negotiation process). The long turnaround time created missed opportunities to work with industry sponsors and for patients to participate in clinical trials.

Participants in the workshop identified the critical pieces of information a study team needs to provide to initiate negotiation, and they moved many of the necessary institutional approvals to an earlier point in the process while eliminating some unnecessary approvals altogether. Additionally, they designed an intake form that virtually walks those involved in initiating the request through each step in the process by building in visual cues and simplified instructions. In addition to rolling out the new process, metrics to show the process's full effect on the target goal of thirty-four days will follow. In the short term, we don't need metrics to know we've already improved. People now know where they fit and what they need to do with respect to others. With the process redefined, the relied-upon workarounds, excess processing, ping-pong e-mails, and other inefficiencies are no more. When we do get the metrics, we expect them to prove what we can already sense—these changes have significantly sped up the execution of clinical trial agreements, allowing participants to enroll more quickly.

"I am thrilled the team tackled this project," says Dr. Blythe Thomson, a principal investigator from hematology and oncology. "It's challenging to work with industry sponsors when our turnaround time is so long, and the delays can mean that we lose the opportunity to enroll patients who would benefit from new drugs."

Another prominent CPI endeavor at SCRI involved workshops for equipment processing and material handling that improved efficiency and reduced waste in animal care services. As a result of these CPI events, animal care services reduced TAT for sanitizing animal cages and bottles, improved the flow of materials and delivery of services, and increased the safety of animal care personnel.

To ensure that the process improvement initiatives encompassed all process steps in both areas, vivarium staff organized two workshops to address (1) the organization of the cage wash area and removal of wasteful work; and (2) the standardization of work, flow of materials, and safety of staff.

There were four phases in both workshops: assessment, planning, execution, and follow-up. The assessment and planning phases were approximately three weeks long, the workshop itself lasted three days, and follow-ups were conducted thirty and sixty days after each workshop to ensure that gains were sustained and that there was an opportunity for continuous improvement.

The first workshop was organized by all five vivarium staff with input from researchers who use the vivarium; the second workshop team consisted of two vivarium staff, a safety representative, and a researcher; and both workshops were facilitated by a project manager. Team members were recruited by the vivarium director, who championed the project to senior management and provided material and financial resources.

The first workshop incorporated the principles of 5S in the cage wash area. This led to the development of a visibility board to indicate the rate of cage changes. With the schedule displayed on the visibility board, staff members could pace their work throughout the week, leading to better inventory control and less stockpiling of inventory.

Another workshop focused on further reductions in the frequency of cage changes, using rodent feces as a "biologic signal." Prior to the event, all cages were changed at seven days, regardless of the number of animals housed within the cage. A clinical trial event was conducted to measure bedding conditions in cages containing from one to five mice maintained for a period of fourteen days without a cage change. Based on the study, the team concluded that cages containing one mouse could be changed at fourteen days, cages containing two to three mice could be changed at ten days, and cages containing four to five mice or litters could be changed at six days. This effort further enhanced operating efficiencies while reducing costs, resulting in our having one of the lowest costs-per-rodent compared with peer institutions.

The workshops at the animal care facility had an immediate beneficial impact on its operation: the teams improved the quality of the macro environment, facilitated the movement of materials, increased safety, and enhanced customer service. And staff members are now visually able to determine when they reach capacity in the dirty and clean cage areas through the use of 5S, standardization, and visual cues. Importantly, a culture of improvement has taken hold, empowering technicians to make changes to increase safety and employee engagement, reduce turnaround time, and increase in macroenvironmental quality. And, as the vivarium at SCRI grows, CPI tools and techniques will help ensure the continuation of streamlined and standardized operations.

In late 2008, leadership of the hospital and research enterprises came together at an annual retreat to talk specifically about the practical applications of CPI within various components of Seattle Children's (clinical, academic, and research). Following the retreat, SCRI leadership sensed a new readiness among research leaders to apply CPI to their work. As a result, the academic and administrative leaders of SCRI determined that the time was right to foster CPI more deliberately within the institute, and they decided to build SCRI's own CPI infrastructure. In the summer of 2009, a CPI research department was launched with two full-time equivalents (FTEs) and a part-time FTE from the University of Washington funded by the Institute of Translational Health Sciences (ITHS) at the University of Washington School of Medicine.

One of the first projects undertaken by the new research CPI department involved tackling a nonclinical problem. Using the A3 problem-solving tool, we addressed the issue of ordering, distributing, and standardizing office supplies on six floors at two locations per floor (twelve locations total). The problem was that there was no reliable method for users to order supplies or to know which supplies were usually stocked, or for the supply distributor to know when supplies were low, when to order, or when to monitor inventory.

Using A3 methods—which engage people in collaborative, in-depth problem solving that addresses the root causes of issues—the team conducted 5S on all supply areas; the process started with the two new floors, determined "par" levels and made them visible, placed general supply lists and resupply forms at each location, and posted and communicated supply lists online. Weekly 5S audits showed compliance with 5S standards; and, overall, with rare exceptions, the project has been seen as a successful improvement by research staff.

Another A3 project involved improving the study binder process within the CCTR. A staff member was spending approximately thirty minutes for each study binder, creating them for each site that participates on a given study. Through A3 methods, we were able to reduce the time spent by 50 percent, to fifteen minutes each, by eliminating some of the unique information on the covers.

When we asked the Five Whys during the problem analysis, a common discovery was made: no one had asked if the information was necessary. The old process was in place because that's the way the staff member was trained to do it when she began nine months before. After discussion with the study managers, it was agreed that some of the information wasn't really required. Over the last three quarters, the staff member created two hundred binders, at thirty minutes per binder, for a total of one hundred hours. This 50 percent time reduction would save nearly fifty hours over three quarters, or nearly seventy hours over a year. Once a new study begins, the new process will be tested.

The added benefit of these two projects is that the staff members involved have been imbued with the spirit of continuous improvement, and they continue to look for other ways to eliminate waste. Introducing staff to the A3 method has been a great incentive to do more.

The research CPI (RCPI) department's overall goal is to roll out CPI and other improvement projects within and across SCRI, building on the successes of the IRB, the PCRC, and the office of animal care. With the intention of introducing CPI to all departments at SCRI, our approach is to begin with "the basics" across the research institute. That means the following:

■ Establish foundational and consistent understanding of CPI basics and language.
■ Begin use of basic CPI tools (5S and A3) for small, incremental improvements.

- Create visibility and communication boards to increase awareness of CPI work.
- Identify the approach for the SCRI value stream work, including the development of standards or guidelines for establishing the patient as the customer in the research institute and for identifying key value streams within research. Research value stream architecture has been designed and the first research value stream will be launched this summer, focusing on translational research and moving discoveries from bench to bedside more rapidly.

We are very early in the adoption cycle of CPI methods throughout SCRI. We have the advantage of having had our investigator faculty, for the most part, at the hospital during the early CPI years, albeit observing from afar. As a result, the faculty is not totally unfamiliar with the concepts of CPI, but it is rather unfamiliar with the practical application of these methods within our labs. "How will CPI make my life easier or save me money?" is a just-below-the-surface, yet very relevant, question from our faculty.

Despite the natural skepticism, some SCRI investigators clearly understand how CPI can apply to their world. Science is conducted collaboratively. Successful research is often about how to undertake standard work, communicate efficiently as teams, and produce an accurate research product. Principal investigators (PIs) are frequently involved in multicenter trials and face the issues of standardizing work among disparate sites. In addition, all investigators face the rigors of grant submission. They realize their work would be greatly improved by removing "waste" from the grant-writing process. And, ultimately, all our researchers are focused on how quickly they can apply their study to the clinical world. In frequently used nomenclature, how can we reduce the time from bench to bedside, or, more accurately, how can we more rapidly get advances into clinical trials and Phase III studies?

CPI can be the means to this end.

A very relevant example is the way that Toyota used its methods to rapidly bring the original Prius from concept to reality. As explained in *The Toyota Way*, the first part of the Prius project was not defined as a hybrid vehicle project. There were two goals:

- Develop a new method for manufacturing cars for the twenty-first century.
- Develop a new method of developing cars for the twenty-first century.

By using Toyota's principles of creating flow, leveling the workload, and stopping the process to ensure high quality and standardization, the Prius team designed a development process that allowed the Prius to be completed in record time.[1]

Toyota believes that the most important outcome was "making fundamental innovations in its product development process that "are being used for all vehicle development." The company also says that the returns on the Prius project are priceless and the investment is almost trivial. The importance of the Prius was the learning."[2]

These principles can be applied to all aspects of our research setting.

We are sharing our CPI story with key academic partners such as the ITHS at the University of Washington School of Medicine. The ITHS supports translational research—research that improves human health by leading to discoveries that will eliminate human disease. ITHS strives to create an environment in which business principles can inform scientific development. It has begun to apply CPI principles to reduce waste in translational research, and a member of the ITHS management team, Havivah Schwartz, PhD, is a member of the SCRI CPI group.

In an early collaboration between SCRI and ITHS, CPI principles were employed to improve the process of scheduling visits for Clinical Research Center (CRC) research subjects at the University of Washington. Researchers were dissatisfied with the scheduling process, including the excessive lead times to schedule appointments and a high rate of no-shows. Through this effort, the CRC stabilized staffing assignments, making the workload more predictable and reducing overtime costs. The CRC also lowered the number of no-shows from 21 percent to 14 percent. The result was a more transparent system that allows unit managers to make more informed decisions. And the increased efficiency among staff members allows them to better meet the needs of researchers.

Impressed by the results achieved by the ITHS, leaders at the National Center for Research Resources (NCRR) began to explore the application of "lean" principles to their work at the NIH. Despite the influx of over $10 billion to fund research through the 2009 American Recovery and Reinvestment Act, there has been a downward trend in NIH grant funding and a strong emphasis on achieving efficiencies in the research arena. The NCRR has demonstrated a commitment to learning CPI tools and methods and to applying those principles to its work, with the overall objective of improving collaboration, reducing waste, and creating standard work and reliable methods.

Our experiences within the ITHS and the NCRR demonstrate that there are a number of practical applications of CPI within the research enterprise. It is still too early in the application of this improvement method to claim unqualified success, but the initial interest at local, regional, and national levels shows long-term promise for adapting CPI to the clinical laboratory setting.

SCRI leadership is united in its belief that there are great opportunities to improve the processes supporting research—namely, the IRB process, the grant submission process, and the vivarium. And it makes sense to initially prove the concept of CPI by improving research support processes because once the concept is proven to our research faculty, they, as with their clinical colleagues in hospital departments, will clamor for CPI support in their labs to help improve their processes.

From the beginning of our CPI efforts, the SCRI leadership recognized that creating a culture of continuous improvement would require a strong commitment from investigators. They perceived that the easiest way to ensure that commitment was to consider the investigator as the "customer." Starting from this perspective enabled them to engage skeptical investigators who believed their world is different from that of their clinical colleagues in much the same way that Boeing employees believed their world is different from that of Toyota employees.

But this question of "Who is the customer?" is more complex for researchers than it first appears. For our early work at SCRI, we defined the customer as the investigator. But if you define the customer as the one who ultimately pays for services, our research institute would identify the customer as our largest funder, the NIH. When you speak to leaders at the NIH, they define the customer as Congress (or, if pressed, taxpayers). But ultimately we returned to the concept that it is the patients who are the customers, the patients who are looking to our researchers to develop cures and improve outcomes. A significant achievement of SCRI leadership has been the identification of the patient as the customer.

We continue to build momentum for applying CPI to research. At our 2009 leadership retreat, the faculty and executive leaders of our hospital gathered with the investigative and administrative leaders of the research institute to continue discussions about the application of CPI within the research enterprise. Much of the discussion at the retreat was focused on the role of research within clinical value streams. Presentations were given by two research center directors on how they envision applying CPI principles to their work. The conclusion was that rather than trying to "patch" research work flows onto existing clinical value streams (e.g., cancer and operative services), a more strategic approach that includes research in value stream visioning and implementation needs to occur. This is an indication of increasing support for greater alignment between the clinical and research realms. While this seems logical and hardly noteworthy, it can't be emphasized enough that this type of thinking and collaboration is, indeed, truly transformational.

At the same leadership retreat held one year prior, a key clinical and research faculty leader was disheartened at how CPI seemed to be conveyed with almost evangelical fervor, without sufficient data or metrics to support the zealous enthusiasm of her clinical colleagues. That same leader today is a strong advocate for CPI, having gone through advanced training and having presented her CPI efforts at this year's retreat.

Indeed, the research enterprise is an ideal environment for not only applying the principles of CPI but also studying the outcomes, defining the metrics, measuring the results, and publishing the findings in order to encourage replication elsewhere. In the months and years ahead, we expect to undertake numerous CPI training and improvement events, and we have created a sense of urgency and hardwired participation by creating an institute-wide goal to complete up to sixteen CPI events this year. To accomplish these goals, it is critical that our lead investigators be engaged in our CPI processes. Currently we are actively recruiting our research center directors and other PIs to complete training in CPI principles and leadership. Many of our key leaders have been enthusiastic participants in our training programs and will soon travel to Japan to learn from some of the most advanced "lean" organizations in the world.

We are convinced that CPI must become an integral component of our "institutional DNA." And, because of our commitment to an integrated approach to quality, cost, delivery, safety, and engagement in research, we believe we can—and will—achieve essential cures for our patients and families.

Note

1. Jeffrey Liker, *The Toyota Way* (New York: McGraw-Hill, 2003).
2. Jeffrey Liker, *The Toyota Way,* (New York: McGraw-Hill, 2003), p. 62.

Chapter 19

Integrated Facility Design at Seattle Children's Hospital

Michael Boyer, MBA, PhD
Principal
Joan Wellman & Associates

Lisa Brandenburg, MBA, MPH
Chief Administrative Officer
Seattle Children's Hospital

Joan Wellman
President
Joan Wellman & Associates

Strategic analysis of Seattle Children's Hospital's (SCH) market position and patient access challenges in early 2006 pointed out the need to expand accessibility and services offered to the rapidly growing "Eastside" of the Seattle metro area. The board approved the building of a clinic and surgery center off of the main campus in Bellevue, Washington, in order to improve access to pediatric subspecialty services, create additional capacity for the main Seattle campus by shifting outpatient clinic volume and procedures to the new building, increase SCH's presence for Eastside growth, and improve inpatient referral volume. The facility would be designed to support urgent care, specialty clinics, outpatient surgery and recovery, infusion, imaging (including MRI), a lab, and a pharmacy, with a 240-space parking garage.

Lisa Brandenburg arrived on the scene at SCH's shortly after the board's decision and was handed the assignment to "get Bellevue built." Shortly thereafter, Lisa had a conversation with Pat Hagan, SCH's COO, which went something like this: "We've done CPI [continuous performance improvement] in almost every area of our enterprise, except facilities. Let's design and build this facility using Toyota methods. When can you go to Japan?" Before she knew it, Lisa was bound for Japan with SCH's CEO and other members of the senior team to participate in a factory production preparation process (3P).

Upon returning from Japan, Lisa and her executive leadership colleagues agreed to approach the design and construction of this new facility in a new way, staying true to the CPI philosophies and building on what the team had learned in Japan. Lisa laid down the challenge: deliver a facility that meets customer demands, occupies a smaller footprint, uses fewer design and build resources, is constructed in less time, and reduces the total ownership cost. To achieve these results, a very different process was needed.

Early estimates for the Bellevue project indicated the facility would need 110,000 square feet at a cost of $100 million to meet the desired program needs. The response to that estimate was simple: cut the square footage by 30 percent, reduce costs to $75 million, but keep the program requirements the same. As if the challenge was not great enough, the board of directors subsequently asked for an additional reduction to a $70 million total cost level or the project would be put on hold.

In the end, the seventy-five thousand square foot (a 32 percent reduction) Seattle Children's Bellevue Clinic and Surgery Center opened on time (July 20, 2010) and under the $70 million budget by $3.5 million. This is the story of how this was accomplished by SCH and its partners.

The Approach

As a new space design for an efficient facility was envisioned, so was the supporting design process. The traditional approach of industry benchmarking, parametric sizing, protracted user group input, and the separation or siloing of the owner, project manager, architect, general contractor, and subcontractors was purged and replaced with a concurrent set of design activities through a sponsor and project management (PM) group, a facilities team, and a core team. The sponsor and PM group maintained strategic direction and removed barriers. Included in this group was SCH (owner), Joan Wellman & Associates (lean counsel), the Seneca Group (design manager), NBBJ (architect), and Sellen Construction (general contractor). The facilities team provided guidance on specific design and construction issues and connected the owner, architect, and contractor throughout the project. The core team acted as stewards of the lean principles, assured alignment as decisions

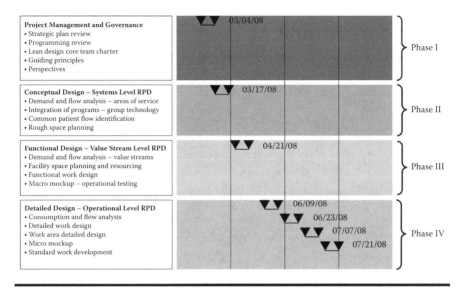

Figure 19.1   Core team process. The design phases and milestones where the core team worked to represent all stakeholders in the design process and ensure lean principals were applied throughout.

were made, and defined the intersection between the functional work design and the physical construction. The core team integrated strategic plans and daily operations by blending user and designer desires from inception to delivery. Core team members acted as advocates and champions, subject matter experts, and inspired designers responsible for meeting project targets and assuring success.

The process of design for the core team spanned four phases that included (1) a project management and governance phase, (2) a conceptual design phase, (3) a functional design phase, and (4) a detailed design phase. The overall core team project phasing is shown in Figure 19.1.

Phase 1: Project Management and Governance

The purpose of the project management and governance phase was to assure alignment on time frame, select the core team membership, and develop solutions or countermeasures for the issues that would impact core team launch. A key element was the interview and selection of the architect and the general contractor. Joan Wellman & Associates (JWA) collaborated with SCH in the selection of the core team and the internal project manager, charter development, and sponsor expectations. An initial data set was gathered that included process lead times and cycle times, resource requirements, and specific medical specialty requirements.

The governance activities established the core team's roles, responsibilities, norms, and agreements, and solidified the project expectations. A set of lean guiding principles was developed to assure core team alignment in project purpose, method, and outcome. A summary of the guiding principles is shown in Figure 19.2. The core team operating norms and agreements and metrics were set.

Next, considerable time was spent with the core team to understand the hospital's strategic plan. The process allowed the core team to fully understand the corporate strategy behind the project; become grounded in the data, logic, and policies that formed the project assumptions; and align with the performance parameters that would guide future decisions. Questions regarding the project timeline, whether primary or ancillary support services would be shared or dedicated, initial space estimates, demand estimates, and facility performance requirements were answered. Ultimately, the core team had to understand and "buy into" the strategic planning assumptions in order to define the facility's ten-year programming requirements.

In addition to strategy review, the project team conducted an analysis of the current operating conditions. The voices of the patient, family, provider, and staff were recorded through a series of structured interviews and gemba walks in the current outpatient facility. This phase ended with core team feedback regarding what had worked well on similar projects, what should be avoided, and what should be improved for this project. With the project established and governance issues resolved, the group was ready for conceptual design.

Phase 2: Conceptual Design (System Level)

The conceptual design phase was accomplished through a five-day integrated design event (IDE) that delivered a conceptual design or theoretical description of a facility that achieved the guiding principles. This overarching conceptual model provided a consistent vision from the strategic plan through to construction. The core team's involvement in this five-day event ensured that its members were the "keepers of the design concept" from early inception to the operation of the facility on move-in day.

During conceptual design, a work flow analysis was performed that considered the type of service demanded; the patient, family, staff, and provider routings; the lead time and cycle time of each process; and the associated resource requirements. Utilizing group technology (a methodology that balances cycle time, customer demand characteristics, and resource use similarities), the integration of programs yielded common routings and the logical grouping of similar services with shared resource solutions. From this work, common patient flows or value streams were identified and confirmed against the facility's program requirements. For example, the procedure-centric clinic specialties of ophthalmology, otolaryngology, dermatology, urology, and plastics would share space, while the longer cycle time and consulting nature of pulmonary, neurology, psychology, and adolescent medicine would be collocated. Likewise, the shorter cycle time clinic visits of urgent care,

Values / Beliefs / Philosophies

➢ The design is Patient/Family/Staff/Provider centered.
➢ The facility is organic and adapts with the future – it is not obsolete upon opening.
➢ Environmental Sustainability is considered and permeates all design and construction decisions.
➢ The facility creates a unique experience as a healing environment.
➢ Children's is an academic medical center with Bellevue in support of this intent.
➢ Patient safety is paramount.
➢ "Customers" include patients, families first. Our design must also support staff, and providers, Bellevue community.

Assumptions

➢ The space / structure is designed with future flexibility in mind. Facility barriers to change are minimal.
➢ The multiple usage of available space is maximized and all spaces are considered candidates for multi-use. The exam rooms are universal and are designed for rapid reconfiguration and multi-use.
➢ Space is a function of need and is owned by the Common Patient Flow.
➢ The design maximizes the multidisciplinary model of care and supports the clinical research and teaching mission. Each service will determine the academic model that is appropriate.
➢ The facility is designed for high throughput (capacity and process meets demand).
➢ The clinical space is maximized and the office space is minimized utilizing a lean perspective.

Principles

➢ The Value Stream contain multiple services and processes to drive effectiveness and efficiency. The clinical services are physically embedded within the flows.
➢ Standardization is the source of efficiency and flexibility and is the foundation of improvement.
➢ Simple designs with fewer components make for reliable service. The larger the system scope, the less reliable the system. Simple is always better, processes must be intuitive, complexity is a veiled type of waste.
➢ The space is right sized to the task (monuments are avoided) recognizing that too much space is an enemy and drives waste.
➢ Build tents, not castles – flexibility is built in to allow for rapid reconfigurations
➢ There is a line of sight and visual management created that promotes flow and identifies abnormal conditions at a glance.
➢ 5S principles and infection prevention are high considerations in design – an ounce of prevention is worth a pound of cure (detection).

Concepts

➢ Continuous Flow Theory with the management of variability is used to achieve high throughput service. A pull system is fundamental to continuous flow and is used to minimize blocked or congested patient flow through the facility
➢ The work cell concept is utilized and promotes single piece flow and dedicated services.
➢ The concept of sub assembly production is used as it improves flow and throughput.
➢ The facility utilizes the modularization of internal components and the placement of modular components for future flexibility.
➢ The flow has 'One way in / One way out' at the system level and the 'same exit and entrance' at the work cell level. Materials enter from outside of the cell and handoffs are minimal. Location of services to entrance / exit must consider the process, service provided and hours of operation.
➢ Supplies, tools and equipment are at point of use and move from the dock to fingertips without storage.
➢ Flexible walls / partitions can be used so that exam rooms and team rooms can be created as required.
➢ Wayfinding is clear and apparent.
➢ There is point of care testing within the surgical suites.
➢ There are open area clinics with line of sight to exam rooms. Documentation / dictation will occur in the exam room. There are multi-use conference huddle spaces available for the Team Room function. There are Simple Cells / Complex Cells with Huddle Space
➢ Pre-op and Phase I and II recovery are the same space. Families are in this space.

Figure 19.2   Bellevue Project guiding principles developed by the core team.

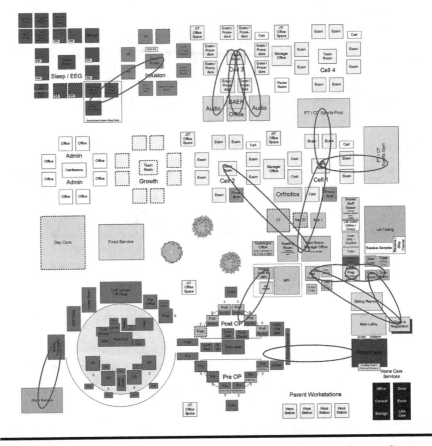

Figure 19.3 Conceptual design. Lean concepts were used to analyze and recommend floor layout to minimize space.

general surgery, gastroenterology (GI), nephrology, and cardiology led to the grouping of these specialties. These services would traditionally occupy separate and larger spaces. The conceptual design is shown in Figure 19.3.

Participants in the conceptual design IDE were asked to think "out of the box," without the square footage or building footprint constraints. The IDE outcomes from this phase included (1) a definition of patient flows that addressed the performance needs of the facility, (2) a performance specification and capacity analysis for each identified common patient flow or value stream, (3) a conceptual space design with room allocations in support of the value streams, and (4) a rough space plan with block diagrams and a schematic of the "seven healthcare flows." An example of the conceptual design with multiple flows is shown in Figure 19.4.

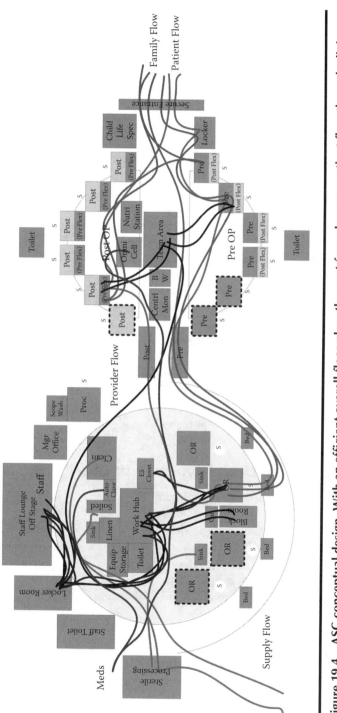

Figure 19.4   ASC conceptual design. With an efficient overall floor plan, the next focus became patient flow through clinics.

Phase 3: Functional Design (Value Stream Level)

During the functional design phase, the overall utility of the facility was defined. The constraints and requirements established adjacencies and necessary connections between value streams, resulting in an overall stacking and space plan. Through the construction of and experimentation with macro mockups, the group demonstrated how the value streams would operate, resources would be utilized, and people would interact in the proposed space. The realities of the structural and mechanical limitations were introduced at this point to ensure that the realities of the site, code, and other constraints were recognized.

During a five-day functional design IDE, the core team physically modeled seven healthcare flows in action so that a descriptive text of the functionality or operational composition of each value stream could be generated. The seven healthcare flows were patients, families, staff, supplies, equipment, medications, and information.

A full-scale "macro" mockup allowed the team to test space shape, size, and adjacencies. The mockup walls were easily repositioned to test new ideas within seconds. For example, the core team mocked up virtually all of the surgery space as part of the macro-mockup functional design. After experiencing the full-scale mockup, the team substantially changed the initially accepted two-dimensional paper design. Repeated scenario testing of the seven healthcare flows with stopwatches and simulated patient, family, provider, and staff "actors" demonstrated the strengths and weaknesses of the design. In addition to the mockup, a discrete event computer simulation of the value streams supported decision making regarding space relationships, final adjacencies, and functional affinities. An example photo of one of the macro mockups is shown in Figure 19.5.

Phase 4: Detailed Design (Operational Level)

The detailed design phase was completed through a series of highly focused IDEs, combining the best thinking of staff, patient families, and designers. The purpose of these micro-IDE sessions was to define the working-level detail (e.g., interior equipment, services, work surfaces, storage, and utilities) for each area. Using "7 Flows of Medicine" and waste analysis, the IDE participants generated interior room details. Figure 19.6 shows the output of the detailed design event for a clinical floor. An example photo of a room interior is shown in Figure 19.7.

From IDEs to Construction

The use of lean thinking did not stop when the IDEs were completed. Far from it! For example, when it came time to do construction detailing, three-dimensional modeling and further mockups and test fits were used along with weekly design workshops with experienced leaders from all disciplines. During construction, offsite

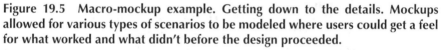

Figure 19.5   Macro-mockup example. Getting down to the details. Mockups allowed for various types of scenarios to be modeled where users could get a feel for what worked and what didn't before the design proceeded.

prefab of facility components improved cost and schedule performance. A triparty contract agreement was used to align the owner, architect, and general contractor with a mutually beneficial common goal and shared "risk pool." This arrangement promoted teamwork and alignment in a way that traditional contracting had not and set the tone from the beginning that infighting and poor cooperation would only lead to everyone's misfortune. Lean construction principles were applied throughout the construction period, including the use of "pull planning" with subcontractors. The cumulative results of these innovations are described below.

The Payoff

The Bellevue project met the organizational goals for cost reduction, space reduction, and on-time delivery. The space reduction from 110,000 square feet to eighty thousand square feet was achieved primarily by (1) the successive review of the mocked-up physical space by the core team, and the core team's agreement to minimize space requirements through multipurpose use; (2) data-driven capacity analysis based on lean processes, not current practice; and (3) physical mockup and computer simulation of patient, provider, and staff flows to strip unnecessary square footage and travel distances that did not support efficient activities. The traditional approach of using industry benchmarks was rejected, and a zero-based

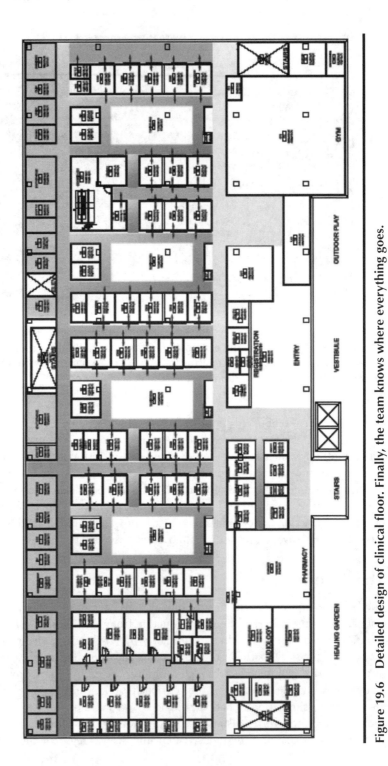

Figure 19.6   Detailed design of clinical floor. Finally, the team knows where everything goes.

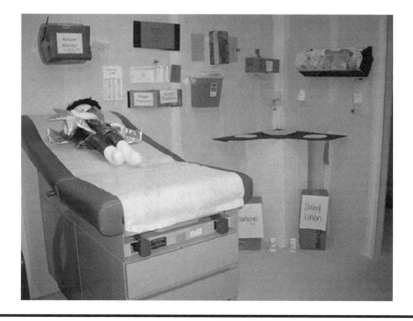

Figure 19.7 Exam room interior. As detailed design concludes, lean principals are part of the design and nearly every detail has been considered. There should be little uncertainty or surprises at this point.

methodology challenged all current-state baselines. The volume data, process flow analysis, and functional descriptions justified the requested space, not the personal or experiential preferences of the users.

One of the key validation measures of the success of the integrated project delivery or lean design and build project is the cost performance. The target value design was set at $45 million and performed at $40 million. The cost model was based on benchmarks, while the target budgets were established through team collaboration. Each discipline had ownership of the costs and tracked its individual budget. Budget status was shared weekly and collaborative cost management caused a reduction, as shown in Figure 19.8.

How does the Bellevue project compare to other projects of similar size and scope? Table 19.1 shows a comparison of key metrics to demonstrate the success of the lean approach.

It is well known in the design and build world that the amount of change activity over the life of a project and response time for the acknowledgment and resolution of issues are major drivers to total project costs. In reference to Table 19.1, an RFI is a request for information generated by the general contractor, a CIW is a change in work produced by the architect, and an owner-requested change (ORC) is written by the owner. There was a stark contrast between the Seattle Children's

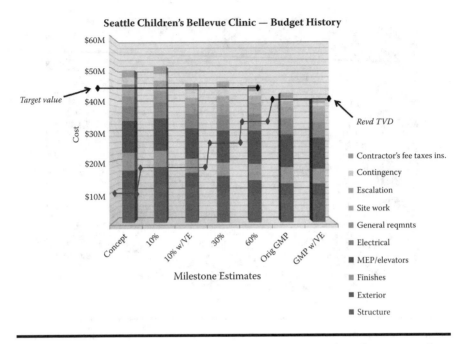

Figure 19.8 Cost target achievement. Estimating categories of cost at various points in the design process. Lean principals drove down cost. *Source*: **Courtesy Jeff Giuzio, partner, Seneca Group.**

Bellevue Clinic's (SCBC) change activity and that of the comparison project. Also, the number of submittals (confirmation by the contractors to the architect's specs) is shown in Figure 19.9. The submittals indicate the relative ambiguity of the design and incompleteness of the information as each stage on construction progresses. The low number of submittals received (primarily at the front of the project) was a demonstration of the high quality of the design. This had a strong positive effect on lowering the cost. The rapid turnaround of the submittals also helped maintain excellent schedule performance.

The RFIs are requests from the general contractor and indicate the level of project rework. The RFI performance shown in Figure 19.10 was startling because of the low quantity, which further demonstrates the robustness and collaboration of the design and build processes.

The coordination of the design and build groups from the very beginning of the project, with fewer change requests occurring early in the process, helped keep the project plan well within schedule. Figure 19.11 shows the days ahead of schedule resulting from the integrated facility design approach.

Opening day of July 20, 2010 could have been accelerated ever further if required by the owner. Again, this metric was another indicator of a successful process and solid leadership.

Table 19.1 Metrics Comparison to Similar Project

Metric Description	Seattle Children's Bellevue Clinic	Similar Project
Completion date	June 2010	June 2004
Project duration	14.5 months	18 months
Gross square feet	186,000 sq. ft.	152,362 sq. ft.
Ambulatory surgery center	73,100 sq. ft	78,065 sq. ft
Parking garage	112,000 sq. ft	74,297 sq. ft
Total construction cost	$40,273,684	$33,544,682
Cost per square foot	$216.53	$220.16
Quantity of requests for information (RFIs)	78	608
Quantity of changes in work (CIWs)	37	39
Quantity of owner-requested changes (ORCs)	18	102
Total change order (CO) amount ($)	$1, 500,000	$2,566,160
Total CO amount (% of total)	4%	7.6%

Critical Leadership Implications for Facility Development

Seattle Children's Bellevue Clinic gave the partners an opportunity to collaborate in very new ways to achieve remarkable results. The following are reflections on the "must haves" for successful integrated facility design.

Lean Experience

The integrated facility design (IFD) process is best used in an organization that already has lean thinking as part of its operational philosophy and a natural way of thinking. The belief that much of what the processes contain is waste; that single-piece continuous flow of work is the goal; that waiting and idle resources are waste; that too much space is waste; and that travel, multiple handoffs, and searching should be reduced are foundational building blocks for an IFD process to deliver

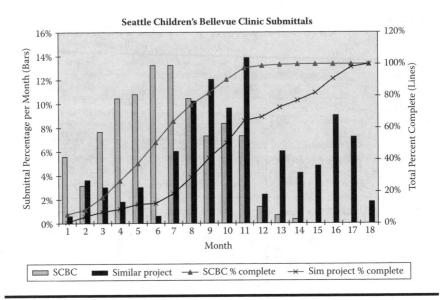

Figure 19.9 Submittal frequency. Lean design principals reduced the ambiguity in later months of design and drove the design to be completed sooner than by traditional methods. *Source*: Courtesy Jeff Giuzio, partner, Seneca Group.

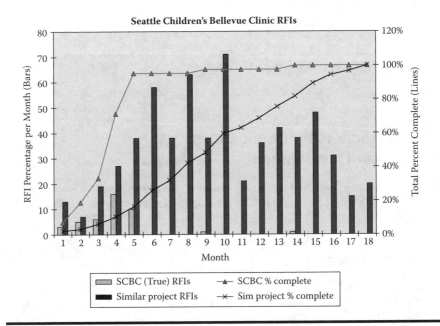

Figure 19.10 Request for information (RFI) frequency. Do you know what you want? With lean design principals, you do, and rework required during design is vastly reduced. *Source:* Courtesy Jeff Giuzio, partner, Seneca Group.

significant results. Attempting to do IFD and lean design in an organization without prior experience with lean would likely fail.

SCH's CPI experience and knowledge helped resolve many design issues. Any of the issues could have been resolved differently if thinking had not been guided by a number of key lean concepts. For example, the principle that all of the space should be flexible and usable for multiple purposes helped the core team break down the traditional departmental thinking and generated designs with more standard and shared spaces. The idea of "building tents, not castles" (a phrase coined by chapter author and book editor Joan Wellman for lean facility design and adapted from work of Hedberg, Nystrom, & Starbuck[1]) brought in a deeper understanding of flexibility and rapid reconfiguration in contrast to hunkering down into one's own space. Initially, few believed that too much space was an enemy until they saw how it promoted excess travel time and impaired "line of sight." The lean principles permeated the mind-set of the participants from concept to construction so much so that waste was equally attacked in the design process and in the physical product.

Project Leadership

It is crucial to have strong, experienced leadership guiding the project. This process changes how people perform their work. The leader needs to continually bring the team back to their guiding principles and objectives over and over again and not allow the work groups to slip back into "traditional" facility

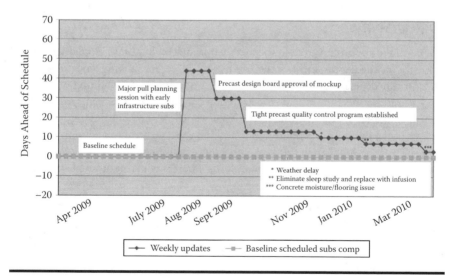

Figure 19.11   Days ahead of schedule. Less rework and less uncertainty mean faster results and a favorable schedule variance. *Source*: Courtesy Jeff Giuzio, partner, Seneca Group. Unpublished intellectual property of the Seneca Real Estate Group Inc.

design or decision-making practices. For example, it was a foundational principle that the determination of the number of clinic rooms required for various specialties should be based on verifiable data (i.e., expected volumes, cycle times, and work-in-progress [WIP] calculations). There was a tendency to make the room decision based on personal beliefs ("I think this is how many I need" or "I need more than I have") or on architectural planning calculations guided by industry benchmarks. This tendency requires leaders to rely on quantitative analysis and computer simulation models when demonstrating that the building is "big enough." Strong and experienced operational leadership paired with strong facility-building leadership are critical in order to "stay the course" with lean thinking.

Core Team

The core team should be composed of the organization's best lean thinkers rather than populating the team with the "usual suspects" needed for political acceptance. The core team must "own" the design rather than simply react to the architect's design. In the Bellevue project, the core team lived the project from concept to becoming members of the operations team. Team members knew that they were accountable as stewards of the design from beginning to end. The core team needs to include all key parties from the start, including the architect, the general contractor, and other key construction partners.

Logical Sequence

It is common for groups to rush to a detailed layout prematurely. Applying a logical sequence for the development of the end user space meant moving from an abstract, unconstrained perspective to a detailed design by progressively adding constraints. Understanding the clinical and surgery center functional requirements, establishing critical adjacencies, and defining operational workflows before bringing in the constraints of the building and building site allowed the core team to design the building to fit the work rather than fit the work into a preconceived notion of the building. This may not always be feasible, but when building a new site it is an optimal approach.

The Value of Mockups

Mockups are frequently used during the design process, but rarely at the scale done for this project. The importance of mocking up not only individual spaces but also the relationship between spaces is critical to lean design and can lead to considerable breakthroughs. In the Bellevue project, mockups promoted early rapid prototyping, and participants often made their spaces smaller, changed traditional adjacencies, or completely changed their design thinking after "seeing and using" their paper design brought to life. Renting empty warehouse space for large-scale mockups was worth the investment, resulting in an improved design, reduced change order activity, and minimal friction between owners and architects. In the traditional design process, the parties would be looking at blueprints and attempting to resolve conflicts or downsize without truly understanding how the proposed space would function.

Alignment of Incentives

As discussed earlier, a triparty contract agreement was used to align the owner, architect, and general contractor with a mutually beneficial common goal. A contingency fund was established so that if common goals were met, the pool would be split three ways. As shown in Figure 19.12, the design team performance contingency (DTPC) line represents an acceptable project but without the distribution of an award. The initial team target line represents full incentive distributed. The "actual DTPC use" line shows that almost the entire contingency was received. It should be noted that there was also a risk element that balanced the reward. It was possible for the project to go above the DTPC line and for all parties to be required to fund the overage if costs were not controlled.

While an integrated form of agreement requires significant effort to develop, the payoffs in cost reductions resulting from collaborative decision making and integrated problem solving are considerable.

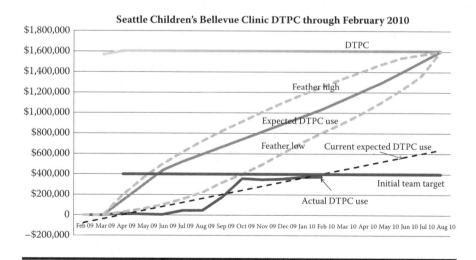

Figure 19.12   Triparty agreement pool. Sharing the risk and sharing the reward. Owner, architect, and general contractor all benefited financially by participating in the lean process. *Source:* **Courtesy Jeff Giuzio, partner, Seneca Group. Unpublished intellectual property of the Seneca Real Estate Group Inc.**

Conclusion

Not everything was perfect. It was said many times that "we learned as we progressed." The group did not "make it up as we went along" but rather traveled together on a project of new ideas and discovery as guided by a reliable process. The lean, healthcare, project management, architectural, and construction expertise converged on new problems and solved them as they arose. For example, a traditional equipment-planning process was layered on top of the lean design structure. In retrospect, equipment planning should have been integrated into the work early on. In the end the equipment budget was met, but it required more energy to complete than if integration had been comprehensive.

The project targets and methods were strategically driven from beginning to end. Traditionally, similar projects are viewed by many as a facilities responsibility and cost reduction expectations are expected to be generated well after the concept and functional decisions have been solidified. In this project, the new process changed the role of the facilities department, forcing much earlier and much deeper joint decision making with operational leaders in the room. While these were not uncomfortable changes, given SCH's history with CPI, they were nonetheless changes that required modifications to past practices.

SCH set the culture and expectation of excellence and the way work would be done. This approach changed the job for everyone, especially the architects and contractors in relationship to the owner's involvement. The core team became intimate with the design and "owned it," a role usually played primarily by the architect. The adjustments were not "drama-free," but when the team successfully emerged on the other side, there was agreement that the old way would never be used again.

Deeper education on the lean principles was needed by all team members. For this project, the traditional sequential or "waterfall" model of design development was replaced by an integrated or iterative methodology. Concurrent engineering or the parallel and overlapping processing of conceptual, functional, detailed, construction, sustainability, and life cycle design activities was not understood by all and caused conflicts. Selecting a core team with lean experience was not enough. Process experience with the lean concepts was an insufficient replacement for specific lean design and concurrent engineering knowledge. Also, there was the belief that the non-SCH team members could learn as the project progressed, but the mismatch in levels of lean understanding caused friction and delay. The architects and contractors were selected because of their lean experience, but as the project unfolded more education was needed than initially imagined.

"We Did It!"

The Achilles' heel of traditional facility design with user groups has been the inclusion of a select few, resulting in design disagreements by the eventual operational residents who were never asked. The process used throughout this project was very transparent. Great effort was made to solicit constant feedback at every decision point. With newsletters, daily updates, open houses, mockup tours, structured interviews, surveys, and countless tie-in meetings, every avenue of outreach was employed. The input was incredible. Patients, families, providers, and staff were involved every step of the way. The goal was to exhaust the users with requests for feedback and then ask them again. The results were worth the effort. Hundreds of people "touched" the design in some way. The outcome is truly the product of a shared vision.

Although the quantitative evidence demonstrates undeniable success, some of the emotional aspects spoke louder. The sense of accomplishment—"We did it!"—is palpable. Core team members frequently expressed their enthusiasm for being included in the project. Other non-SCH team members saw this as one of the best projects of their careers. Still others keep asking, "When are we going to do this again?" Such comments are the reward for the lean leader.

Notes

1. Hedberg, B.L., Nystrom, P.C., & Starbuck, W.H. "Camping on Seesaws: Prescriptions for a Self-Designing Organization". *Administrative Science Quarterly*, March 1976, Vol. 21, p. 41–65.

Chapter 20

Leading Cost Reductions in Healthcare

Tamra Kaplan, PharmD
Chief Operating Officer
Long Beach Memorial Medical Center

Michael Boyer, MBA, PhD
Principal
Joan Wellman & Associates

Despite near universal interest in healthcare cost containment, overall costs continue to spiral upward. Healthcare costs have grown on average 2.4 percentage points faster than the GDP since 1970. With almost half of healthcare spending used to treat just 5 percent of the population, many policy experts believe new technologies and the spread of existing ones account for a large portion of medical spending. A recent Kaiser Health Tracking Poll found that more than half (53 percent) of Americans say their family cut back on medical care in the past twelve months because of cost concerns. They are doing this by relying on home remedies and over-the-counter drugs rather than visiting a doctor, skipping dental care, and postponing the healthcare they need. Beyond actual financial hardship due to medical care, nearly half of Americans (45 percent) report that they are "very worried" about having to pay more for their healthcare or health insurance.

There are many factors affecting the healthcare cost picture. The U.S. population is aging, and because older people have more health problems and use more healthcare than younger people, population aging will have a small but persistent impact on cost growth in the years to come. Increases in disease prevalence, particularly chronic diseases such as diabetes, asthma, and heart disease, coupled with the growing ability of the health system to treat the chronically ill, contribute to the high and growing levels of health spending. Government subsidies for health coverage also affect cost levels and potentially cost growth. Some argue that the high prevalence of health insurance encourages health technology development because those developing new technologies know that insurance will bear a substantial share of any new costs. Another factor is the small share of healthcare costs that Americans pay out of pocket. This encourages consumers to use more healthcare, leading to expenditure growth.

Another major factor driving up the cost of healthcare is the growth of healthcare providers. Expansive healthcare systems that offer acute care hospitals, specialty facilities, clinics, labs, physician practice groups, and other services are becoming prevalent. While these systems provide many benefits to the communities they serve, they also require a great deal of money to fuel their growth and ultimately place upward pressure on the costs of many medical services.

Faced with this reality, putting one's head in the sand is a poor strategy. Staying true to their mission, MemorialCare is purposefully and directly addressing the escalating costs of healthcare by the application of lean principles.

The MemorialCare Journey

MemorialCare is a five-hospital system on four campuses in southern California: Long Beach Memorial, Miller Children's Hospital Long Beach, Orange Coast Memorial, Saddleback Memorial–Laguna Hills, and Saddleback Memorial–San Clemente. The hospital system employs approximately ten thousand staff with 3,200 medical staff. With approximately $1.5 billion of annual revenue, the MemorialCare mission is to improve the health and well-being of individuals, families, and our communities through innovation and the pursuit of excellence. MemorialCare began its lean journey in 2006 with focused learning and research. It was recognized by senior executives that a continuous improvement culture with a focus on eliminating waste would complement the existing pursuit of excellence in providing high-quality patient care services.

The executive support for continuous improvement through the implementation of lean principles was strong. The multiyear roadmap is shown in Table 20.1. The improvement efforts began with pilot projects in an eight-room surgical area, a breast center, and an outpatient imaging center.

From a corporate perspective, financial resilience continues to be a core competence. Through the application of lean thinking, the goal was to influence the culture, adopt a continuous improvement perspective on healthcare processes, and reduce the cost of providing exceptional care while maintaining patient safety. The strategic financial focus is shown in Table 20.2.

Table 20.1   Multiyear Roadmap

Year	Theme	Key Outcomes
1	Establish foundation.	Common understanding. Infrastructure established. Point improvements through RPIW and 5S events Identify and select key value streams (latter half).
2	Connect the dots.	Value stream improvements. Lean leaders in place. Fully functioning MC*21MS resource office. Daily management system in place to sustain gains. Lean priorities are tied to annual goals and strategic plans.
3	Bottom-line results.	Value stream improvements. Restructure MC*21MS resource office around value streams. Attack structural barriers.
4	Enterprise focus.	Replicate and extend value stream work. Include key suppliers.

Getting Started with 5S

Initially, the organization acclimated to the lean principles of the Toyota Production System through a series of 5S workshops. The surgical areas chosen for this work were in need of organization, and in their current state they were a source of frustration for many of the staff and surgeons. Excess inventory and patient care supplies were removed, and space was created in areas that were viewed as impossibly overcrowded. Frontline staff were empowered to improve their own workspace and make it more productive. The wastes of searching, traveling or movement, and waiting were greatly reduced, and the employees had a positive opinion of the lean principles as they applied to workplace organization. Early wins encouraged people to participate and influenced senior management to do more and go farther. The new 5S'ed areas worked better, things were easier to find, and the cultural effect was positive.

Table 20.2   Strategic Financial Focus

FY10 Financial Resilience
Ten-Year Strategy
MemorialCare will enjoy a strong financial position that allows us to fulfill our overall system vision and mission while successfully addressing cost pressures.
Five-Year Strategy
Preserve and improve payor mix, and achieve benchmark Medicare LOS and performance on other financial metrics for MemorialCare (e.g., *earnings before interest, depreciation, and amortization* [EBIDA]; and days cash on hand) in order to sustain our A+ bind rating and fund strategic initiatives for growth and deployment.
FY10 Initiatives
Implement system-wide utilization management collaboration.
Achieve Year 3 targets for MC*21MS (lean).
Refine systems to support financial rigor.
Review and maximize recovery *audit* contractor (RAC) compliance.
Study and gain education in new care models.
Analyze further case-pricing opportunities.
Set and achieve bold goals for philanthropy.
Achieve multiyear Keane conversion.

Value Stream Management

The next phase of improvement came in the form of value stream management. A number of value stream projects were launched to spread the philosophy and practice of the Toyota Production System. Project teams were assembled and the infrastructure deployed for a radiology value stream, a materials management (supply chain) value stream, and two perioperative services value streams. The support structure through a centralized continuous improvement office was sound. Senior management received in-depth education and coalesced to actively guide the organization forward. The goals of healthcare excellence, patient safety, cultural change, process improvement, and cost reduction through waste elimination were augmented by the financial pressure of demonstrating a return on investment (ROI). The grounding financial reality was the establishment of a savings target for each value stream project. The value streams were held accountable for generating the results and were provided the resources to make it happen. The commitment for savings of approximately $17.2 million over three years is summarized in Table 20.3.

The approach for value stream improvement at MemorialCare followed a process of assessing the value stream, analyzing the current state, creating an ideal or future state, and generating a project plan to achieve the ideal state. The organization applied Rapid Process Improvement Workshops (RPIWs), 5S events, specific topic-focused events, and a collection of related actions to redesign each value stream into the ideal state driven by the expectation of cost effectiveness. The accountability of the value stream managers was not limited to demonstrate improvement only through cost reduction. If cost could be contained while volume increased, success could be claimed.

In the Field: A Perioperative Example

The Orange Coast Memorial Medical Center (OCMMC) perioperative value stream was launched in late 2008, and RPIWs proceeded through each major organizational process in the ideal-state model. From the scheduling and pre-case

Table 20.3   Savings Commitments

	Savings Commitments (in Thousands of Dollars)						
Area	*FY09 Q1*	*Q2*	*Q3*	*Q4*	*FY10*	*FY11*	*FY12*
Orange Coast Memorial perioperative	138	275	288	300	1,000	1,200	1,200
Long Beach Memorial perioperative	171	321	528	734	1,754	3,254	4,200
Saddleback Memorial radiology	31	63	87	111	292	500	500
Point improvements	76	76	76	76	303	303	303
Saddleback Memorial breast center			248	248	495	990	990
Total	416	735	1,225	1,468	3,844*	6,247*	7,193*

* FY10, FY11, and FY12 are projections.

function, to admit, to preoperative, to intraoperative, and finally to postoperative, the employees analyzed their own processes for waste and evaluated potential improvement opportunities.

The project plan was translated into dollars in support of the cost reduction targets. The workshop groups uncovered wasteful processes and opportunities to do more with less. During the workshops, there was a real excitement about making the work environment and processes better.

Concurrently, there was a growing fear that the newly designed methodologies translated into someone losing their job. The people were reminded of the commitment made by the organization to maintain a person's job if improvements demonstrated that their job was no longer needed. This value stream developed a formal method of redeployment for displaced employees. The excess labor was reduced through attrition, growth, and natural job movement of the staff. There was staff satisfaction found in creating a better way to provide excellent patient care with the fewest resources. The goal was to make things better, and the workshop groups delivered. Figure 20.1 shows the projected savings (gray) and the actual accumulated savings (black) through the end of 2009.

The perioperative value stream is currently working on holding the gains and refining the new processes. Daily management has been essential in sustaining an unrelenting cost reduction perspective.

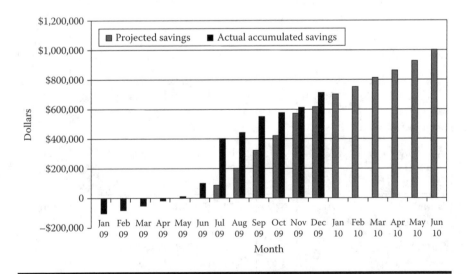

Figure 20.1 Accumulated value stream savings for Orange Coast Memorial Medical Center (OCMMC) periop versus accumulated savings. Cost savings from redesigning wasteful processes and properly staffing each organization without layoffs.

In the Field: Emergency Department Example

The MemorialCare Long Beach emergency department (ED) serves 92,600 patient visits per year. With a left without treatment (LWOT) rate of 6.8 percent and a length of stay (LOS) average of 511 minutes for admitted patients, there was a strong business case for applying lean principles to this value stream. The ideal-state value stream map is shown in Figure 20.2.

The initial project activities began in January 2010 and will proceed through December 2011 as the value stream transitions into a strong continuous improvement mode. The accumulated savings for the ED value stream are shown in Figure 20.3.

The emergency department is positioned well for the change it is embracing. The ED culture is adaptive and accustomed to change. Leaders in the ED have embraced a project plan that calls for significant change, including work in (1) initial patient contact, (2) patient triage, (3) internal communication, (4) ancillary testing, (5) disposition and discharge, (6) a fast-track pod, (7) a main patient pod, and (8) a pediatric pod.

Leadership Challenges with Cost Reduction

Leaders of the perioperative and ED value streams have multiple challenges to face as they forge ahead.

Resistance to Change

Regardless of the adequacy of the initial launch actions and the sound infrastructure, the radical changes being implemented in the ED and OR value streams result in staff feeling a combination of loss and fear about "What's next?" Value stream leaders respond to staff by increasing participation, providing thorough education, facilitating the process, and negotiating for win–win solutions.

In spite of this response by value stream managers, staff can easily feel manipulated or coerced. In fact, some of the ideas put forward by value stream managers just did not seem feasible from the standpoint of staff. Concerns about feasibility, as well as fear of the unknown, are often interpreted by managers as "resistance."

High-performing staff are some of the first to point out process waste, inefficient policies, and high levels of variation in the productivity and effectiveness of the staff as a whole. These high performers often welcome process changes that make those who "don't pull their weight" more transparent, even if it means that fewer people may be needed in the process.

MemorialCare took the approach of recognizing the dangers of labeling staff responses as "resistance to change," and instead developed targeted actions for

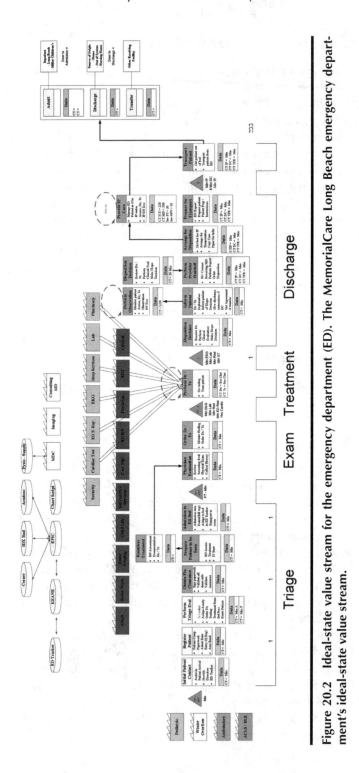

Figure 20.2 Ideal-state value stream for the emergency department (ED). The MemorialCare Long Beach emergency department's ideal-state value stream.

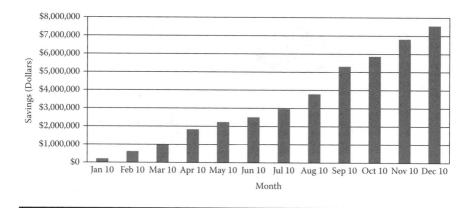

Figure 20.3   Long Beach Memorial Medical Center (LBMMC) accumulated value stream savings for the ED (anticipated).

each unique situation. For example, if the value stream work resulted in a role change for some staff, there was a direct, specifically designed action to support the role change. If the value stream efforts indicate that job losses are probable, then the leadership team must uniquely and specifically manage the labor reduction issue.

Labeling staff pushback as "resistance to change" makes it hard to problem solve due to an overgeneralized and inaccurate diagnosis. Identifying the true issue and then dealing with the effect directly are much harder, but vastly more effective than simply labeling staff responses as "resistance." MemorialCare recognized these facts and committed to manage each issue, looking for the root cause of staff concerns and responding to each unique situation.

Labor Component of Total Cost

MemorialCare's value stream leaders have the right things in place: a sense of urgency, a guiding coalition and meaningful vision, a robust change process, and a sound support system. They realized early on that cost reductions couldn't be achieved without major challenge of the status quo.

Using the Toyota Production System as a model to "rethink" the status quo has been useful, but not without its challenges from staff. The most frequent criticism was the belief that patient care was much more complex and variable than automobile manufacturing. Many discussions occurred to underline that the thinking and approach to waste elimination were the reasons to use the Toyota metaphor, and that the use of the metaphor in no way implied that people are like "steel and paint."

It was understood that the total cost structure of the value streams was quite different than the Toyota cost model or those of other manufacturing-based industries.

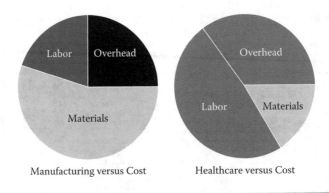

Manufacturing versus Cost   Healthcare versus Cost

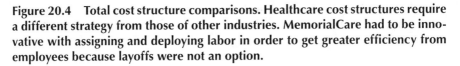

Figure 20.4   Total cost structure comparisons. Healthcare cost structures require a different strategy from those of other industries. MemorialCare had to be innovative with assigning and deploying labor in order to get greater efficiency from employees because layoffs were not an option.

Figure 20.4 shows a comparison of the cost structures for a manufacturing value stream and a typical value stream under study at MemorialCare.

From the cost structures, it is clear that the majority of the cost reduction would come in one of two ways: a reduction of labor (e.g., productivity, premium labor, attrition, and redeployment) or an increase in demand (maintaining the same labor basis). For MemorialCare, the reduction of material costs was a lesser element in affecting the financial position of the organization. The material costs were highly related to the labor costs and would be addressed, but the cost targets could not be achieved by material cost reductions alone.

The timing and logical choices for labor redeployment and adding volume were challenges. If the headcount of a value stream is reduced prior to the initiation of process improvements, the motivation to streamline the tasks and activities out of necessity is high, but then there are risks to patient safety and staff satisfaction with this approach. It is also extremely difficult to right size the staff prior to performing the analysis of determining the optimal staff level.

The collaboration during RPIWs by the people doing the work proved to be the most effective way of determining the best staffing level. Yet if the headcount is reduced after the lean principles are applied and those doing the work determine the right sizing of the work group, the employees have now threatened their own personal livelihoods. Value stream leaders had to continue to reiterate that no one would lose their jobs as a result of RPIWs with the caveat that job responsibilities might change.

When opportunities for labor reduction are identified, MemorialCare has responded by (1) reducing overtime; (2) assigning the extra labor in support of more improvement projects; (3) brining the work from marginal suppliers to be done internally; (4) utilizing flex time, or reducing the work week for all employees; (5)

increasing demand and growing business volume; and (6) holding the excess labor until attrition brings the labor requirements in line.

Current Culture and Perseverance

Culture is an effect, not a cause. It is a result of doing the hard work of leadership and making decisions that serve the organization mission in a way that is consistent with organization values. The employees at MemorialCare view lean implementation as a measure of the integrity of the leadership. At first, they wondered if lean was another "program of the month" or a permanent way of thinking and acting. The workshop results have been significant, the cost reduction targets have been met, and the processes have been streamlined, but the work has become harder—doing more with less. As is typical in other industries, the MemorialCare culture is not one of unlimited self-sacrifice in terms of working oneself out of a job. The culture of self-protection combined with the difficulty of large system change makes cost reduction a thorny leadership challenge. There is also the legitimate fear that the improvements may not yield the expected gains, so employees often resist the new methodology. From this vantage point, the organization's ability to persevere under this leadership challenge is essential.

The change process demands authentic leadership. Authentic leaders have a deep sense of purpose for their leadership. Authenticity includes standing behind one's words. Cost reduction leadership at MemorialCare has tested the authentic leader's resolve. The authentic leader consistently behaves in alignment with his or her core values, acts as a steward and servant of the people, and leads with head and heart while building an enduring organization. In relationship with cost reduction, the MemorialCare leadership understands the risks of making a commitment to employees when the environment demands significant cost restructuring, job reassignment, and difficult labor decisions.

In the current economic climate, cost pressures demand a sophisticated level of management decision making and leadership guidance. MemorialCare raises lean implementation issues to the highest level: an oversight committee consisting of the system and campus CEOs, COOs, and CFOs. This group provides insight, counsel, and key decisions and often does the hard work that others can't do. The oversight committee asks that all leaders model authenticity, including forthright accounts of the impact of ineffective processes and excess resources, and that leaders make hard decisions with absolute transparency. Staying true to the mission and values of the organization in the face of fear and threat to the status quo is key to MemorialCare's success. MemorialCare leaders realize that the challenges ahead require the perseverance to "stay the course."

The bold goal for MemorialCare is to "achieve a cost of providing care at or below Medicare reimbursement rates by 2014." This means reducing expenses by $2,800 per discharge with the lean principles at the center of the fight. Guiding the organization successfully forward requires a substantial commitment to the following: (1) the change must be led by the executive team—they must be the change they expect; (2) the development of a multiyear road map and staying the course; (3) maintaining an investment mentality against shortsighted decisions to assure financial resilience and goal achievement; (4) the cultivation of internal leaders at all levels to produce a solid foundation for continued success; (5) wisely selecting the areas of improvement and effectively resourcing and supporting the value streams to generate momentum and timely wins; (6) constructing an ROI basis at the start and holding the organization accountable to the commitments, setting the stage for high performance; (7) devoting the necessary time for assessment and planning; and (8) making the successes and learnings highly visible to protect the investment and encourage a culture of discovery and improvement.

In the initial stages of lean implementation, the activities and projects will be challenged. Knowing that the healthcare system in the United States is at a turning point, staying patient-centric and maintaining an appreciation of the employees are the soul of this organizational effort.

Chapter 21

Back from the Brink: The Jefferson Healthcare Turnaround

John Nowak, RN
Performance Improvement Officer
Jefferson Healthcare

Teresa Deason
President
Lean Synergy & Solutions, LLC
Lean Consultant,
Joan Wellman & Associates

The Jefferson Healthcare story is about passionate people working to save their community healthcare system. Yet, people can't make up for poor processes forever. Given their tight budget, they could no longer solve their process problems by adding more people. So, why did they decide to embark on a lean journey? Survival! And how did they turn their "false start" into a "turnaround story"? They stayed the course!

Jefferson Healthcare (JHC) is a critical access hospital located in Port Townsend, Washington, a beautiful seaside city two and one-half hours from Seattle, separated by Puget Sound. Jefferson County is home to a diverse population of thirty thousand and is frequented by tourists year-round. With the goal of providing a broad range of services to the community, Jefferson's leadership was facing a "perfect storm" in healthcare with decreasing reimbursement and increasing costs. (See Sidebar 21.1.)

SIDEBAR 21.1

JEFFERSON HEALTHCARE AT A GLANCE

- Twenty-five-bed critical access hospital.
- 75 percent of our business is outpatient.
- Average daily census is 12.7.
- Annual budget is about $75 million.
- 525 employees, 305 FTEs.
- The emergency department (ED) has about ten thousand visits per year.
- The district employs most of the local providers (about twenty) in rural health clinics.
- Largest employer in Jefferson County.

In early 2004, several of Jefferson's key managers were trained in Toyota Production System (TPS) fundamentals for a week with the hope of improving internal process efficiencies and patient and staff satisfaction. There were obvious financial constraints, so the hope was that they could go it alone, without experienced mentors or coaches.

Once they emerged from training, the managers were excited and enthusiastic about the possibilities for improvement. The technical aspects of TPS are straightforward, and, more important, they parallel the "art and science" of medicine. Much to their dismay, however, the TPS trainees were met with intense resistance throughout JHC when they returned to Jefferson Healthcare and began to apply what they learned in training.

The trainees consulted with JHC CEO Vic Dirksen to determine if TPS was the appropriate change management tool. Dirksen had not been through TPS training and didn't feel capable of providing realistic advice. He also recalled a previous reengineering project, which had engaged eleven people for six months but never substantially improved patient care or profits. Like many organizations, these well-intentioned projects simply soaked up resources instead of producing the expected results.

At this point, Dirksen decided to attend lean leader training. Afterward, he was convinced that TPS would provide a methodology and mind-set for systematic change that could sustain itself over time.

"I realized we had only dabbled at lean," remembers Dirksen. "You can't say that you are doing lean just because you have read a book or attended a seminar. It was not very effective until we decided to commit the resources and hire a coach."

Now it was up to Dirksen to provide the organization with a clear directive that TPS was not optional. He started with the hospital's strategic leadership group (SLG), which includes the CEO, COO, CFO, CNO, and human resources director. He gained a commitment from this group that TPS would be the methodology tool set for improving quality and decreasing cost at JHC. The SLG agreed to invest in TPS, and it decided to hire a coach to guide TPS implementation.

This was the turning point for Jefferson Healthcare. The hospital's leaders did three very important things: they engaged experts to guide the lean journey, they established an internal lean resource office (LRO) with the leader reporting to the CEO and added to the SLG, and they agreed to empower the staff for owning the processes.

Jefferson Healthcare invested significant resources in its lean resource office. JHC is a small organization (about three hundred FTEs), and the LRO consists of 3.8 FTEs. This small team has been empowered by the organization to champion lean improvements in all areas of the organization. The leader of the LRO has also been asked to link strategic initiatives to lean workshops and targets.

Once the decision was made, there was no going back. The hospital leaders felt certain that this would be a powerful approach that would turn their organization around, even though staff had often waited out other "change" systems, believing that JHC executives and managers would eventually shift course. The only question now was where to start in order to bring the entire team into the brave new world of lean enterprise.

The first target of opportunity was the JHC laundry.

The cramped laundry room used to be a dirty and disorganized place. The staff responsible for keeping things running smoothly was disillusioned and always behind in its work—and with good reason. Piles and piles of laundry were being dumped on the doorstep each day with no rhyme or reason. Indeed, no one knew when the laundry was coming in, when it had to be ready, or where it was supposed to go. As a result, bins and bins of sheets, towels, uniforms, and patient gowns simply sat and never got cleaned. Things got so bad that some of the dirty laundry at the bottom of the heap became moldy and had to be thrown away.

Confronted by this dysfunction, JHC's leaders were a heartbeat away from outsourcing the total laundry operation to an outside company. Jobs would be lost as a result of that decision. Fortunately, JHC embarked on the lean journey that helped drive systemic change throughout the hospital.

Working together, an outside consultant and internal lean resource office helped bring to the surface a magnitude of issues and improvement opportunities inside the laundry. And, collaborating in a workshop, the laundry's team members focused intently because they were deeply concerned about the future of the laundry. The weeklong workshop also included some of the laundry's internal customers (ACU RNs, the ED tech, and the radiology manager) (See Sidebar 21.2.).

SIDEBAR 21.2
TPS WORKSHOP ROLES AND RESPONSIBILITIES
Process Owner

- Has ongoing responsibility for managing the process to get optimal results
- Ensures measures are in place and monitors measures

  - Conducts follow-up audits and meetings
  - Is accountable for the achievement of agreed-upon objectives

Process Sponsor

  - Champions process improvement and convenes the management guidance team (MGT)
  - Models the spirit of improvement
  - Ensures resolution of cross-departmental issues
  - Supports process owner to ensure commitment of resource representatives

Management Guidance Team

  - Represents the cross-functional teams and models the spirit of improvement
  - Ensures resolution of cross-departmental issues

Resource Representatives and TPS Tiger Team

  - Attends workshop as needed to provide support, advice, and guidance in respective areas of expertise

Before they really got going, the workshop attendees agreed to overhaul JHC's laundry facility, and they set the following targets:

- Reduce the work-in-progress (WIP) by 50 percent.
- Reduce the lead time by 50 percent.
- Reduce laundry costs by 20 percent.
- Improve employee and customer satisfaction by 50 percent.
- Establish standard work.

After a day of TPS training and learning, the workshop attendees fully grasped the amount of waste embedded in the current laundry process; in response, they drafted a vision statement—and the goal was to adopt the values contained in the statement by the end of the workshop week.

The vision statement was crisp, clear, and concise: "Our laundry team works in a safe and efficient manner, utilizing steady flow and standard work. We produce quality linen to satisfy our customers while working in a well-equipped environment that is adequately staffed, promoting good morale."

The workshop team then focused on several processes within the laundry. To begin this phase of the exercise, the team separated value-added steps from non-value-added steps.

The subteams in the workshop then prioritized the work for the rest of the week. The top projects included the following:

- Implementing a one-piece flow work cell
- Measuring customer demand and establishing par levels
- Improving infection control processes
- Establishing ergonomic standards to avoid employee injury
- Establishing, documenting, and training in standard work
- Increasing staff productivity with staff schedules that meet the rate of demand for laundry services

The team managed to meet or exceed the targets for the workshop while overcoming multiple challenges. The process owner/department manager was challenged to get employees who were not in the workshop to support the team's ideas, and the LRO was challenged to get the facilities team to build a table and hang the production control board in short order.

By the end of the week, the vision was realized—and the results were impressive. The team had established a starting point, which the organization could build upon. And today, other departments at JHC are learning about key TPS principles—such as one-piece flow, visual systems, and daily management—by studying the laundry operation. (See Table 21.1, Figure 21.1, and Figure 21.2).

One of the most important successes here was the fact that the laundry team decided to voluntarily continue daily audits to ensure that gains from lean improvements could be sustained; and, after two years, the audits continue (See Figure 21.3). Indeed, the laundry's daily management system (DMS) includes a daily huddle, a review of the previous day's audit, and a production control board, which is based on customer demand.

But even after JHC's early success with TPS workshops, such as the laundry project, there were still large numbers of the staff who resisted the new process; their hope, of course, was that the organization would give up, eventually change direction, and move on to a new program or plan.

But JHC's leadership stood firm behind its commitment to TPS.

"When we aligned behind TPS and all agreed that was our method for improvement and change," recalls Dirksen, "then staff started to get on board."

Adds Paula Dowdle, JHC's COO, "We made it absolutely clear that TPS was our method for change and improvement. There are other methods that might work, but we told staff that we had selected this one and that we were going to be the best we could be at using TPS."

The next step was wider engagement. Within the next few months, all SLG members had participated in a TPS workshop, and there was enthusiastic support after everyone had seen firsthand how transformational these workshops were for the organization. In addition, all leadership team members at JHC were encouraged

Table 21.1   Laundry Workshop Results

Measure	Before	After	% Improvement
Number of steps	28	18	33%
Lead time	2.5 hours	1.75 hours	30%
Value-added steps	4	4	0%
Value-added time	14%	22%	33%
Number of checking steps	1	1	0%
Number of queues	4	1	300%
Number of work-in-process	29 bins	9 bins	200%
Staff satisfaction	15%	50%	230%
Customer satisfaction	30%	85%	41%

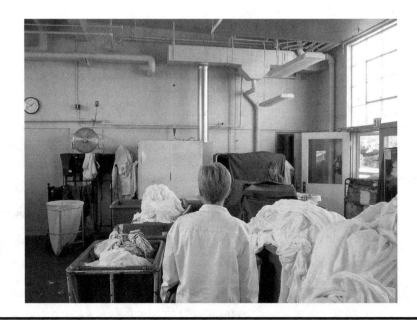

Figure 21.1   Laundry before. Facing the possibility of being outsourced, which would result in a reduction in force, the laundry was the logical place to begin the "proof of concept."

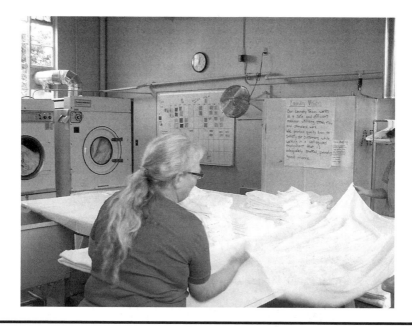

Figure 21.2 Laundry after. Despite multiple challenges, the team went to work and managed to meet or exceed the targets for the workshop.

to attend workshop report-outs to show support for TPS as well as for the teams doing the work during the workshops.

Staff began to see the leadership team participating in workshops and even supporting workshops when they weren't directly involved. As things progressed, it became clear that the leaders were really "walking the walk."

As the leadership team became more involved in workshops, it helped drive accountability throughout the organization. Leaders were coached on how to ask questions during report-outs so that workshop teams would push for breakthrough improvements. And, during postworkshop sustaining meetings, when workshop owners were asked in a public forum why results had not been achieved, a powerful message was delivered to everyone that leadership was serious about achieving objectives.

"It was difficult at first to ask the hard questions," says Dowdle. "But as an organization we gained the discipline to do it, and when we started to see the results we were getting, we were convinced of the importance of speaking up."

The organization's commitment to TPS also extended to the board of directors. This alignment was significant because Jefferson Healthcare is a public hospital district, governed by a five-member board. Board members participated in workshops and routinely attended workshop report-outs. Involvement at this level provided still more support for JHC teams doing the work of improvement.

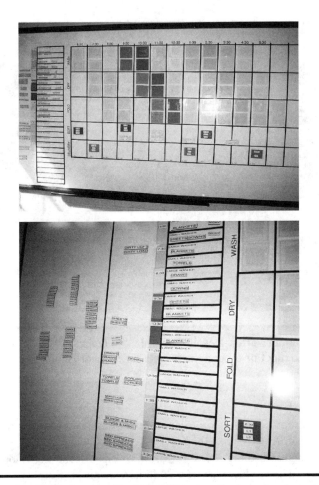

Figure 21.3 Production control board. Still today, the laundry department is "on tour" for other departments to learn about key TPS principles: one-piece flow, visual systems, and daily management.

One board member was cautious about TPS. He was invited to participate in a workshop to improve patient access to providers. After being present for the workshop week, he changed his point of view, and declared himself impressed with the potential of TPS. This reversal helped influence all of the board members; and four out of five board members have since participated in TPS workshops.

As the work of TPS continued in the JHC organization, staff involvement at the department director level became critical to overcoming general staff resistance. Directors were usually involved as "process owners" and were responsible for assessing and planning workshops with the lean resource office. When it comes to TPS today, JHC now has broad acceptance and deep skills at the director level. This evolution stems from the SLG's ability to coach directors to meet or exceed workshop targets.

But as important as the commitment of leadership is in an organization, the real work of TPS is ultimately completed at the staff level. And the staff at JHC has driven the success of TPS by being involved and engaged in workshops. The JHC organization's small size allowed more than 40 percent of the staff to participate in workshops during the first two years. This level of involvement has helped JHC reach a tipping point, where enough staff has been involved firsthand in workshops and sideline critics have a hard time getting traction.

Staff satisfaction surveys are routinely completed pre- and post workshop at JHC. All of these surveys have demonstrated increased staff satisfaction—not only for the staff participating in the workshop, but also for the staff in the departments affected by the workshop. This increase in staff satisfaction helps shape the culture so that it can accept change; it also silences staff members who are skeptical or resistant to change.

Workshops in the first year were structured by the lean resource office to include one or two staff members who were "actively disengaged." Almost all of these skeptics were converted by participating firsthand in the TPS process. When they returned to the workforce and lauded the process, it was powerful for the rest of the staff to hear former critics who were now supportive of TPS. Communication about the workshop success and system-wide reporting of workshop results definitely helped reduce resistance.

One of the more remarkable transformations at JHC involved participation by providers; indeed, nineteen of twenty clinic providers employed by JHC have been involved in a workshop.

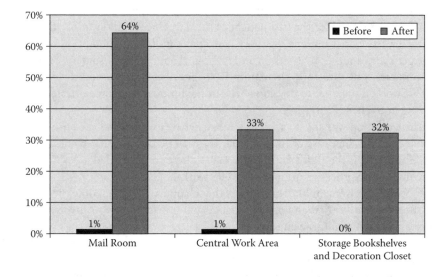

Figure 21.4 Staff satisfaction in three areas before and after 5S workshops.

"For the thirty years that I've been here," explains Dirksen, "we've tried many methods to involve providers in process improvement. But we haven't been very successful. Lean has been a wonderful tool that has allowed us to get providers to partner with us to solve problems and improve processes."

Adds Dr. Joe Mattern, a provider in one of the JHC clinics, "Even though we work together every day, we do not usually sit down to talk about our process. TPS allows us to talk in an intentional way about how we do our daily work. In the two years we have been participating, we have made real improvement in our process."

Providers who have participated in JHC workshops have improved their workflow, increased the access they provide to patients, developed a standard visit template for all of their offices, and developed and delivered many other enhancements. Workshops involving providers are typically cross-functional, thus combining providers with staff, resulting in improved communication.

JHC works with employed and nonemployed providers. After hearing about the successes of employed providers, nonemployed providers chose to use TPS tools to improve their process as well.

For example, Dr. Dimitri Kuznetsov, chief of surgery, who is not employed by JHC, decided that the operating room (OR) should conduct a workshop to help with preoperative (preop) readiness for patients. His goal was to improve on-time starts. The lean resource office initially discouraged him from being overly aggressive in what could be accomplished in one workshop due to the multiple issues that can cause late starts. Yet Dr. Kuznetsov was determined to use TPS to make a difference. He became a co–process owner with Florida Rue, director of surgery. Together, during the planning phase and throughout the week of the workshop, they supported the team and encouraged them to challenge the status quo.

The team members participating in the OR workshop decided to attack the problem of late starts for the first patient of the day; their solution revolved around improving two processes: one that packages a patient's information prior to the day of surgery, and another that sets up and lays out the morning of surgery. Surgeons, preop nurses, OR directors, circulating RNs, anesthesia staff, and provider office staff all worked together to develop a streamlined process to remove waste and get the patient to the OR on time.

The workshop was able to achieve Dr. Kuznetsov's vision, and the on-time start rate for the OR's first case of the day went from 14 percent to 91 percent in ninety days. Even better, the staff's enthusiasm about these results fueled a desire to continue improving processes utilizing the TPS workshops.

Process improvement like this implies that change will impact only the process. But the hard truth is that any process change will impact the *people* involved in the process and, as a result, the culture.

What is culture?

It is the people side of any business. It includes the urban legends, unwritten rules, staff behavior, and current routines. And, indeed, it is the hardest and most complex component of moving to a lean enterprise.

To facilitate this complicated cultural change, JHC established the lean resource office early in its lean journey. The LRO became "control central" for measuring, planning, coaching, and directing the organization in lean principles. And the LRO manager is an officer-level position at JHC that is also responsible for conducting ten to twelve workshops a year.

Running these workshops can often be difficult for the workshop facilitator. During workshops, staff may mask resistance by not fully participating or not following ground rules. The workshop facilitator must deal with these behaviors directly and quickly, usually by talking with the recalcitrant person during the quiet moments of the workshop. Process owners can also balk at fully accepting responsibility for the workshop results. Again, the workshop facilitator must help the process owner understand his or her role as a champion for change.

Every workshop is designed to support and empower a specific team, so if the workshop facilitator is unable to influence appropriate behavior, the sponsor and/ or the MGT must quickly address the issue. This is a key test of the organization's commitment, a reflection of whether it will stay the course, and a signal to the staff that "no" is not an option. Members of the MGT may also be new to the principles of TPS, so they, too, must be coached about modeling the behaviors necessary to keep process owners and team members accountable.

Here's a good example of the challenging behavior that took place during some of the early TPS workshops at JHC. One of the workshops was designed to enhance flow in provider offices, and in the middle of a session a clinic director became very frustrated with the concept of working in teams. It became clear that she was unable to model the necessary behavior of a process owner. During the workshop, she had a conversation with the process sponsor, insisting that TPS was not the right way to manage change. The sponsor did not cave in and told her that JHC would continue to use this method to improve patient care. The director decided to submit a letter of resignation. Instead of negotiating for her to stay, it was agreed that it would be best for the director to leave the organization. This was a critical moment of truth, and it sent a very clear message that TPS was—and would continue to be—in place at JHC.

Moments of truth like this reinforce the fact that TPS has brought a substantive process of improvement to JHC, unlocked creativity within the organization's culture, and demonstrated that ownership of critical core processes is in the hands of the staff and directors—not the leadership group. The role of leadership is simple yet critical: support and encourage significant process changes. (See Sidebar 21.3.)

SIDEBAR 21.3

KEY INSIGHTS FROM JHC

- Have patience and stay the course.
- Be clear that there are no "exempt" departments.
- Teach managers to have difficult conversations.

■ Decide that TPS is a condition of employment.
■ Take quick action with those who undermine the process improvement work.

"The sign of good leaders at JHC," explains Dirksen, "is that they are hardly recognized as being part of process change—the team members make the changes on their own." This bottoms-up approach stimulated new accountability at JHC, and the LRO increasingly used TPS tools to help the organization hold staff and managers to a higher standard.

But the transition was not an easy one.

For many years, JHC had used different improvement methods, and, as a result, there were often no standards for completing projects on time or at a certain quality level.

The new accountability system at JHC also required a rigorous and broad-based discipline throughout the hospital. Each workshop included a follow-up task list with due dates and individual responsibilities. Audits were also employed to ensure that staff understood and followed the standard work developed in the workshop. The process owner was responsible for auditing and coaching. These audits were conducted daily for one month, then three times a week for two more months. Measures from the workshop were also required to ensure the workshop hit the targets requested by the management guidance team. Staff was required to report on the audits, measures, and tasks at thirty, sixty, and ninety days.

The intensified organization-wide accountability effort went even further.

JHC developed a system so that monthly workshop progress could be reported at a single meeting. During this monthly gathering called "Big Monday," staff involved in workshops joined with leadership of the organization to hear progress reports on each event. The leadership team worked with workshop leaders and held them accountable for targets and measures; asking the hard questions about progress in a public forum was a very effective tool.

In addition to Big Monday, JHC used a "visibility wall" to display the progress of its workshops. This wall was located just outside the hospital boardroom in a high-traffic area where the public could view it. The wall utilized a "dashboard" that showed the status of audits and measures. It also displayed a "task meter" that showed the status of all tasks for the workshops.

The task meter was another tool that drove accountability at JHC. When it was first added to the board, it did not include visual indicators that showed when tasks were overdue. These visual indicators were added when leadership and the LRO became concerned because many tasks *were*, in fact, overdue. The first step was to color the bar for tasks red (shown as shaded gray in Figure 21.5) if any tasks were overdue. Next, the leadership team was encouraged to talk to process owners if they had tasks that were overdue. Soon, only a few tasks were colored red.

JHC manages process improvement on a daily—as well as monthly—basis. After two years as a value stream, for example, the JHC clinics started using the tools of the daily management system. These tools include a daily huddle and a measurement dashboard, which displays measures that are linked to the organization's strategic goals as well as staff productivity goals. DMS is a powerful tool that brings the entire team together—staff, physicians, and management—to review daily progress as goals are set and reached.

Shifting the culture and reaping the benefits of sustainable long-term process improvements require an investment of time, energy, and money. And this investment—like the TPS journey—must be measured in years, not days, because process change is a generational endeavor.

Bearing this in mind, JHC had to make two key decisions in order to ensure that quality became—and remained—"job one":

- What was the appropriate amount of money to invest in the quality improvement effort?
- How could that investment be leveraged to ensure that the tipping point was reached as quickly as possible?

After considerable thought, calculation, and analysis, the SLG determined that 3 percent of JHC's revenue was a reasonable investment in TPS.

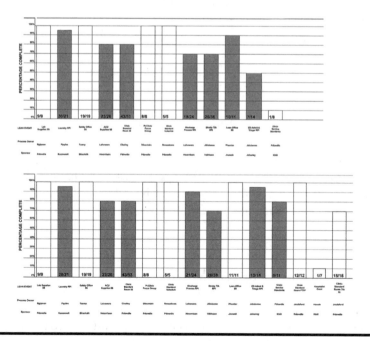

Figure 21.5 Task meters on the lean events dashboard. "When I looked at the board and I was the only event in the red, I was very motivated to complete my tasks" (process owner).

In order to leverage that financial investment, JHC made the decision to hire a coach, or "sensei." Learning from previous experiences and mistakes, the hospital realized that it's easy to veer off course and that the cost of learning bad habits can be damaging—if not devastating.

When preparing TPS budgets, JHC also realized that the largest long-term expense was the cost of staff time that allowed full engagement in lean activities. The time investment by leadership can also be very demanding, especially in the early stages of process change, when everyone is learning. JHC's leaders believe that the average executive should spend a minimum of five hours per week on lean improvement.

Looking back, JHC has learned a host of lean lessons—some of them the hard way. This acquired knowledge has helped the hospital spread the plan, do, check, and act (PDCA) mind-set throughout the organization, and it's also clarified which steps result in less than desirable outcomes.

When establishing the lean resource office, for example, it's worth considering the following:

- Make the leader of the LRO part of the executive leadership team, and be sure he or she facilitates a minimum of six workshops per year.
- Hire a coach or sensei to teach the fundamentals.
- Develop full-time fellows to be lean experts; engage the best and brightest.
- Support the LRO with leadership enforcement.

When it comes to the TPS workshops:

- Follow the standard work as instructed by the sensei.
- Ensure early successes.
- Determine what pace the organization can absorb; test the system.
- "Don't just plan—*do*." A few workshops can be focused on planning, but the majority should implement a new process by the end of the week.
- Build a core following of lean advocates who become TPS champions.

When it comes to lean leadership:

- Don't play with multiple methodologies; make a decision and then stay the course.
- Understand that leadership has to learn, too, and will need coaching.
- Intervene with weak leadership early on; have the difficult conversations.
- Teach managers to have the difficult conversations.
- Ensure there are no "exempt" departments or individuals.
- Expect accountability and put systems in place to make it transparent.

- Be consistent; there will be pushback, but "no" is not an acceptable answer.
- Give time to those who cannot understand or accept the TPS methodology; they will eventually self-select out.

Changes to culture, increased accountability, and improvement are all important TPS results—but the ultimate reward here is better care for patients, and JHC got this point loud and clear during one of its workshops.

Patients having an acute heart attack in Jefferson County before the workshop faced complexity, delays, and uncertain outcomes because six organizations were involved in an uncoordinated process. During the workshop, the JHC team examined that process and tried to make it better by establishing a cohesive system that worked better. The team's vision statement for the workshop was "Joining resources to save heart muscle."

The team started by looking at the size and geography of Jefferson County, and developed a standard for when patients should go directly to Harrison Hospital in the Bremerton, Washington, area, about a sixty-minute drive from Jefferson Healthcare during rush hour. Team members also added a new protocol to the EMS system, which allowed medics to administer clot-busting drugs to patients en route to Harrison.

Within a few months of the workshop, the local newspaper published a letter from the daughter of a patient who had been treated using the new protocols. Her father had completely recovered from a heart attack.

"[My father] was treated in the ambulance with a new emergency protocol that resulted in his complete recovery after he received a new stent to repair a 90 percent blockage," said Karen Nelson in her letter to the editor. "We found out later that he was the first resident of Jefferson County to benefit from an innovative new emergency protocol relating to rapid response to cardiac events. Many lives will be saved under this new protocol because of the conviction and leadership of Vic Dirksen, executive director of Jefferson Healthcare, and Gordon Pomeroy, vice chief of East Jefferson Fire Rescue, as well as a large group of professionals whose names we do not know."

In the end, as Karen Nelson indicates below, TPS is really all about making the lives of patients better. And, from top to bottom, JHC knows that TPS is the tool set that allows the hospital to fully realize and achieve its core value of "intentionally patient-centered care."

To put it simply: TPS has helped JHC create a culture of accountability while pointing it toward a much brighter and healthier future.

SIDEBAR 21.4

New Emergency Cardiac Protocol Saves Lives

On June 26, my eighty-eight-year-old father had a heart attack. We called the paramedics as soon as we realized what was happening and they quickly arrived at his home in Kala Point. He was treated in the ambulance with a new emergency protocol that resulted in his complete recovery after he received a stent to repair a 90 percent blockage (see "'Clot buster' brings help for hearts," [Port Townshend, Wash.] *Leader*, June 24).[1]

We found out later that he was the first resident of Jefferson County to benefit from an innovative new emergency protocol relating to rapid response to cardiac events. Many lives will be saved under this new protocol because of the conviction and leadership of Vic Dirksen, executive director of Jefferson Healthcare, and Gordon Pomeroy, vice chief of East Jefferson Fire Rescue, as well as a large group of professionals whose names we do not know.

Our family wishes to extend its sincere appreciation and gratitude to the group of paramedics and health care professionals who provided such stellar medical treatment. Our community is extremely fortunate to have access to an emergency procedure for cardiac victims that will ensure the best possible chances of survival. In deep appreciation to all those who participated in the successful effort to implement this new life-saving strategy for Jefferson County residents,

Karen Nelson
Port Townsend

Note

1. *The Port Townsend & Jefferson County Leader*, July 20, 2009; RPI on Heart Attack treatment which included Jefferson Healthcare Emergency Dept, local and county EMTs, and the Harrison Hospital's Cardiac Cath Lab.

Glossary

Andon: A visual and/or audible communication system indicating the current status of a process.

Batching: The mass-production practice of making large quantities of a part regardless of customer or process demand; causes excess inventory and process waits, and masks errors and their root cause.

Buffer resources: A small but sufficient amount of inventory (people, material, space) to meet customer demand when customer ordering patterns, or takt times, vary.

Cells: A process approach that uses groupings of equipment, tools and people organized to perform an entire sequence of a process in one continuous physical location (cell). A well-designed cell can increase the flexibility of operations and produce a variety of products in smaller and smaller quantities. It reduces operating costs and improves the utilization of people as variation in volume and mix occur.

Changeover: The process of readying workspaces or machines for the next job. A component of "set up".

Continuous flow: The ideal process state where customers are provided what is needed, just when it is needed, and in the exact amounts needed. Continuous flow is synonymous with just-in-time (JIT).

Continuous improvement: A philosophy by which an organization looks for ways to always do things better. The gains made through continuous improvement activities are generally incremental, small-step improvements that lead to significant improvements over time in the quality, cost, delivery, and safety of an organization's products and processes, and the engagement of its employees in the work of the organization.

Continuous Performance Improvement (CPI): Seattle Children's Hospital's adaptation to healthcare of the Toyota Production System, CPI is a philosophical, long term approach to continuous improvement. CPI focuses on improving results for the benefit of SCH patients and their families, and on supporting the people of SCH in their work.

Cycle time: The time that elapses from the beginning of a process to completion of that process. Cycle time is measured, not calculated.

Defect: A defect in a product or process is an error that has moved beyond where the error occurred. Risk and cost increase as defects move further along in the process.

Error: Any deviation from a specified process or expected outcome.

Error proofing: A means of eliminating errors before they occur

FIFO: First in, first out (FIFO) is a work-control method used to ensure that the oldest work (first in) is the first to be processed (first out).

Five Whys: Ask "why" five times whenever a problem is encountered in order to identify the root cause of the problem and to avoid merely addressing the symptoms. By asking why and answering each time, the root cause becomes more evident.

Flow: The progressive achievement of tasks along the value stream so that a process or product proceeds one step at a time, timed to customer demand.

Gemba: Japanese term that means the "actual place" where work is performed.

Heijunka : See "load leveling"

Just-in-time (JIT): A system which ensures that customers receive only what is needed, just when it is needed, and in the exact amounts needed.

Kaizen **(Continuous improvement):** Small daily improvements performed by everyone. Kai means "take apart" and zen means "make good." The goal of kaizen is the total elimination of waste.

Kanban: "Kanban" means "to put away and to bring out" or "signal" and is a cornerstone of the just-in-time pull system. A Kanban communicates upstream precisely what is required (in terms of work specifications and quantity) at the time it is required.

Lead time: Lead time is the total of all cycle times within a value stream, including waste. It is the total time between customer order and customer receipt of a product or service.

Lean: A shorthand term for continuous improvement.

Load leveling or *Heijunka:* Balancing the amount of work to be done (the load) by time and by worker in balanced proportions based on customer demand and product or service variety.

Monument: Any process or technology that necessitates batch processing.

Muda: See waste

PDCA: Plan-Do-Check-Act, or Plan-Do-Study-Act; the Deming Cycle

Plan-Do-Check-Act: Plan-Do-Check-Act (PDCA) is an iterative, four-step problem-solving process; a structured cycle of process change. One might think of it as the layperson's scientific method. Plan means to prepare for and design the change; Do refers to implementing or trialing the change and observing what happens; in Check the results are analyzed; and Act, determine next steps based on the analysis, which then leads back to the Plan step, and so on.

Poka-yoke: A mistake-proofing device or procedure to prevent errors.

Process: A sequence of operations (consisting of people, materials and methods) for the design, creation and delivery of a product or service.

Processing time: The time a product is actually being worked on in design or production and the time an order is actually being processed. Typically, processing time is a small fraction of cycle time and lead time.

Pull: A system in which nothing is produced by the upstream supplier until the downstream user signals a need.

Push: Conventional work in which services or products are created based on schedules and availability of materials regardless of need downstream. It results in batching and the waste of inventory.

Quality, Cost, Delivery, Safety, and Engagement: QCDSE. The framework for continuous performance improvement at Seattle Children's Hospital. By removing waste from processes and systems, SCH seeks to improve the Quality, Delivery, and Safety of its care and services. Through the elimination of waste, as Quality, Delivery and Safety improve, Costs are reduced, and Engagement of faculty and staff improves as barriers and obstacles in their work are removed.

RPIW: Rapid Process Improvement Workshop

Rapid Process Improvement Workshop: An important tool of continuous improvement, particularly at the beginning of an organization's journey. The workshop consists of several days of focused learning, process mapping, waste removal, and process redesign with the intent to implement process changes by the end of the workshop. Multiple disciplines and multiple levels of faculty, staff, and management are involved in an RPIW, leading to enhanced Engagement. PDCA is critical post-workshop to assure continuous improvement.

Reliable methods: Reliable methods are consciously developed, consistently followed, and evaluated for capability. Reliable methods must have an identified owner to audit performance and uniformly maintain the methods as standard.

Root cause: The ultimate reason for an event or condition.

Sensei: A teacher with a mastery of a body of knowledge — in this case, CPI philosophy and methods.

Set-up time: The entire time it takes a process to switch from producing one part or service to another. Defined as the time from when the last step of process A is completed to the start of the first step of process B.

Seven Flows of Medicine: Patients, Staff, Medications, Information, Supplies, Equipment, Families

Single-piece flow: A process in which work proceeds one complete step at a time without interruptions, re-work, or waste.

Spaghetti diagram: A map of the path taken by a specific product, person, or piece of information as it moves through the value stream, so-called because the route in an unimproved process typically looks like a plate of spaghetti.

Standard work: The application of time to reliable methods.

Standard work combination sheet: Defines the order of actions that each worker must perform within a given takt time. Illustrates the relationship between the processes manual time(s), automatic time(s), walking time(s), waiting time(s) and the takt time.

Standard work in process: Minimum inventory that is necessary to perform the job safely and successfully within a given cycle time. (SWIP)

Standard work sheet: A visual control tool to help the worker, team leader and manager maintain a standardized operation routine. It details the motion of the worker and the sequence of actions. Serves as a guideline for workers and supervisors to show where and in what sequence operations are completed in the work area.

***Takt* time:** The pace, or rhythm, of customer demand. Takt time determines how fast a process needs to run to meet customer demand. Takt time is calculated, not measured and may be longer or shorter than cycle time. To calculate divide the total operating time available by the total quantity required by the customer. Takt time is expressed in seconds, minutes, hours or days.

Team charter: A document that describes the elements of an RPIW. It includes, but is not limited to, the following elements: 1) a clear definition of a team's mission, 2) a statement of team members' roles and responsibilities, 3) a description of the scope of the team's responsibility and authority, 4) project deadlines, 5) workshop metrics and targets, and 6) expected deliverables (outcomes).

U-shaped cells: A U-shaped, work area layout that allows one or more workers to process and transfer work units one piece—or one small group—at a time.

Value added: Defined from the perspective of the customer. An activity that transforms the fit, form, or function of a process or product. An activity that, if the customer knew you were doing it, they'd be willing to pay for it.

Value-added percentage: The percentage of the total lead time that is spent actually adding value to a product or service. To calculate value added percentage, divide the total value added time by the total lead time.

Value-added time: Time during which an action or process changes the fit, form or function of the process and a customer would be willing to pay for if they knew you did it.

Value stream: A collection off all the steps (both value-added and non-value added) involved between customer order and customer receipt of the product or service.

Value stream leadership: Responsibility for the customer experience throughout the value stream, with an emphasis on relentless process improvements within and between the "silos" through which a product or service must transit.

Value stream map: Identification of all the specific activities (including waste), from the perspective of the customer, that occur along a value stream of a product or service.

Visual control: The placement in plain view of all tools, parts, work activities, and indicators of system performance, so the status of the system can be understood at a glance by everyone involved. This includes the use of color, signs and clear lines of sight in a work area. Visual controls should clearly designate what things are and where they belong. They should provide immediate feedback as to the work being done and its pace.

Waste (also known as *muda*): Anything within a value stream that adds cost or time without adding value. The nine most common wastes are 1) processing, 2) correction, 3) search time, 4) transportation, 5) wait time, 6) space, 7) inventory, 8) complexity and 9) under-utilized people.

Work in Progress (WIP): Items (material or information) waiting between steps in a process

5S system: A method for removing excess materials and tools from the workplace and organizing the required items, using visual controls, such that they are easy to find, use and maintain. 5S stands for: Sort, Simplify, Sweep, Standardize, and Sustain (definitions follow).

Sort: The first activity in the 5S system. It involves sorting through and sorting out items, placing red tags on these items, and moving them to a temporary holding area. The items are disposed of, sold, moved, or given away by a predetermined time.

Simplify: The second activity of the 5S system. It involves identifying the best location for each item that remains in the area, relocating items that do not belong in the area, setting height and size limits, and installing temporary location indicators.

Sweep: The third activity of the 5S system, involving a regular physical and visual sweep of the area to identify potential problems. Keeps the area and equipment in good condition.

Standardize: The fourth activity in the 5S system. It involves creating the rules of maintaining and controlling the conditions established after implementing the first three S's. Visual controls are used to make these conditions obvious.

Sustain: The fifth activity of the 5S system, where a person or team ensures adherence to 5S standards through communication, training, and self-discipline.

Index

269